SWORDS AND PLOUGHSHARES

Swords and Ploughshares

Patrick J. O'Mahony

Sheed & Ward
London

ISBN 0-7220-8740-3

Nihil obstat: David McLoughlin, S.T.L., Censor
Imprimatur: + Maurice Couve de Murville, Archbishop of Birmingham, 4 July 1986

Published in Great Britain in 1986 by
Sheed & Ward Ltd,
2 Creechurch Lane,
London, EC3A 5AQ

Book production Bill Ireson

Filmset by Fakenham Photosetting Ltd, Fakenham, Norfolk
Printed and bound by A. Wheaton & Co Ltd, Exeter, Devon

Acknowledgements

In writing this book I have enjoyed the help of many. To all I am most grateful. I am indebted to the Commission for International Justice and Peace for making the drafts of the Pastoral Letter of the United States bishops available.

My thanks to Peggy Hirons who typed the script and Colette Ware who read the work in spite of her lecturing and teaching commitments. But no words can express my gratitude to Professor W. Hollenweger for his kindness, patience and inspiration. Without him this book would never have been attempted.

Contents

Introduction

The marvellous achievements of technology do not provide the meaning of life and death nor do they ensure justice, peace and respect for human life. On the contrary, along with the benefits of technology, which are usually measured in economic productivity, have come the problems of environmental danger, economic disparity by the concentration of power and wealth, the rapid growth of the arms race and the ever-increasing nuclear arsenals which threaten the very survival of man and the planet. The aim of this book is to identify these dangers and to demonstrate that while technology does not in itself ensure justice and peace, its achievements can be used by man at the service of these values.

Throughout the twentieth century, there has developed both nationally and internationally, a clearly discernible trend towards bureaucratization, the concentration of wealth and power, and the increasing recourse to social and physical coercion. In spite of the many declarations of the United Nations, the violation of basic human rights has become accepted practice in many parts of the world. The battle for survival is waged by millions, yet money and resources are wasted in millions, particularly by the production and sale of the technology of death.

Not only does the nuclear threat hang over the world, but there have been more than a hundred wars since the Second World War resulting in many more deaths than for the whole of that particular war. Every year illiteracy increases and with all this are the many prevalent forms of political tyranny and human enslavement. Similarly Australian Aborigines and the African Bushmen, as well as other ancient cultures, suffer by losing their cultural roots while acquiring few of the benefits of Western "development". These examples are listed not only because they are symbolic of the much larger confrontation but because political prisoners, the Aborigines and the Bushmen were part of the writer's work in his quest for peace.

Meanwhile, the nation-State with its claim to absolute sovereignty, is a problem of massive proportions. How can humanity cope with these challenges and how can man live with the technology of death?

In *Part I*, the problem is stated and the question of direct and indirect killing is examined. It is hoped to show that not only is direct killing of the innocent morally unacceptable, but that indirect killing can also fall into this category. This is particularly significant where modern warfare and the arms race are concerned and, as we shall see, where indirect killing is intrinsically connected with the nuclear weapon. The question of how man can live with the technology of death is analyzed. One of the major obstacles to world unity, interdependence and peace, is the nation-State concept which has been the concern of the World Council of Churches and the Papal and Conciliar documents. Is there not a better way of organising people so that justice and peace can be more effectively promoted, in keeping with the fact that we are one people and this one planet is our home? Cannot the new technology be used to serve peace and unity rather than be a cause of suffering and destruction? Above all, does this new question of the nuclear bomb demand new attitudes and answers? It is claimed that the present organisation of society, together with prevailing attitudes, lend themselves to the ever-spiralling arms race which threatens all and indirectly kills many.

In *Part II*, the various responses to the nuclear threat are treated. Down through the history of the Church, Christians were faced with two options in regard to war, namely that of non-violence and the just war position. From the earliest days of the Church, there is evidence of Christians who were pacifists. However, modern thinkers are anxious to emphasise more than ever that the just war position begins with the same presumption as the pacifist position, namely, the love of one's neighbour.

In *Part III*, the problem of war-making in a nuclear age, which was highlighted in Part I, is re-examined and the vision of peace is outlined. A new attitude to war and peace is necessary in our time which, in turn, requires a massive educational programme. The Church has a much greater role to play in this effort.

It will be shown that frequently the Church's contribution to peace-making has been regarded with some suspicion. In fact, much more can be done to teach people to think "world" as well as "parish" and thereby enable religion to make a more positive contribution to peace. Oftentimes, the contrary seems to be the case. This means, in fact, that while the Church is situated locally, it must be more than ever conscious of its universal thrust because the local Church is, in fact, the universal Church incarnated in this or that particular place. Indeed if the universal Church is ever to play its true universal role it will do so through the local Church.

Furthermore, the question of peace is examined with particular reference to its political and religious aspects. This eventually entails a reflection on the dynamics of peace-making which involve the motivation of self-interest and self-preservation, world order and planetary unity as well as the power of education. It is hoped to demonstrate that mission and worship have complementary roles in this educative process of promoting peace and that it is possible by liturgy and action to change minds and hearts, thereby making a Christian community more outward looking to the world God loves.

In conclusion it is suggested that only by new attitudes to war and peace can man live with the technology of death. But this requires a change of mind and heart whereby, not only Christians but all people are educated to work for the peace and the unity of the international community. That entails helping all to see that the world is really one community rather than a collection of competing nations. Indeed at the most down-to-earth level of self-interest, the planet must be considered as interdependent, not only in the systems of air, land and water, but also in its people. The international community is, in fact, the family of God, which is loved infinitely by Him. It is imperative to try to teach that we cannot love less than the Creator. If this vision of unity – which is not only a vision but a hard and inescapable fact – can become part of the common insight of all the inhabitants of the planet then we may find that, beyond all our inevitable pluralisms and fragmentations, we can just achieve enough unity of purpose to build a safer and more human world.

SWORDS AND PLOUGHSHARES

PART I

The Technology of Death— The Problem Stated

CHAPTER ONE

Direct and Indirect Killing

This chapter has a three-fold purpose. Firstly, it attempts to provide an explanation of direct and indirect killing. Secondly, it explores the question of death in the Third World, and whether there is responsibility for indirect killing which arises from omission. It reflects on the moral implications of the diversion of resources to armaments, which in turn is connected with killing. Finally, it aims at demonstrating that national sovereignty or security, unless subordinated to the international community, facilitates the new war technology in direct and indirect killing. In short, it seems that national sovereignty of *itself* and especially when in conflict with internationality, is not a suitable organisation to monitor and control the new technology so that the right to life is promoted rather than infringed.

THE PROHIBITION

Christian teaching on human life arises from the belief that it is a precious gift from God and, therefore, there is a divine commandment to respect it. This life is a great gift and, as so often with gifts, it brings responsibilities with it. It is a talent which we possess as a steward; it is to be developed, fostered and actively protected. That is why medical care is necessary and, in some countries, available. We are morally obliged to have recourse to it if necessary for the normal preservation of health "up to the point it becomes futile, or where it would itself involve burdens that the patient need not feel obliged to undergo".[1]

Killing
The inviolability of human life has always been of paramount importance for the security and safety of the individual and

humankind. The principle of respect for human life has been formulated traditionally as: "Thou shalt not directly kill the innocent." This principle, which also applies to suicide, has a rational basis which is explained by Plato in the *Phaedo* when he argues, in the person of Socrates, that man is not completely his own master. He belongs to God and his life is a sacred trust of which he must not dispose before the time chosen by divine decree.[2] Not only that but Plato gives a lucid explanation in *The Laws* of the various classes of homicide.[3] The gift of human life is so precious in God's sight, and should be in our sight, that God protected it with a strict moral commandment which is found explicitly in the New Testament (Mt 5 : 21). Recent scholarship shows that the formula of the 5th (6th) Commandment of the Decalogue "not to kill" was in its Israelite setting not comprehensive. It existed in a community which had capital punishment and in which war was permitted and even commanded. It has been claimed that the verb used, *Rāsah*, refers to "illegal killing inimical in the community".[4] Nevertheless, this view is not without its critics.[5] The Old Testament basis of the prohibition is indicated in Yahweh's words to Noah (Gen 9 : 6):

He who sheds man's blood
shall have his blood shed by man
For in the image of God man was made.

The revelations of Yahweh as Lord of life and death underline the limitations of human lordship over other people, especially in matters of life and death.

Much of Christian teaching about respect for human life is common to post-biblical Judaism.[6] There is a fairly developed casuistry on medical subjects in the rabbinic response. Killing an innocent person "whether he is healthy or about to die from natural causes" is legally codified as murder. Human life is of infinite worth so that any fraction of it is reckoned to be of infinite value and a patient on his deathbed is considered as a living person in every respect. "It is forbidden to cause him to die quickly . . ."[7]

Cessation of heroic methods to prolong a lingering life, with no hope of recovery, may be sanctioned.[8] In short, Judaism teaches that "killing any innocent person, whether he is

healthy or about to die from natural causes, is murder".[9]
Furthermore, this right to life is codified in Article 3 of the
Universal Declaration of Human Rights (1976).[10]

Killing and the New Testament

In the New Testament, the prohibition of homicide is taken for
granted by Jesus and the Apostolic writers which Jesus and his
disciples repeated on a number of occasions.[11] In his letter to
the Romans, Paul treats these moral principles as valid for all
and available to all through their consciences (Rom 1f, 13 : 9ff).
The central and moral directive of the New Testament, and the
one to which all others reduce, makes killing unthinkable (Mk
12 : 28–34). The response of love to the neighbour demands
respect for his actual existence as a necessary basis for the
development and expression of love. Not only may one not kill
but, as followers of Jesus, one must love one's enemies (Mt 5 :
21). Since man through Christ is the son of the Father and
brother of Christ and his fellow men, all murder is now
fratricide.[12]

There is no conclusive argument that Jesus intended to
exclude all exceptions, although it is more difficult to justify
them. The acceptance by Jesus of the State authority and its
formal justifications by Paul (Rom 13 : 4) seem to indicate,
according to some experts, the possibilities of exceptions.[13]
However, others have reservations about this interpretation.[14]
The weight of the New Testament does make exceptions difficult. While the early Christian writers were conscious of their
Old Testament heritage, they had difficulty in accepting the
pre-Christian exceptions of war and capital punishment.
Moreover, they explicitly rejected direct abortion.[15] The fact
that they endorsed martyrdom demonstrates that they were
aware that human life could, and in some circumstances
should, be subordinated to higher values.[16] But even this was
debated as to whether martyrdom was something of value in
itself or tolerated as an evil for the sake of a higher value. All the
same it is hardly possible to deny that the laying down of life in
the face of the higher demands of charity or duty may not be
within the responsibility of the individual. Responsibility requires that he take account of all the moral values in the
situation and of the relative force of these values. In such a
situation there may be a value greater in importance than life

itself. The surrender of one's life for this value may be an act of
the highest generosity and courage. Scripture, itself, has indica-
tions to this effect when Jesus speaks about a man "laying
down his life for his friends" (Jn 10 : 11, 15 : 13) and St Paul
speaks of "daring to die for a good man" (Rom 5 : 7).

Although there is some ambivalence which shows itself here
and there in Christian writing, it is true to say that the consensus of early Christians was anti-militaristic in that it was
against taking of life even by soldiers or the State. It was only
after Constantine that Christian writing countenanced Christian participation in war. Up to then Christian agapé (love)
transcended the highest in Judaism and Hellenism.[17] Even
during the first centuries of the Constantine era, the Church
Fathers, while making adjustments to the "Just War" theories,
kept pacifism as an absolute rule for monks and the clergy and
took up rigid directives for non-violent conduct in private life.
For example, Ambrose and Augustine did not condone killing
in self-defence outside of military or public service.[18] St Basil
abandoned the general objection to war but still had grave
aversion to bloodshed[19]; a point indicated by the Methodist
theologian Paul Ramsey in his classical work *War and the
Christian Conscience* (1961).[20] St Basil just about admitted
there could be a distinction between war and murder but he
recommends abstention from Communion for three years if
hands were unclean because of the war effort. Nevertheless,
Ramsey claims that the change of attitude in Christian thinking
from pacifism to the just war position was not a fall from the
original purity of Christian principles; it was merely a change
of tactics. The basic strategy of Christians remains the same.
The just war was caused by the demands of Christian love and
service of the neighbour who was attacked. Consequently, it
was the love or agapé which was the motive for the just war as
well as pacifism. What would Jesus have the Good Samaritan
do if he came upon the person while he was still under attack?[21]

Charles E. Curran observes that Ramsey too easily justifies
war in the name of agapé when it is a question of defending
others.[22] Though Ramsey insists that the central point is concern for one's neighbour, Christian agapé would never allow
one to kill an aggressor on the basis of self-defence, and that is
why Augustine found killing in self-defence morally
unacceptable.[23] What is more, Aquinas, while allowing self-

defence, also believed that the person under attack could not intend to kill his assailant. The objective intention of the action and its direction must not be towards the death of the aggressor but to his incapacitation.[24] Needless to say, this point will be reintroduced later, but for the present it is sufficient to state that from the beginning of the Old Testament right down through the New Testament and the early Church, there was a clear rejection of the killing of the "innocent" – a word neatly defined by Bonhoeffer as...

> ... any life which does not engage in conscious attack upon the life of another and which cannot be convicted of any criminal deed worthy of death.[25]

However, in Catholic theology, emphasis is not placed on the word "conscious" in the case of an unjust aggressor. Whether the assailant is formally or consciously attacking does not really matter. For example, a material unjust aggressor such as a drunk or a madman may be equally repulsed and, if necessary, killed. Formal guilt was not relevant.[26]

As the years went by, exceptions to the principle were defended by theologians; these did include self-defence. The other two exceptions were war and capital punishment. Indeed, Karl Barth feels that we have strayed "far from the Commandment of God" in so easily allowing these exceptions and that the highly exceptional circumstances in which war and capital punishment have been allowed, have indeed been trivialised.[27] However, Barth agrees that the exceptions are universally defended even though they do involve direct killing in three cases: the killing of the unjust aggressor; of the enemy soldier; and of the criminal. The reason is that they are no longer entitled to normal respect for human life. In other words, the assailant or criminal is no longer an innocent person. It has been pointed out by some that the capital punishment situation is very much like the *Lex talionis* of the Jews, which is a life-for-a-life punishment (Ex 21–22).

Direct and Indirect Killing and the Principle of the Double Effect

An evil effect of an action is imputable if the action need not have been performed and the evil result was foreseen, at least in a confused way, and could have been prevented. In the world in which we live many actions have mixed results or side effects. To live and act at all it is necessary to accept, without willing or intending them, the unacceptable evil consequences of our (necessary) good actions. The technical analysis of such actions is known as the "Principle of the Double Effect". There are two qualifications to the use of this principle in matters concerning life and death which should always be considered if the principle is to be used responsibly:

1. Is there any other alternative action where there is no evil effect?

2. How far are individual or social acts of omission, which result in evil effects like death, simply ignored or regarded less important than positive action?[28]

Indeed, evil effects resulting from omission are also imputable if they are foreseen in some way, could have been prevented, and a solid reason was present why they should have been prevented. Some have put this in another way, stating that evil effects due to omission are imputable when there is the ability, the opportunity and the reasonable expectation to act.[29] The application of the principle of the double effect has been used by moralists justifying killing of civilians in war. It is interesting to note that the Working Party of the Church of England used this principle when investigating the question of nuclear warfare.[30] The deaths are not directly willed but rather are the unavoidable consequence of an act justified in itself, e.g. the bombing of a military target. Moreover, we cannot describe the moral character of an action merely in terms of its results or its motive. It is not enough to say Nagasaki stopped the Second World War. Actions cannot be judged except in the totality of their morality, i.e. of the circumstances, the action itself, the good and the evil effects, the intention of the agent and the reason why the action was placed in the first case. And so it is that the principle of the double effect simply states that an evil consequence may be permitted (if it cannot be prevented) but not directly intended, in certain clearly defined circumstances. It goes without saying that the action itself must not be evil and the good effect must follow from the action at least as immediately as the evil effect. That means that the good effect does not come as a result of the evil effect, otherwise one is doing evil that good may come (Rom 3 : 8). Furthermore, there must always be sufficient reason to justify allowing the evil result, when it cannot be prevented.

The Working Party of the Church of England gives the interesting example of the doctor who cannot employ chemotherapy for cancer without causing some unwanted side effects. These are not intended but merely permitted; they can be described as incidental or accidental. The Report goes on to describe the principle by saying:

> One is justified in permitting incidental evil effects if there is a proportionate reason. It is presumed that if there were any less harmful way of achieving the desired good, one would take it.[31]

However, it must be admitted that the phrase double effect can be mystifying and yet, in most of our lives, there are side effects to many actions in addition to the result aimed at. When it comes to matters of life and death it should be understood that the principle does not mean that death can be caused as long as it is not intended. Nor does it mean that the side effect is less heinous than when it is intended. A practical example in modern times is the blowing-up of banks knowing that there are innocent people within. One cannot argue that because one does not intend to kill the innocent people here, there is no moral blame. In fact, responsibility for the death of the innocent in such a case is just as clear as if they had been deliberately shot. However, when an action is placed that is not directed at another's death, placing it may be justified if there are means or necessities of sufficient weight which would provide a valid reason for risking or allowing death as a side effect. Without such an excuse, foreseeable killing is either murder or manslaughter. There are two classic examples given in medical ethics which exemplify this thinking. One is the justification of removing the cancerous womb,[32] even though it contains an inviable foetus, on the grounds that delay would gravely endanger the mother's health, and that the death of the foetus is merely permitted but not intended. Here there is a justifying reason. The action is neutral or good, i.e. the surgery, and there is a good effect (the health of the mother). The second case is a much more difficult situation and has caused endless controversy amongst moralists. It is known as the case of the tubal ectopic foetus.[33] The pregnancy is located in the fallopian tube; delaying treatment could cause rupture and haemorrhage and seriously endanger the mother's life. Here also the foetus is inviable and there would be grave danger in waiting for viability. It is now generally accepted that the tube is a pathological case and, consequently, can be treated as such, even though it automatically means the death of the foetus. The action of its nature is directed at the pathology and the death of the foetus is not willed but permitted. Moreover, the reason for operating is a good one.

However, this reasoning has been challenged by moralists of various persuasions. Some have claimed, such as Grisez, that the evil effect (namely the death of the foetus) is as immediate as the good, the health of the mother, and that in practice the act is indivisible from which comes its justification.[34] It does require considerable sophistication to distinguish this procedure from other non-acceptable cases of direct therapeutic abortion, at least where the Catholic Church is concerned. Indeed the matter was referred to Rome in the last century for consideration. In reply, the Holy Office limited the operation to the case of viability.[35] The result was a more extensive debate on the difference between direct and indirect killing. Eventually one expert, after widespread consultation throughout the medical profession, came to the conclusion that the tube was, in fact, pathological and, therefore, could be treated as such even in the case of inviability, and that the majority of moralists within the Catholic Church would follow that reasoning.[36] It is true that, in borderline cases, such as the ectopic foetus, the texture of the argument of the double effect may appear threadbare but, in any area of human action, the moral colouring shades right across from white to black. On the borderline is an indistinguishable texture where moral decision hesitates. All the same, some have grave reservations about this type of reasoning, classifying it as mechanical or artificial.

Bernard Häring, the German moral theologian, would adopt a completely different line. In the case of killing of the unborn, he says, an attack is made on the right of the foetus to live.

The physician should do his best to preserve the foetus in the case of ectopic conception but, as soon as it becomes certain, as is normally the case, that intervention is mandatory to save the mother and there is no chance to save both by waiting, then intervention does not directly deprive the foetus of the right to live since it already has no chance to survive.[37]

For Häring, then, it is a question of saving one or letting both die.

The double effect principle is being submitted to further scrutiny by others. Paul Ramsey for example tries to establish a similarity between the war situation and the foetus. In war, he says, it is not the guilt of the soldier but rather his combatant role; a function which is the basis for *incapacitating* him. This is like the solution proposed by Aquinas in the case of defence against the unjust aggressor.[38] Ramsey applies this to the situation where mother and foetus may die unless the foetus is incapacitated. It is important to note here that both for Ramsey and Aquinas one cannot intend to kill the aggressor. One can only intend to *incapacitate* and, in this case, according to Ramsey, the foetus is in the position of the material unjust aggressor.[39] The objective intention of the action and its direction is not towards the death of the foetus but towards the incapacitation of the foetus from what it is doing to bring about the death of the mother. But Catholic teaching does not accept the use of the unjust aggressor model on the basis that the foetus could not be in such a position. Once again, there has been intensive argument amongst Catholic moralists such as Lehmkuhl,[40] Sabetti and Aertyns, and has only subsided with the findings of Bouscaren.[41]

Yet even today, conflict situations of life and death, especially in regard to war and pregnancy, are vigorously debated by people such as the philosophers, Bruno Schuller, W. K. Frankena and others.[42]

The debate about direct and indirect killing is relevant to my subject because of the morality of collateral damage to civilian populations. Nevertheless, I believe that the proponents of the different positions in this debate reach the same conclusions about the point at issue. One view holds that the *directly intended object* in such an attack is the destruction of a military target and that civilian deaths are *unintended indirect consequences*. According to this view, one is still bound by the traditional interpretation of the principle of the double effect, to weigh the evil consequences which indirectly accompany the attack against the good effects which flow from it. Even, therefore, if one argues that collateral damage to a civil population is indirectly voluntary, the judgement about proportionality between the two effects must still be taken into account. The other school of moralists in the debate take a different approach in their treatment of intention. They argue that one cannot determine what an agent intends without taking all the foreseen consequences into account. If the agent chooses to perform an action whose good effects are proportionately greater than are the evil ones, this school would judge that the evil consequences are not the object of the direct intention. If, on the other hand, the foreseen evil consequences are proportionately greater, then the direct object of the intention is evil. In other words, for the second school, the direct intention cannot be determined apart from a judgement of proportionality. Interestingly enough, both schools, therefore, evaluate the morality of collateral damage by assessing the proportionality between the evils of loss of life, plus possible escalation, and the goal of defending justice. Therefore, both schools come to their conclusion by different routes and, as we will see later, find that the significant damage to life and population centres is morally unacceptable.[43]

However, this point will be taken up again in the following chapters. Suffice it to say here that while experts argue about what constitutes indirect killing, they nevertheless agree that all direct killing of the innocent is impermissible.

THE THIRD WORLD AND INDIRECT KILLING

By the end of the 1960s it was realised by the United Nations that human rights are indivisible and that civil and political rights are interconnected with economic progress and other human rights. Up to that time the activities of the United Nations in this area seemed to be carried out in an isolated manner with little interchange between economic development, social progress and human rights.[44]

Rich World – Poor World
Gradually the world has begun to struggle to attain its unity, but, at the same time, is paradoxically bedevilled with all sorts

of fragmentations. Justice and human rights are becoming master ideas in modern society. Another great movement in our time is the fact that this quest for justice and human rights is now on a world scale – the social issue is now global.[45] So there is a moral concern focused on the dignity of the human person, that all people have a claim to the basic conditions that are necessary for an acceptable human existence. Hence a notable feature of human rights is their universal character and this is automatically accompanied with a universal responsibility for their universal implementation.[46]

Rights and responsibilities are inseparable yet there is practically an infinite gap between the idea and the action.[47] The North Atlantic countries comprising largely of the white Christian and post-Christian people, and comprising between one-quarter and one-third of the world's people, enjoy 80 per cent of the world's resources and trade, 90 per cent of its services – shipping, banking and insurance and nearly 100 per cent of the capacity for research.[48] At the same time, the majority of the world's people live in undeveloped places. Some 800 million people, more than one-third of the total population of the developing world, live in absolute poverty. That is to say, they live at the very margin of existence with inadequate food, shelter, education and health.[49] Unfortunately, the great divide between the North and the South seems to widen and the majority of the world's people, therefore, are not able to attain the fundamental human rights to eat, to health, to literacy and to life.[50]

A few nations of the industrialised world have escaped from this condition, for the time being at any rate, and this small segment is wealthier than any that previously existed. This fact stirs emotional protest amongst peasants and peons, among fellahs and coolies, among negro migrants and ghetto dwellers. It already underlines the violence of post-colonial protest in South-East Asia or the anti-feudal stirrings in Central America and along the Andes. Another factor is that policies do exist in aid, trade and other strategies but governments and politicians seem to lack the political will to implement them. There was no sense of urgency or haste in Santiago in 1968 when the Second United Nations Conference for Trade and Development (UNCTAD 2) pledged 1 per cent of their Gross National Product to aid the poor countries.[51] This was later to become 0.7 per cent; the pledge has been honoured by only a few.

The quality of British aid is being diluted by the pursuit of trade related objects at precisely the point when it had started to take a few faltering steps towards improvement.[52] Not only is the aid limited in quantity but also in quality because much of it is tied. Of all the limitations on aid, the tying of aid to purchases in the aid-giving country is one of the most serious. The Pearson Commission stressed that "the use of tied aid also tends to interfere with trade among the developing countries".[53] That was a long time ago. However, at present most British aid is tied to the purchase of British goods. In 1980, 63 per cent of bilateral aid was fully tied and a further amount partially tied – the highest proportion of any country in the Organisation for Economic Co-operation and Development (OECD).[54]

Again in 1976, UNCTAD 4 adopted an Integrated Programme for Commodities (IPC) designed to improve prospects for developing country exporters but, six years later, the heart of the IPC, The Common Fund, remains unratified. Most commodity agreements are under pressure and world prices of several commodities have fallen to an all time low.[55] Yet, as the Brandt Report showed, 12,000,000 children under the age of five years died of hunger in 1978.[56] Some people see an explosive factor in this situation and others have compared it with the pre-revolutionary period in France where the French underprivileged were known as the Third Estate; today the hungry millions are known as the Third World.

Lessons from Scripture
There is continuity from the Old Testament right down through the New Testament concerning the responsibility of helping the needy.[57] The obligation to share with the hungry is clearly underlined. As well as caring and sharing, the importance of justice and human rights is spelt out in Isaiah.[58] Indeed Jesus identified himself with the message of Isaiah when he preached in his home town (Lk 4 : 18ff). In the early Church, it is recorded that relief was sent to the victims of famine (Ac 11 : 27–30), and St Paul speaks of balancing what is our surplus or affluence against the needs of others (2 Cor 8 : 1–5, 9–15). Help should be given not only generously but also cheerfully

(2 Cor 9 : 6–15), and, in consequence, is blessed by God. Luke tells us the futility of making possessions and wealth our main goal. There is no security in them, even if we are affluent (Lk 16 : 19–31). Hoarding and avarice were certainly problems, according to Jesus (Lk 12 : 15–21). The parable of Dives and Lazarus is now seen by some writers as typifying the great divide between the rich North and the poverty stricken South.[59] It is difficult to reconcile the policies and reactions of the North with the fulminations of the Epistle of St James (Jas 2 : 1–17). Moreover, St Paul reminds us that our care for our neighbour means love for the whole human race which, in fact, is a prophetic statement in regard to the interdependence and unity of the international community (1 Thess 3 : 11–13). Furthermore, Jesus taught that we should feed the hungry and give drink to the thirsty (Mt 25 : 31), and by serving our neighbour we are, in fact, serving Christ himself (Mt 25 : 40).

Paradoxically, there is a climate of indifference in the North, which is Christian and post-Christian. In spite of their religious protestations, there is no doubt about it that contemporary Christians are extremely rich in relation to the rest of the world for they alone live in the wealthy lands from San Francisco to Moscow. This is a situation that past history has never confronted. Never before has wealth been so concentrated while there is massive starvation in the rest of the world. All the same, because of the vast array of communications today, for the first time in history "the brotherhood of man" has a technical and physical meaning. The Bible does not pose man with a choice between God and the world but rather summons all to affirm both, and, together with the Creator, serve mankind and creation. It is because people are soul and body, and very much part of this world, that they can dare to say "Thy Kingdom come" and be deeply concerned with justice and peace and political action.[60] All are called to inaugurate that Kingdom "where weapons of war become agricultural implements and all men live in peace and economic independence".[61]

Jesus said "Feed my lambs, feed my sheep" (Jn 21 : 15–17). This text includes much more than the needs of the body and mind but it can be argued that the greater includes the less. The strange thing is that mankind has never before had such ample technical and financial resources for coping with hunger and poverty. If the resources available in the North Atlantic countries were used through the structures of politics, education and media, millions of human beings could be saved from death by starvation, oppression and malnutrition.

Robert McNamara, President of the World Bank, in his 1973 address to the Board of Governors summed up these points in a fitting manner when he said:

> All of the great religions teach the value of each human life. In a way that was never true in the past, we now have the power to create a decent life for all men and all women. Should we not make the moral precept our guide for action? The extremes of privilege and deprivation are simply no longer acceptable. It is development's task to deal with them. You and I – and all of us in the international community – share that responsibility.[62]

Omission and Responsibility

The moral responsibility of the people in affluent nations to the starving millions has been carefully argued by a number of experts.[63] What ought we to do about this massive hunger, probably one of the greatest problems of all time? And what moral responsibility have people in the affluent countries?

Brandt's contention that the rich cannot survive alone and that they depend on the South for new markets, new consumers and future employment, underlines the point that it is in the interest of the rich to help the poor. Apart from the case of mutual interest, Brandt also claims that because of the unity and solidarity of the international community, the matter of world poverty is a question of distributive justice and human rights and, therefore, for this reason, the rich world should help the poor South.[64] Few people realise the full dimensions of world hunger which results in about 10,000 deaths daily and causes millions of people to be malnourished. What kind of responsibility, therefore, have the rich nations for so much pain, death and suffering? Most of the writers on this question agree that it is a serious moral issue, but Joseph Fletcher and Gareth Hardin demand that aid for the poor be conditioned by a programme of birth control. Indeed, Hardin argues that giving aid is futile unless control of reproduction is introduced.[65] Fletcher goes further and claims ...

> ... to give developmental assistance and food relief, either one without reckoning the cause or without counting the cost, is irresponsible i.e. unethical.

He concludes quite categorically that aid causes even "more starving bodies".[66]

Fletcher fails to appreciate that the population explosion is not just a question of more births, but also of less deaths. The fact is that, in many places in the Third World, an explosive growth of population has followed from the conquest of major epidemics. Again, the control of the grosser forms of contamination is often ahead of full-scale diversification of the economy. If one compares this situation with nineteenth-century England, one finds the population growth had slowed down to about 1.5 per cent a year, that is to say, industrialisation reached the people before public health so that people lived "better" before they lived "longer". In the Third World the opposite is often the case, and so there is an increase in population but not an improvement in the standard of living in the developing countries. In spite, therefore, of evidence of rising birth rates, there is also the factor of longer life expectancy that has to be taken into account. Moreover, the whole psychological mentality in the developing countries towards population growth is radically different from the affluent North. Children are sometimes considered to be the only investment poor people possess, so that in their senile days there are more hands on which to depend for support; and also, because of the infant mortality rate, which is very high, more children have to be born so that some will survive. However, this point did not find support in the Pearson Commission.[67] In any case, it is a well known fact that economic advancement brings about a less explosive growth. This is not to say, however, there is no room for effective family limitation programmes.[68]

Others disagree with Fletcher and a number of them like Rachels, Singer, and Narveson argue that food production could contain and even eradicate hunger.[69] While Fletcher argues that India has already exceeded its carrying capacity, Rachels concludes just the opposite. Watson claims that the over-riding principle of equity demands equal sharing of food and one writer makes the point more sharply by stating that the rich countries became affluent by commissively wronging the very nations that are racked by starvation; Michael Slote pertinently asks whether such nations can keep their goods and let people die or remain malnourished, especially when these nations are partly responsible for the poor countries' plight.[70] The principle is put forward by Singer that people are morally bound to prevent something bad happening if they can do so without sacrificing anything of "comparable significance". So, the affluent minority, since they could help the needy without substantial loss, are obliged to do so.

William Aiken and Onora O'Neill emphasise the right of the hungry against those who had an unfair share of the world's goods.[71] O'Neill asserts that a person's right not to be killed may sometimes be violated when the killing is indirect and not intended. She proceeds to argue a case of omission where indirect killing is imputable. She states that if a company invests in an undeveloped country and manages its affairs so that a high level of profit is repatriated, while the minimum wages of the labourers are lowered to such an extent that survival is endangered, then this company is responsible for the indirect deaths that are caused.[72]

Where people die because of this policy, she says, "then those who establish that policy are violating some person's rights not to be killed". O'Neill then proceeds to demonstrate that investors and management have corporate responsibilities for these indirect effects.

It goes without saying that religious organisations and churches have corresponding obligations where investments are held in companies which operate in countries like South Africa. This situation was faced by the Roman Catholic archdiocese of Birmingham in 1977 and 1980 when it analyzed its total portfolio of £1,250,000 and disinvested, as a result, from 13 multinationals.[73]

Other writers are primarily concerned with the moral obligations of people in affluent nations. Aiken and O'Neill emphasise the rights of malnourished people against those in rich countries. Therefore, when assistance is provided, it is not something which affluent countries can choose to do, or even are required to do, it is something owed to those who are hungry:

> The needy must no longer supply reasons why they should be helped ... Rather those who can assist the hungry must explain why they are not acting. It would no longer be morally acceptable merely to let people die and then claim moral innocence.[74]

Aiken finalises his argument sharply:

> No longer would it be taken for granted that as long as you do not harm someone directly, you are morally blameless. This applies to the drowning child, the accident victim case and especially the world hunger issue. Inaction, the omission to act, must be justified when the need of another is extreme (to the point of death).[75]

The burden of the proof, therefore, according to this argument, is on the "haves". All the same, while writers differ on their methods to establish a moral duty to aid the starving, they do generally agree there is a duty.

Vatican II makes a similar point when it urges both individuals and governments to remember the sayings of the Fathers: "Feed the man dying of hunger because if you have not fed him you have killed him."[76]

Additionally, when one considers the negligence which causes the wastage and pollution from industrialisation that threatens the very biosphere, the moral obligations of the affluent countries to the rest of the planet and its people become significantly greater. Garratt Fitzgerald, the Irish Prime Minister, has pointed out (1979) that human kind is facing:

> An important turning point in the development of its corporate moral sense about the maldistribution of wealth, not merely between individuals within States but also between people in different States.[77]

It is of particular interest to note the definition of health given by the World Health Organisation (WHO). It notes that the following principles are basic to happiness, harmonious relations and security of all peoples:

> Health is a state of complete physical, mental and social well-being and not merely the absence of disease or infirmity. The enjoyment of the highest attainable standard of health is one of the fundamental rights of every human being without distinction of race, religion, political belief, economic or social condition. The health of all peoples is fundamental to the attainment of peace and security and is dependent upon the fullest co-operation of individuals and states.[78]

It is beyond doubt that the majority of the South could not come under this definition. It is a matter of fact also that many of the millions who die every year from disease and malnutrition could be saved because "for the price of one jet fighter (twenty million dollars) one could set up thousands of village pharmacies".[79]

The Problem of Conversion

It may seem unnecessary to lay stress on this point but, like most revolutions in the history of mankind, it has happened gradually enough to have escaped the notice of many, both in the developed and developing worlds, yet rapidly enough to be quite astonishing in the long perspective of world history in which exploitation of man by man was the norm, and the concept of social justice at either national or international level was confined strictly to the level of religious precept and almost never extended to the practice of ordinary life. A similar point was made by Edward Heath:

> One of the most remarkable things about the period since the Second World War has been the speed with which the world has become a community. The sad thing is that many people are still unwilling to accept this to be the simple truth.[80]

It is now becoming clear that we are not talking so much about nation-States and the rights of people within their country, but of a global society in which there is an international community all entitled to basic human rights, such as the right to live, to eat, to health and literacy. The moral imperatives of the past are becoming the physical necessities of the present if the human family is to survive. In other words, all the warnings of the prophets of the Old Testament are becoming more and more relevant.

As to the question of population, underlined by Fletcher and Hardin, few would deny its importance. Indeed the Brandt Report recommends expanded and more effective family planning policies, but also mentions that economic development itself leads to a reduction in population and "that what is done to meet the challenges of poverty, ill health and hunger is a primary contribution to checking excessive population".[81] One is reminded of the slogan during Population Year: "take care of the people and the population will take care of itself".

There is no doubt that the population problem should always be kept in perspective, but too often this one aspect is used as a scapegoat for many other causes of lack of development and pursued as if it were a panacea. It would be irresponsible to deny that it is an important factor, but it is only one factor in the many complexities of development. Population policies, land and social reform, aid and trade are all important. They are not mutually exclusive and should be pursued as an integrated policy.[82]

In conclusion, one is not attempting to argue that there is any kind of absolute moral difference between killing and letting die. Whereas some instances of letting die are morally equivalent to killing and, therefore, impermissible, there are other cases of letting die which are morally acceptable as in the case of failing to use "extraordinary treatment" in the case of a very senile person with a terminal illness. When "letting die" is classified under the label "omission", the consequences of omissive behaviour are morally imputable because there is the *ability* to act, the *opportunity* and the *reasonable* expectation that one should act. For this reason, it would follow that the writers who claim that the rich are morally responsible by omission for indirect killing in the Third World have a very strong case because omission is not mere non-doing. Something not done is *omitted* if it ought to have been done or was reasonably expected. As Aquinas succinctly said: "It is both possible and necessary for the agent to act and yet he fails to do so."[83]

THE TECHNOLOGY OF DEATH

Armaments and Killing

One of the greatest threats to life and its quality is war and the preparations for war:

> The relationship between armaments and development is still very much in the dark. The prospects which might open up, if only part of the unproductive arms spending were turned to productive spending on development, are only slowly dawning on people.

Thus says the Brandt Report in its opening observations in the chapter "Destruction or Development?"[84] Even a fraction of the physical and human resources spent on war, if diverted to the wise support of life, could solve many human problems. The Brandt Report gives a number of factors which are quite startling in this regard:

1. The military expenditure of only half-a-day would suffice to finance the whole malaria eradication programme of the World Health Organisation, and less would be needed to conquer river blindness, which is the scourge of millions.

2. A modern tank costs about one million dollars; that amount could improve storage facilities for one hundred thousand tonnes of rice, and save four thousand tonnes or more annually. One person can live on just over one pound of rice a day. That same money could provide one thousand classrooms for thirty thousand children.

3. For the price of one jet fighter (twenty million dollars) forty thousand village pharmacies could be set up.

4. Again one-half of one per cent of one year's military expenditure would pay for all the farm equipment needed to increase food production and approach self-sufficiency in food deficits in low income countries by 1990.[85]

It is also a terrible irony that the most dynamic and rapid transfer of highly sophisticated equipment and technology from rich to poor countries has been the machinery of death. Furthermore, the impact of the arms trade on the spending decisions of developing countries, oftentimes for junta or government prestige purposes, means less money for basic necessities for the ordinary poor people.[86] The Brandt Report assessed the annual military bill at over 450 billion United States dollars, while official aid counts for less than 5 per cent of that figure.[87]

History's most expensive arms race is also proving to be the most costly in terms of world security and the ever-present threat is a nuclear catastrophe on a scale that would end all life. Additionally, about 500,000 (approximately 20 per cent) top scientists and engineers are now involved in military research and production.[88] Global expenditure on military research development in 1980 reached about 35,000 million dollars, which is about one-quarter of all the money spent on research and development in the whole world. Indeed, just two countries, the United States of America and the Soviet Union, accounted for 85 per cent of this military research, while France and Britain make up about 5 per cent.[89]

Lightning advances in technology make the weapons of today grossly destructive of civilians as well as the armed forces that are involved.[90] In local wars since 1960 at least 10,000,000 people have died, more civilians than soldiers.[91] On this subject, which is of such importance for humanity, official records are notoriously silent. It is evident that modern weapons are responsible for more killings direct and indirect. This is apart altogether from the fear created by the stock-piling of nuclear weapons equivalent to about 16,000 million tons of TNT, which is an overkill capacity to destroy the world and its people many times over, and to say nothing of radiation and genetic damage that would follow. Already there is a prospect of thirty to forty nations being in a position to produce nuclear weapons in the next twenty years. Had the huge sums of money, which were spent on nuclear weapons of destruction, and which are produced by all sorts of sophisticated technology plants, been used for peace and development, millions would not have been killed either directly or indirectly in war itself, or left to die by omission in the poor countries. To change these trends it would be necessary to have greater political will on the part of governments influenced by a vast lobby in each country.

> Disarmament will only come if people – political leaders, citizens and activists in political and social organisations change the direction of policies which have led to the arms race ... More aid and other measures aimed at helping developing countries will come if people to a greater degree adopt and act upon internationalist values – the equality of man; the need to eliminate poverty, mass unemployment, disease, hunger and illiteracy; the desirability of bringing the benefits of science and technology to everyone.[92]

To put it another way: the test of our progress is not whether we add more to the abundance of those who have too much; it is whether we provide enough for the ones who have too little. We have forged ahead with our nuclear arms and with the development of sophisticated killing devices with scarcely any thought of our actions, and without any serious reference to the majority of mankind. The East–West confrontation has clouded the far greater problem of the North–South divide. Most people are aware of some of the great benefits of modern technology to people, especially in the world of modern medicine, such as anaesthetics in operations, preventive treatments, drugs and other resources where technological progress has contributed well to human progress or human flourishing, but it is a sad fact that these benefits are available to relatively few, while so much science and technology is devoted to the weapons of death.

Killing and the nation-State

Jonathan Schell's book *The Fate of the Earth* (1982) helps us to focus on this by describing carefully the result of a nuclear exchange.[93] In his concluding section, Schell suggests that the only way to avoid the consequences is through abandonment of the nation-State concept as the major organising form of human society.[94] But this could only be accomplished in intermediary stages. Structures like the European Economic Community (EEC) could be the first faltering steps towards an international community. What is more, the Church and indeed multinationals which transcend national boundaries could have a big part to play as stepping stones to the international community. What the United Nations attempts in the temporal order, the Church should be in the spiritual order. Its vocation is to remind nations and people that they are one community, that is to say one family of God. As Schell puts it: "Nuclear powers put higher value on national sovereignty than they do on human survival."

The nation-State concept now seems to provide too small a framework for the human community and its unity, and it goes without saying that the nation-State is not essential to human existence. It is merely a particular way by which people are organised and the people that make up the group are more important than the framework or organisation that contains them. Whatever about the nation-State in the past, with its advantages and disadvantages, it does not seem to be a suitable framework for the future because the human community, in these dangerous times, has to emphasise more than ever its indivisibility as children of God and its vulnerability on this planet.[95] Schell believes that just as people have been sacrificed for the nation-State or have sacrificed themselves for it in the past, it certainly can happen also in the future since this concept has been so central in our thinking in politics, economics and indeed religion. Many would consider Schell's thinking as bordering on the Utopian and unrealistic. Yet to Ice Age man the nation-State concept itself would also seem to be Utopian. History tells us, and we have no other criterion, that countries which now have national governments were in the past riddled with internal strife. To them, national institutions of civic justice, which seemed Utopian, are now a reality. Schell contends that governments still acting within a system of independent nation-States, and formally representing no one but people of their separate sovereign nations are driven to try to defend mere national interests with the means of destruction "that threaten not only international but inter-generational and planetary doom".[96]

The world now has to decide whether to reject national sovereignty and "war" and institute global political arrangements that would arbitrate international disputes. Whatever people might think, the world is in fact choosing the course of attempting to refashion the system of sovereignty and to accommodate nuclear weapons.[97] For Schell, at any rate, the whole agonising dispute between the unilateralists and the multilateralists is merely a case of treating effects rather than causes. In fact, we have to face the serious position that as long as we have a world society organised in its present fashion, then these effects will be the natural outcome. In other words, we should never have reached this point, and the sooner we dismantle the system, the safer and better for everyone.

It is of interest here that Brandt also indicated the need for an international instrument to strengthen the role of the United Nations.[98] Perhaps its role could be extended to monitor all science and modern technology which is now a prior concern of human kind, a point hinted at by Paul VI in his 1965 address to the United Nations in his plea for world peace.[99] If then, as Schell says: "the institutions and passions of nationalistic sovereignty retain their domination"[100] and, therefore, are likely to ensure the world's destruction, there is an extra incentive for implementing the thoughts of Duchacek, namely submerging territorial nationalism by the "irresistible tide of universalism".[101]

The power of technology to mould and stamp life or destroy

it completely, demands more than ever social accountability which should be in direct proportion to the potential of these new powers. A serious attempt should be made to ensure that this new science and technology should be placed in the service of human rights and the liberty and dignity of all people. Few will doubt the value of national governments in the past; by mediation and authority, they have brought order, stability and indeed justice to their people by legislative, executive and administrative powers. It should not be beyond the imagination and power of modern man to translate these institutions of civic rights and justice, which have been so necessary locally and nationally, to an international level, though some would claim that this would demand world government. In this way, the new science and technology could be used, not just for a few but to serve the needs of the global society and thereby protect the rights of all people to live in peace and security, and with a standard of living that is in keeping with the dignity of the human person made in the image of his Maker. The human community should strive to insist that the energies and resources of technology be redirected into less destructive channels; more calculated to prevent disease and to improve the quality of life. There is a yearning in the world for its unity, in spite of violence and fragmentation, and it would certainly seem that some sort of instrument, which is bigger than the nation-State, and with international standing, is needed to demand this social accountability from technology and to prevent the misdirection of its resources.

A start of sorts was made in Europe. The EEC was conceived as the beginning of an answer to the self-destruction and deepening crisis of the twentieth century in Europe. The architects wished to discover some wide context in which to live and work at peace; hence the Common Market was designed to interweave commercial processes of different nations and in that way lose the will to tear each other apart and thereby avoid fratricidal war. This was a serious attempt in building the world's first, functioning, post-national society. But a division which was virtually unheard of when the Treaty of Rome was signed – the division between the developed "North" and the developing "South" – has moved forward to the centre of the world's agenda of survival. The world has moved on. Has the EEC moved with it? Will the post-imperial, post-Christian nations, gathered or gathering in the EEC look outwards to their fellow men? Their cultures at least are rooted in a Gospel by which the judgement of God is called down upon those who feast and fill their barns with highly protected cereals and edible fats – while leaving Lazarus to starve at Dives's gate. Perhaps one of the greatest challenges to the community is to add to its task of European pacification the new dimension of planetary justice and peace. An example of how this might function is found in the Supra National Court in Strasbourg where human rights are concerned. In the meantime, if we are to prevent direct or indirect killing, and serve man totally and everywhere, then we have to move from loyalties that are merely nation-centred to loyalties which have as their centre the planetary society.

Perhaps the nation-State problem could be solved by retaining it as an entity within, and subordinate to, the international community, just as local authorities and councils function within the nation-State. In other words, both concepts are not mutually exclusive. In fact they are complementary. All this has been recognised by serious thinkers like More, Bacon, Hobbes, Locke, Kant and Hegel, and Mazzini who said that in order to have internationalism, one must create nations.[102] Nevertheless, it is essential to remember that people are subjects not objects, ends and not means only, and there is no more consoling belief than that we are one family, with one Father, and this one planet is our home. More than ever, all religions and all peoples need to reflect on this broader horizon. Our human solidarity compels us to see the unbreakable connection between the love of God and the love of our neighbour. In this light, killing is fratricide and the deprivation of humanity is a scandal. People are God's children and because of their uniqueness are more important than the shape or group or organisation that contains them. True religion rejects the idea of jingoism or nationalism for its own sake and also the belief that some are born poor and others rich, and that the poor must attribute their poverty to the Will of God when, in fact, it is the injustices...

... between men which are our real problem to be resolved by man, knowing that Christ wants us all to live humanly as befits men, neither sub-humanized by misery, nor dehumanized by riches.[103]

The question of particularism and universalism is raised in Biblical thinking in God's dealing with people and the choice of Israel. The choice is not to be understood exclusively, but inclusively, she is chosen because all are being chosen.[104] Israel is the special case in which the election of all people is to become visible and tangible. So Israel has the burden and grace of election to bear, so that a universal salvation might dawn at last for *all*. It is striking that Jesus limited his activity and that of his disciples, initially at least, to the nation of Israel. It emphasises the link between the nation of Israel and the world. In short, Israel's role or vocation was to be an example – "the light to the Gentiles and a witness to God in the world".[105] This lesson of two thousand years ago has still important implications for our time if direct and indirect killing are to be avoided globally.

Finally, it would be remiss if this chapter failed to acknowledge that the World Council of Churches (WCC) demonstrated its acute awareness of the danger of "national security" or sovereignty back in the middle of the last decade.[106] In the Fifth General Assembly of the WCC in Nairobi its subject was "The World Armaments Situation". It alarmed the Churches into an awareness of growing militarism. In his address to the United Nations First Special Session on Disarmament in 1978, the General Secretary of the WCC, Dr Philip Potter, emphasised the need for new perspectives and elements in the arms situation. In particular, he challenged the prevalence of the concept of "national security" identifying it as a main source of fear and mistrust between nations and peoples. At its meeting in Kingston, Jamaica (1 to 11 January 1979) the WCC Central Committee received the report of the Commission of the Churches for International Affairs (CCIA)[107] which dealt with two basic factors of militarism:

1. The competition of the super-powers and the prevalence of the doctrine of national security.

2. It is the prophetic duty of Christians to unmask and challenge idols of military doctrine and technology in the light of the Christian vision of Justice and Peace. Such idols include:
   – the doctrine of "deterrence" which holds millions of hostages to the threat of nuclear terror and has led to the development of still more terrifying weapons of mass destruction;

– any doctrine of national security that is used to justify militarism and the arms race;
– the doctrine that "qualitative improvements" in military technology will result in reduction of arms...[108]

Only recently, the Working Party on nuclear weapons and the
Christian conscience, under the chairmanship of the Bishop of
Salisbury, which had its origin in the General Synod of the
Church of England (1978) also expressed grave reservations
about the adequacy of the "sovereign State" as a basis for
international relations:

> Many factors in recent history have called in question the adequacy
> of the concept of the sovereign State as a basis for international
> relationship ... One of the chief claims of the sovereign State in
> past centuries has been that each nation has a right to pursue its
> own interests, even if this infringes the rights of others, and to do
> so even by means of armed force.[109]

CONCLUSION

Even though there is some ambivalence here and there in early
Christian writing, the consensus of early Christians was anti-
militaristic and anti-killing.

After Constantine, Christians countenanced Christian participation in war but, even here, some of the Fathers, while
making allowances for the "Just War" theories, kept pacifism
as an absolute rule for monks and clergy. While there was some
argument about killing in self-defence, later, at any rate, it was
justified and so also were capital punishment and war.

It is an alarming fact and a challenge to all, especially Christians, that for the first time in history, the brotherhood of man
has a technical or physical meaning. Never before has the
planet been sufficiently united by technology for people to be
neighbours or nothing. But this proximity makes the earth a
very small place and, oddly enough, because of the advance in
modern warfare and especially because of the new kind of
warfare that is involved with nuclear weapons, man is more
vulnerable than ever. Never before has one part of mankind
enjoyed such an affluent life-style; never before has mankind
been capable of total destruction of itself and the planet. It is
strange logic which justifies vast expenditure on weapons of

total destruction while tolerating, according to one estimate, that 800 million people live in a state of absolute poverty. To direct vital resources to killing directly and indirectly, rather than to development and peace, is a contribution to anarchy and annihilation, rather than to the promotion of peace and progress. The scandalous expenditure on armaments and the menacing threat of nuclear weapons deprive many and threaten all.

Contemporary Christians are extremely rich in relation to the rest of the world. The national communities in which committed and nominal Christians form the vast majority have indeed sufficient resources to prevent starvation throughout the world. Yet the rich North has not stood out as a catalyst and world poverty has not been a vote catcher. Nor has there been collective or political will to redirect technology to the service of the international community. It has been pointed out, and will be developed again in later chapters of this book, that there is no escape from our involvement in this most serious situation because God did not build the human body for starvation. As such, this is a political, economic and religious challenge because we are one community and have a responsibility for our neighbour.

It is evident that modern weapons are more vicious and destructive of human life and more responsible for direct and indirect killing. In the past, war could be morally acceptable provided given principles were upheld. It is questionable whether those principles will now apply to nuclear weapons which, in the opinion of the writer, are not only different in degree but also in kind. This point will be further analyzed in the following chapters.

The present organisation of the international community lends itself to the ever spiralling arms race in conventional and nuclear weapons and, therefore, promotes direct and indirect killing by enormous waste, war and expenditure. The question arises what are we to do about it, how can Christianity address itself to this problem?

PART II

Responses

CHAPTER TWO

Pacifism and the Just War

In the preceding chapter, direct and indirect killings were analyzed and particular attention was given to the principle of the double effect, which is most relevant to war. In this chapter, it is now appropriate to discuss the moral choices in the nuclear debate which have caused conflicting conclusions to emerge within the Church about the use of coercive force in a nuclear age. Both the pacifist tradition and the just war position have played their part in the history of Christianity. Today, as ever, the options are sincerely debated and in particular, the National Conference of Catholic Bishops (NCCB) in America, and in England the Church of England have reflected deeply on the just war theory in regard to the nuclear problem.

FORMS OF PACIFISM

Universal and Selective Pacifism

In recent years many people have advocated unilateral disarmament; they have sometimes been called pacifists or selective pacifists.[1] They are of the just war tradition but find that, while some of the wars of the past could be justified by the principles of the just war, the soundest Christian response to nuclear weapons is to renounce them as morally unacceptable. According to Roszak, nuclear pacifists belong to the same historic ethnic tradition as the supporters of the just war theory, except that they differ in their approach to nuclear weapons.[2] In fact they use the tradition to demonstrate that nuclear war could never be justified.[3] Therefore, they argue that nuclear disarmament is the only alternative to suicidal annihilation. Additionally the arms race should be denounced as it usually leads to war and retaliation, which is inherent in modern warfare and contrary to the Love of Christ.[4] Gordon Zahn charges the just war teaching, on which we have relied so much in the past, as abstract and anachronistic in its conception,[5] a point rejected by Ramsey because modern political systems need the just war theory because:

> It states the limit beyond which war as such, becomes in itself a wholly non-human and non-political activity and the point beyond which military force becomes senseless violence and our weapons no longer weapons of war.[6]

However, there is some agreement between the just war thinkers and the nuclear pacifists on the question of means of war:

> If non-combatants are directly attacked or if there will be far more damage to non-combatants than any probable good that might come from waging war, attacks on non-combatants are immoral.[7]

Nevertheless, the emergence of a visible and articulate pacifist movement within the Christian community in recent years is one of the most significant forces shaping the moral argument about nuclear policies today. Indeed the pacifist challenge to the accepted tradition has become central for the Church as a whole. It reminds all Christians that the original just war question implies that non-violence is the Christian *norm* and that war or force could only be moral by way of exception if at all.[8]

The Non-Violent Tradition

As was noted in the previous chapter, the consensus of early Christians was anti-militaristic, based on Christ's teaching on love of one's neighbour. This witness to non-violence and Christian pacifism runs down through some Church Fathers through Francis of Assisi to Dorothy Day, Martin Luther King, Donald Soper and Trevor Huddleston. Universal pacifism maintains that any use whatever of military force is incompatible with the Christian vocation.[9] This vision is not passive about injustice and the defence of human rights; rather, it affirms and exemplifies what it means to resist injustice through non-violent methods.[10] Today, Christians who are convinced of the necessity and value of non-violent methods of the defence of others and self-defence, seek to demonstrate its usefulness on a wider scale.[11] They indicate that the complete renunciation of the use of violence has been witnessed in Christian tradition from the time of Jesus to the present day. How much the pacificism of the early Christians was totally based on agapé is, of course, a matter of dispute. It has been suggested by some writers that there were other motives which forced the early Christians to withdraw from political and military affairs.[12]

Early Christians, according to Ramsey, avoided military service because soldiers were obliged to worship the emperor and this "refusal to commit idolatry may have been the main motive..."[13] Again it is suggested that early Christianity enjoyed exemption from military service, not because of any conscientious objection to warfare as such, but rather because of their objection to fighting on the Sabbath.[14] Furthermore, the early Christian community was a "small mutual aid society and with little or no responsibility for the political community as a whole".[15] Consequently they had no accountability for the organisation and administration of society, a situation which changed after Constantine. Other writers outline the Christian expectation of the Second Coming and, therefore, their reluctance to get involved in the life and structures about them.[16]

After 180 the situation began to change. Roman soldiers became Christians and Christians served in the army. Finally, the more the army took over the function of a police force, the less problematic army service became.[17] After Constantine, when Christianity became the official religion of the Roman Empire, the situation changed rapidly. Again Christians saw the growing invasion of the Barbarians as not only a threat to the Empire, but to Christianity itself. Therefore, their attitude to war changed.[18]

All the same, while granting the point of these writers, that such motivations influenced early Christians, there can be no doubt, as was indicated in the preceding chapter, that Christian pacifism in the first two centuries was, in the main, a consistent deduction from the new foundation laid by Christ in the lives of men, for a new kind of exercise in intention and practice, of love for every man for whom Christ died.[19]

The non-violent posture in the history of Christianity has always posed a substantial challenge to the whole Christian

community. Those espousing non-violence have called upon
the Church to see this charism as an imperative for all Christians. Some Christian communities, like the Quakers and the
Church of the Brethren, have officially taken this position.

Today, the nuclear problem has, in a very real sense, caused a
re-emergence of support for the pacifist option. From a Catholic point of view this option has been supported by Vatican II
and reaffirmed by the Popes of non-violent witness since the
Council.[20] The Council's clear endorsement of a position of
conscientious objection as a valid Christian position and its call
to evaluate war "with an entirely new attitude" has paved the
way for an extensive investigation into the tradition of Christian pacifism and Christian non-violence. Indeed the statement
in the Council document admits either universal or selective
pacifism. Therefore, an ethical analysis of the nuclear problem,
that seeks its roots in the central religious identity of Christianity, must acknowledge that the values of peace and non-
violence make urgent demands and, as the United States
Catholic bishops stated, this "non-violent tradition must be
part of the discussion".[21]

James Douglass believes that the nuclear age is leading
Christians to a pacifist position through a rethinking of the
question of justice and the just war.

> The basic concern of the just war theory is not that we should make
> war but rather that we should make justice, justice conceived in an
> international sense. War, as the physical factor in the theory, must
> give way to justice as the ruling moral principle.[22]

The Rev J. Bryan Hehir (Director of the United States Catholic
Conference Office of International Justice and Peace Commission) aptly remarks that after the death of Pius XII one finds a
shift in Catholic thought. Conscientious objection was made
acceptable at Vatican II, and pacifism is now a legal Catholic
option.[23]

The theory of the just war which has always affirmed recourse to war under certain conditions and having a necessary
police function in international society, must now, in order to
rule out the injustice of mass murder and global destruction,
act as a brake against all recourse to war. The theory, therefore,
is compelled by its own doctrine to reject nuclear war "as a

possible instrument of justice".[24] Now the conflict between
nuclear warfare (and some would add certain forms of modern
warfare, like chemical and biological weapons) and justice is
the basis of the contemporary argument. That is to say, from
the criteria of the just war theory some Christians are forced to
nuclear pacifism.[25] This, therefore, brings us to an examination
of the theory itself and at the same time reminds us of the
important challenge presented by pacifism, namely, that non-
violence for the Christian is the norm or what some thinkers
call the "prima facie obligation" of non-violence.[26] In other
words, thinkers like Douglass, D. Hollenbach, J. Childress
and James T. Johnson, amongst others, in a number of fine
studies on the just war criteria, remind us that its principles are
not for the legitimising or glorification of war but rather for the
limitation of it. War was to be the exception, even in the pursuit
of justice. War was tolerated in certain circumstances under
well defined principles.[27] When justice and non-violence are
not simultaneously realisable, the theory is willing to grant
priority to justice within narrow boundaries. Accordingly
"pacifists and non-pacifist and Just War Christians have something profoundly in common: a searching distrust of
violence".[28] This thinking is also expressed by the American
bishops:

> Just War teaching has evolved, however, as an effort to prevent
> war; only if war cannot be rationally avoided does the teaching
> then seek to restrict and reduce its horrors...
>   Objection to war – all war – must be the norm for all sane
> people.[29]

Having regard to all this, it is difficult to reconcile the fact that
in Catholic thinking a pacifist attitude as well as conscientious
objection was not tolerated until after the death of Pius XII.
One only has to recall the classic case of Franz Jagerstatter's
refusal to participate in Hitler's wars; he was opposed by the
Catholic Church.

THE JUST WAR THEORY

The alternative moral response, therefore, to pacifism is the
just war position. Both the United States Catholic bishops and
the Working Party of the Church of England use the just war

criteria in their evaluation of nuclear weapons. Both cases will
be considered in the following chapter but, in the meantime, it
will be necessary to examine the origin and principles of theory
itself.

Origin

The moral intuitions to which international law gives legal
expression were first stated and developed in the ethical doctrine of the just war. The doctrine expresses the conviction of a
long line of thinkers and begins with the same presumption as a
pacifist position, namely, we should love our neighbour, and
our enemy is the key test of that love. The thinking does not
seek to legitimise war and still less to glorify it, but recognises
that, in certain cases, armed force cannot be ruled out. Consequently, a refined set of moral categories have been developed
about the possible justification of violence in pursuit of justice.

The major thrust for the full development of a Christian
ethic of war came from Augustine though Ambrose had
already made some contribution who, in turn, followed Cicero
and others. But St Augustine added further dimensions and
conditions. What Ambrose sketched, Augustine amplified. He
was aware of sin and its consequence in history, and war was
one such consequence. War arose from disordered ambitions
but it could also be used in some cases at least to restrain evil
and protect the innocent. Therefore, he claimed it could be
reconciled with Christian belief.[30] Faced with the fact of an
attack on the innocent, the presumption that we should love
and do no harm, even to our enemy, yielded to the command of
love understood as the need to restrain an enemy who would
injure the innocent. Later in his writings, Augustine considered the effects of war and emphasises the aim of peace.[31] He
also stressed that war should be waged only as a necessity.[32]
The just war tradition has been formulated in different ways in
the history of Christianity but the Augustine insight remains
the central premise.[33]

The defence of others was expanded to include self-defence
by Thomas Aquinas and this is referred to in the preceding
chapter. Aquinas summarises the main points of Augustine's
teaching.[34] War must be waged by a legitimate authority and
there must be a just cause and right intention. Moreover, it is
never lawful to kill the innocent. This became accepted in

Christian morality. In war, non-combatant civilians are considered to be innocent and may not be directly attacked. This is
now called the "Principle of Discrimination".[35] In the twentieth century, Christians have used this thinking to articulate a
right of defence for states in a decentralized international
order, where there is no international authority to keep the
peace.[36] In short, Aquinas put into a more structured form the
insights of Ambrose and Augustine. Aquinas was followed in
his reflection on war by Gratian and by the theologians, Francisco de Vitoria and Francisco Suarez. De Vitoria in *De Jure
Belli* emphasized the more significant obligation to preserve
peace and fight only when necessary; whereas, Suarez in *De
Legibus* focuses on the means by which war is conducted. Even
if war is not evil, it can become evil because of the way it is
fought.[37]

Criteria

The just war criteria are broadly expressed in two groups: jus
ad bellum which determines whether the alleged grounds for
the initiation of armed force are sufficiently grave to over-ride
the prima-facie obligation of non-violence; and jus in bello
which governs the means by which war can be morally conducted.

The theory of the just war is posed by the NCCB as three
questions:

WHY? – (For what reasons) can force be used.

HOW? – (By what means) can force be used.

WHEN? – (Under what conditions) can force be used.[38]

JUS AD BELLUM   The norms which will apply in determin-
ing Ad Bellum can be stated thus:

Legitimate Authority—War has to be declared by a legitimate
authority. It can only be justified as an act of justice undertaken
by those in charge of the care of the common good, and public
order, and not by private groups or individuals. There are
serious problems here because of the international character of
the NATO decision making processes. Again, experts fear that
command control and communication (described officially as
C^3) might be interrupted by the effects of nuclear war. In that

case subordinate commanders might be left unrestricted and unrestrained. In this new kind of war there are many vulnerabilities.[39]

The NCCB further notes that the matter of competent authority...

... becomes particularly important in conditions of revolutionary war – an oppressive government may lose its claim to legitimacy. Insufficient analytical attention has been given to the moral issues of revolutionary or unconventional warfare. A Just War framework for conflicts of this nature is sorely needed.[40]

Just Cause—War may be employed only to confront a real and certain injury, such as protection of innocent lives or the securing of justice and human rights. Because of the horrific scale of modern war, some authorities, including the United Nations and the Roman Catholic Church, now limit war to legitimate defence against aggression.[41]

Right Intention—Ultimately, a just and lasting peace, including avoidance of unnecessary destructive acts, must be intended.

Last Resort—Peaceful and other reasonable means must have been tried. Some categories also include a declaration of war – in effect, a way of ensuring that it is the last resort.

Reasonable Hope of Success—There should be reasonable expectation of doing more good than harm, otherwise it is futile to initiate force in the first place.

Proportionality—The damage inflicted must be in proportion to the good expected, otherwise the evil effects will outweigh the good. The values of life, freedom and justice, which are achieved, must be greater than the death, suffering, and social upheaval that the war produces. In today's interdependent world, even a local conflict can affect people everywhere; this is particularly the case where nuclear powers are involved.

JUS IN BELLO   The Jus In Bello criteria judge the morality of the particular means or conduct of war. In other words, they assess the moral behaviour of the combatants. There are really two principles, which are discrimination and proportion. The latter has already been used in the Ad Bellum criteria and also plays an important part in the In Bello context. Discrimination states that non-combatants are innocent people and, therefore, have immunity. That means non-combatants must be immune from direct attack.[42] Proportionality requires that a war must not result in harm and devastation which outweigh the good intended.

This principle of proportionality takes on a special significance, precisely because the indirect or collateral damage of nuclear war, and other forms of modern war, can be enormous. The principle provides a second restraint on such actions. For example, a strategy or tactic may be "disproportionate" even if it is not "indiscriminate" i.e. aimed directly at the citizens. It can be said that these two principles are an application of the more general principles already mentioned in this book, namely that a good end does not justify every means. There are things one should not do even in pursuit of a good aim. Perhaps it might be as well here to examine these two principles in greater detail.

The Principle of Discrimination—As already stated, the principles we have looked at strive to protect the innocent and to confine, as far as possible, the damage of war to those actively engaged in it. The fundamental distinction between combatants and non-combatants is not only upheld by Christian teaching but also by international law.[43] In doing so the law draws upon a deep-rooted moral conviction that it is immoral to attack anyone who is not attacking or intending to attack you. The non-combatant immunity is based on the general moral principle that it is wrong to kill innocent people. To directly kill such people is murder. What the principle of discrimination rules out in war is action that is taken intentionally against non-combatants by armed force; nor can the military objective be achieved by means of their deaths. For example, when there is "blanket bombing" of cities or highly populated areas, the principle of discrimination is infringed.[44]

While it is true that there are borderline cases regarding combatants and non-combatants there are people who are non-combatants like the mentally-handicapped, nursing

mothers and babies who, by any standards, can be classed as
non-combatants no matter how "innocent" is defined. Justice
demands that those who do not make war should not have war
made on them. This does not mean to say that non-combatants
can never be killed in war. Unfortunately, this is often an effect
which is indirect in armed conflict and is considered, as we
have seen, as indirect killing governed by the principle of the
double effect. This question of indirect killing and its extent
brings us to the principle of proportionality in the conduct of
war.

The Principle of Proportionality—It was Francis de Vitoria in
the sixteenth century who underlined the belief in the brotherhood of man and appealed to proportionality in war. A war, he
said, is unjust if it is foreseen that it will lead to devastation and
the slaughter of many people.[45] It requires that an action must
be an appropriate means of achieving the end. A desire to limit
harm is certainly behind the principle. It will be clear that there
are many difficulties in applying this principle because it is so
relative. With regard to nuclear war, major conflict with incal-
culable consequences for the whole world, will be considered
by some people a proportionately greater evil than any good it
was attempting to achieve. The risk of nuclear escalation means
that any application of this principle involves a guess of how
the conflict will develop. The NCCB and the Working Party of
the Church of England claim that any use of nuclear weapons
would fail the test under the principle of proportionality. Thus
Anthony Kenny recently wrote that there could be a considerable difference in the number of casualties involved in a
"counter-force" strategy (that is to say one aimed at military
targets) and a "counter-value" strategy (one in which there
were civilian targets). He quotes figures which indicate that in
the latter case the loss of life in Western Europe would amount
to 215 million dead, whereas in the former approach, this
figure could be reduced to 25 million – and concludes that this
claim...

> ... that counter-force strategy of this kind does not involve an
> attack on civilian populations is like claiming not to be responsible
> for the death of a friend if one shoots a bullet to kill a mosquito
> perched on his throat.[46]

The point Kenny is making is the total lack of proportion in all such killing.

Additionally, it should be remembered that indirect killing, even when it results from legitimate bombing and not intended but merely permitted, can still offend the principle of proportionality. This applies irrespective of which school of theology one follows. If, for example, nuclear bombs are aimed at a military target in a highly populated area, the deaths of the innocent people can be classified indirect but, in reality, they become part of the *direct* killing.

The question is whether it is psychologically and honestly possible to avoid the direct intent of killing which seems to be implicit in the choice of a particular weapon. There comes a point where the immediate evil effects of a given action are so overwhelmingly large in their physical extent and mere bulk, by comparison with the immediate good, that it no longer makes sense to say that it is merely indirectly and not directly intended. Commonsense repudiates any attempt to classify this massive killing as indirect or incidental; no matter how one might wriggle or reason otherwise; these effects must be classified as directly intended.

Moreover, in the above situation, the principle of discrimination is also violated. Some, however, claim that the use of nuclear weapons can be justified in certain situations when the weapons are aimed at military targets and are *limited* in such a way as not to produce disproportionate collateral damage. Furthermore, they claim this does not involve direct attacks on non-combatants and can meet the criteria of the just war.[47] This so called "limited nuclear exchange" did not impress the NCCB nor the Working Party of the Church of England. Both point out the problem of radiation and other disastrous effects as well as the danger of escalation. Indeed it could be added that large scale hostilities in Europe would probably produce unacceptable levels of civilian casualties, collateral damage and huge non-combatant losses. This would also seem to hold even if modern conventional weapons were used.

CONCLUSION

It is clear that the non-violent tradition of Christian thinking would obviously oppose all use of nuclear weapons under any conditions. These weapons simply confirm and reaffirm one of the insights of the non-violent position, namely that Christians should not use violence because it is contrary to agapé (love). They believe that to use violence, even selectively, is an illusion. Besides these universal pacifists who object to all wars, there are, nevertheless, selective pacifists who do object to some wars, such as the Vietnam conflict. In addition, there is now a growing number of nuclear pacifists who would hold that any nuclear war is morally unacceptable. It seems even on just war principles, some Christians, like the NCCB and the Working Party of the Church of England feel obliged to adopt this stance. Some writers believe that this position will lead to a recovery of the early Church's commitment to non-violence. Perhaps all this thinking can be summarised in one question: Can the use of nuclear weapons ever be a reasonable means to the attainment of justice?

CHAPTER THREE

The Ecumenical Response

ECUMENICAL APPROACH

One of the most historic changes in late twentieth-century United States history is the groundswell within the Catholic community against United States militarism and nuclear dominated national security mentality.[1] Some would hold, as in *Commonweal*, that the document the United States bishops prepared, *The Challenge of Peace: God's Promise and Our Response*, is: "The most serious effort the Church has ever made, here, abroad or in the Vatican, to come to grips with nuclear war."[2]

However, the questions concerning the arms race and disarmament, nuclear war and peace, have been a major concern of the Catholic Church, and indeed the World Council of Churches (WCC), over the past 30 years. In the Papal and Conciliar teaching, as well as that of the WCC, these important topics have been hammered out again and again and the concern of the Christian Churches has been expressed to political leaders and statesmen, their own members and indeed all people of goodwill, so that each one can take up the responsibility which is properly theirs as members of the human race, and thereby strive to contribute with discernment and sensitivity to the building of a world marked by peace, freedom and universal brotherhood.

The object of Chapter Four is to analyze the position of the United States Catholic Church and its bishops on these important and complex questions. I will also try, in Chapter Five, to demonstrate the moral perspectives and posture of the Church of England with regard to nuclear deterrence and with particular reference to its working document, *The Church and The Bomb* and the reaction it caused in the General Synod.

Since the statements of the WCC, the Popes and Vatican II have greatly influenced the whole Christian community, it will be useful to consider first some of the major statements that have been issued by these bodies.

The teaching of each body stands on its own merits and the texts are arranged chronologically from 1948 to 1981. From the First General Assembly, the WCC and its different official channels have issued 30 major statements. Likewise, some of the major statements of the Popes, from Pius XII to John Paul II, will be considered and the common trends that appear will be noted, such as the emphasis on peace, on international authority as a peace-keeper, war and especially nuclear war, the arms race and the neglect of the hungry millions. The WCC has called the attention of the world leaders to the responsibility and necessity of working for peace. Indeed the ecumenical collaboration that has taken place between the Pontifical Commission for Justice and Peace (PCJP), on behalf of the Holy See, and the Commission of the Churches on International Affairs (CCIA), on behalf of the WCC has been remarkable and inspiring. They have worked together to alert the whole Christian community during the entire post-Second World War era about these difficult problems. Moreover, they have jointly published a most useful document containing many of the official statements of the WCC, the Popes and Vatican II on the arms race, disarmament and nuclear weapons, to which I am greatly indebted.[3] The efforts of these official bodies will be seen as a serious attempt to inform Christian communities, and others, of the Church's pastoral concern and to . . .

> . . . deepen reflection, instruct consciences and inspire action that will contribute to making this a world in which peace is found by turning away from the arms race, by fostering meaningful disarmament and the peaceful solution of conflicts, by promoting justice, equality and human dignity, and by forging the bonds of mutual respect, confidence and responsibility among nations.[4]

WORLD COUNCIL OF CHURCHES

Preamble to Amsterdam

The study materials prepared for the Conference included a volume on *The Church and International Disorder*.[5] A call is made for an international instrument or authority to act as a referee amongst the nation-States. This is one of the first references that I can discover amongst the Churches regarding the idea of world government. Van Asbeck goes on to suggest that the Church should support this idea and awaken peoples' consciences about it. He states that the United Nations is facing in the right direction but that it needs vast improvement. He also stresses that our salvation in a nuclear age is not in the nation-State concept but in international law.

Accordingly, McFadden, commenting on this work, in an unpublished thesis, says:

> The goals of the Church . . . should include lessening the prestige of national sovereignty (the idolatry of nationalism) and promote an international law between nations.[6]

Indeed he holds that the ecumenical movement can serve as a model and make a considerable contribution in this regard. This point of national sovereignty was again taken up by the Fifth General Assembly of the WCC, as stated earlier (Chapter 1).

First Assembly – Amsterdam (1948–53)

In Amsterdam, September 1948, the First Assembly of the WCC, under the heading "War is Contrary to the Will of God" put forward three broad positions:

1. There are those that hold that, even though entering a war may be a Christian's duty in particular circumstances, modern warfare, with its mass destruction, can never be an act of justice.

2. In the absence of impartial supra-national institutions, there are those that hold that military action is the ultimate sanction of the rule of law, and that citizens must be distinctly taught that it is their duty to defend the law by force if necessary.

3. Others, again, refuse military service of all kinds, convinced that an absolute witness against war and for peace is for them the will of God, and they desire that the Church should speak to the same effect.

> We must frankly acknowledge our deep sense of perplexity in the face of these conflicting opinions.[7]

And so it is that the First Assembly immediately recognised the horror of nuclear weapons and indeed the destructiveness of conventional weapons, as well as some of the agonizing problems that are attached to them. Here the WCC did not consider nuclear and conventional weapons as separate problems. It expressed also: "A strong agreement with the progressive reduction and eventual abolition of all national armaments, including atomic weapons and all weapons of mass destruction..."[8] In its report for 1950–51, the CCIA appealed for generous assistance by rich nations for the poor nations.[9]

Second Assembly – Evanston (1954–60)
In Evanston, 1954, the WCC appealed for:

> The prohibition of all weapons of mass destruction under the provision of international inspection and control along with the reduction of all other types of armaments.[10]

It proceeds to assert that international order of truth and peace would require:

> Under effective international inspection and control in such a way that no state would have cause to fear that its security was endangered, the elimination and prohibition of atomic, hydrogen and all other weapons of mass destruction, as well as the reduction of all armaments to a minimum.[11]

> We first of all call upon the nations to pledge that they will refrain from the threat or use of the hydrogen, atomic, and all other weapons of mass destruction as well as any other means of force against the territorial integrity or political independence of any state.[12]

> We must also see that experimental tests of hydrogen bombs have raised issues of human rights, causing suffering and imposed an additional strain on human relations between nations. Among safeguards against the aggravation of these international tensions is the insistence that nations carry on tests only within their respective territories or, if elsewhere, by international clearance and agreement.[13]

> The Churches must condemn the deliberate mass destruction of civilians in open cities by whatever means and for whatever purpose.[14]

The Executive Committee of the WCC reiterated its conviction of an overall strategy to halt the nuclear build-up and
asked Christians in the states conducting nuclear tests to urge
their governments to *"unilaterally abstain* from testing for a
trial period in order to create the necessary confidence for an
international agreement on this subject".[15] There was, however, disagreement on this statement in the WCC Central
Committee.

In August 1958, the WCC Central Committee Meeting put
forward three proposals:

1. The main concern must always be the prevention of war itself,
   for the evil of war is an offence to the spiritual nature of man.

2. The objectives of a strategy to combat the menace of atomic war
   are interrelated and interdependent, such as ceasing tests, halting production, reducing existing armaments with provision for
   warning against surprise attacks, the peaceful uses of atomic
   energy, peaceful settlement and peaceful change.

3. If persistent efforts bring no sufficient agreement on any of the
   interrelated objectives, partial agreements should be seriously
   explored and, if need be, reasonable risks should be taken to
   advance the objectives which must continue to stand as interdependent.

   Under the third principle, the proposal that governments
   should forego testing for a trial period was advanced as a recognised and reasonable risk.[16]

This statement was widely quoted and used throughout the
world and suspension of tests seemed more and more justified
for the following reasons:

a. To prevent the increase of radioactivity in the atmosphere.

b. To get started on mutual inspection which will be needed in
   other areas of disarmament.

c. To limit the danger of an uncontrolled spread of atomic
   armaments.[17]

Third Assembly – Delhi (1961–67)
The resumption of nuclear tests, as well as any use of weapons
which killed indiscriminately, were condemned and the
Assembly emphasised...

... that the use of nuclear weapons, or other forms of major violence, against centres of population is in no circumstances reconcilable with the demands of the Christian Gospel.[18]

And:

To halt the arms race is imperative.[19]

So that, once again, the Council insists that complete and general disarmament was still the accepted goal. It recognised the struggle for world development "as a great opportunity for constructive action and a sign of hope".[20]

And so it is that development and disarmament were linked explicitly by the WCC early in December 1961, and reference to this had already been made in the CCIA Annual Report (1951).

In an appeal to all governments and peoples in December 1961, the WCC said:

There is a great opportunity for constructive action in the struggle for world development. To share the benefits of civilisation with the whole of humanity is a noble and attainable objective. To press the war against poverty, disease, exploitation and ignorance calls for greater sacrifice and for greater commitment of scientific education and material sources than hitherto. In this common task, let the people find a positive programme for peace, a moral equivalent for war.[21]

Indeed in the same year, Pope John XXIII said likewise in the encyclical "Mater et Magistra".[22] Evidently the message of the WCC and the Papacy is similar and probably explained by some sort of cross-fertilization in Christian thinking which was influenced by the same kind of forces.

No significant progress in disarmament had been made when the WCC Central Committee Meeting (in Enugu, Eastern Nigeria) recognised in January 1965 that there was little hope that the limited Test Ban Treaty could be extended to include underground testing. It suggested steps for the limitation of nuclear striking and delivery power, made a plea to establish nuclear-free zones and prevent proliferation of nuclear weapons, and once again suggested diverting the money spent on arms production to the assistance of the developing countries.[23]

Fourth Assembly Period (1968–74)

This reaffirmed (at Uppsala in Sweden) the Declaration of the Amsterdam Assembly.

It was declared that it was the responsibility of the Churches to press for the prevention of war, to halt the arms race, and the cessation of production of weapons of mass human destruction by chemical and biological means; and, especially, it advocated the abandonment of the initial use of nuclear weapons, probably referring to the established NATO strategy called "Flexibility in Response". Therefore, as early as July 1968, the WCC was prophetically calling governments to foreswear the nuclear first-use.[24]

In August 1974, in the statement "The Economic Threat to Peace", the CCIA Executive Committee (which met in West Berlin) once more drew attention to the world's poor because "resources and skill are lavished on the extravagant and lethal accumulation of weapons of destruction".[25] The statement called upon the WCC member Churches to fully support and work for the establishment of a new international economic order which had been solemnly proclaimed by the Sixth Special Session of the General Assembly of the United Nations.

A memorandum on disarmament issued by the CCIA Executive Committee (during its meeting in Geneva) in June 1975, underlined the over-riding priority given by governments to defence and security. It referred to the arms race, propelled by the arms trade and called for an absolute ban on both the use and production of new and even more sophisticated means of indiscriminate destruction, however nominally conventional.

Fifth General Assembly – Nairobi (1975–82)

In his address to the United Nations First Special Session on Disarmament on 12 June 1978, Dr Philip Potter, as we have seen (Chapter One), once more mentioned the question of national security:

We must challenge the idol of a distorted concept of national security which is directed to encouraging fear and mistrust resulting in greater insecurity. The only security worthy of its name lies in enabling people to participate fully in the life of their nation and to establish relations of trust between peoples of different nations. It is only when there is real dialogue – a sharing of life with life in mutual trust and respect – that there can be true security.[26]

Disarmament is not the affair of statesmen and experts only, but of every man and woman of every nation. We are dealing here with the issues of life and death for humankind.[27]

PAPAL AND CONCILIAR DOCUMENTS

Pius XII (1939–58)

From Pius XII to the present Pope, there have been nearly 80 Papal statements and texts, not to mention Vatican II. The question of disarmament, the arms race, nuclear war and peace have been the major concerns of this time. The teaching of Pius XII is a classical expression of the theology of the just war from Augustine to his own time. He seemed to fit the new weapons into the just war framework – an attempt which still exists among Churches and moralists today.[28] Pius did not seem to think that nuclear weapons were *qualitatively* different in the history of weaponry, nor did he rule out in principle the use of nuclear weapons. Rather he assessed them in terms of the principle of proportionality and the principle of discrimination.[29] In particular he did not support conscientious objection; indeed this had to wait until Vatican II for its justification. So, in his statements, there was no room for the Catholic pacifist position. In his encyclical "Summi Maeroris" Pius emphasised the inhumanity of the new weaponry and speaks of the possibility of its annihilating effects and refers to non-combatants:

Let them all remember what war brings in its wake, as we know only too well from experience – nothing but ruin, death and every sort of misery. With the progress of time, technology has introduced and prepared such murderous and inhuman weapons as can destroy not only armies and fleets, not only cities, towns and villages, not only the treasures of religion, art and culture, but also innocent children with their mothers, those who are sick and the helpless aged.

Whatever the genius of man has produced that is beautiful and good and holy, all of this can be practically annihilated. But if a war, especially today, appears to every honest observer as something terrifying and deadly, there is yet reason to hope – through the efforts of all people and particularly of their rulers – that the dark and menacing clouds which presently cause such trepidation may pass away, and that true peace may finally reign among nations.[30]

At other times, as noted, he also referred to the distinction between combatants and non-combatants though the distinction lacked sharpness.[31]

The waste of resources and energy which the arms race entails is rejected, but Pius states that the use of force to repel an unjust aggressor is a right and a duty. It is, however, limited by proportionality between the means used and the ends achieved.[32] Pius XII was one of the first to be aware of the new situation which signalled the interdependent world and demanded international authority to co-ordinate the interaction of sovereign states – a point already mentioned implicitly in his Christmas Message 1956:

Although the United Nations' condemnation of the grave violations of the rights of men and entire nations is worthy of recognition, one can nevertheless wish that, in similar cases, the exercise of their rights, as members of this organisation, be denied to states which refuse even the admission of observers – thus showing that their concept of state sovereignty threatens the very foundations of the United Nations. This organisation ought also to have the right and power of forestalling all military intervention of one state in another, whatever the pretext under which it is effected, and also the right and power of assuming, by means of a sufficient police force, the safeguarding of order in the state which is threatened.[33]

This point was explicitly supported later by Pope John XXIII[34] and Pope Paul VI.[35]

In his Christmas Message 1954, Pius XII said: "No people, furthermore, could support indefinitely a race of armaments without disastrous repercussions being felt in its normal economic development."[36] And, in his address to the World Medical Association (WMA), he condemned nuclear warfare: "When it entirely escapes the control of man and results in pure and simple annihilation of human life within radius of action."[37]

John XXIII (1958-63)

Like his predecessors, John XXIII denounced the arms race and the stockpiling of weapons, but he introduced a new development. For him nuclear weapons were *qualitatively* different and introduced, therefore, new moral problems. In his Christmas message of December 1959 on his reflections on peace, he mentions obstacles to this gift of God which is peace and lists social injustice and poverty:

> It will be necessary again and again to remove the obstacles erected by the malice of man. And the presence of these obstacles is noted in the propaganda of immorality in social injustice, in involuntary unemployment, in poverty contrasted with the luxury of those who can indulge in dissipation, in the dreadful lack of proportion between the technical and moral progress of nations, and in the unchecked armaments race, where there has yet to be a glimpse of a serious possibility of solving the problem of disarmament.[38]

He stressed the necessity of resolving the contradiction that exists between the spectre of misery and hunger and those scientific discoveries which provide ruin and death:

> On the one hand we are shown the fearful spectre of want and misery which threatens to extinguish human life, and on the other hand we find that scientific discoveries, technical inventions and economic resources are being used to provide terrible instruments of ruin and death.[39]

John is disturbed by the fact that so much is spent on enormous stocks of arms while other places are deprived "of the collaboration they need in order to make economic and social progress".[40] In fact, his encyclical "Pacem in Terris", published in April 1963, was one of the most remarkable documents on social theory to have been published in the history of the Church. He argues that humanity has reached a stage of development where a world government is now required to maintain universal peace.[41]

The encyclical itself is a veritable textbook of fundamental human rights in regard to truth, justice, freedom and brotherly love with their corresponding duties. He stresses the right to life, bodily integrity and the right to means suitable for decent living.[42]

Aid should be given to the Third World without strings.[43] Because of the nature of nuclear war, it can be referred to no longer as a suitable way of restoring violated rights:

> It can happen, and indeed does happen, that clashes of interests develop between states. The solution of these should be sought not in recourse to arms, nor in underhand and deceitful ways, but in a manner worthy of human beings: through mutual appreciation of arguments and attitudes, giving mature consideration to all points, weighing them in the balance of truth and resolving differences fairly.

> Admittedly, the conviction has arisen mainly from a realisation of the terrifying power of mass destruction possessed by modern weapons of war and from a dread of the disasters and frightful devastation which would result from their use; but it leads to the conclusion that in our day, which enjoys the glory of possessing atomic power, it is unthinkable that war can any longer be regarded as a suitable way of restoring rights which have been violated.[44]

Once more, in "Pacem in Terris", he refers to world poverty and the scandal of the arms race:

> Against this we must set the immense grief which overwhelms us as we observe how, in those states which have made the greatest economic progress, gigantic stocks of arms have been assembled and are still being piled up, and that the fullest resources of mind and body are being devoted to the process. The result is that the citizens of these countries must bear heavy burdens whilst other nations go without the help they require for their social and economic progress.[45]

Without ever rejecting the assessment made by Pope Pius XII of nuclear weapons in terms of proportionality, "Pacem in Terris" conveys a much harsher judgement on nuclear war and is obviously taken by the fact that there is a qualitatively new situation.[46] John even omits any reference to the standard principle that nations possess the right of legitimate defence. The nearest he comes to it is when he speaks of nations and deterrents:

> Alas, however, nations are often led by fear to spend astronomical sums on defence. They protest that they do so – and there is no

reason to doubt their word – not with aggressive intentions but to deter others from attacking them.[47]

Whilst he observes the fact that nations spend much on defence, he does not explicitly condone it but goes on to hope "that nations will build up more friendly connections and agreements".[48] In fact, "Pacem in Terris" provides no explicit endorsement of the right of self-defence by people and states. This fact is exceptional.

Since the world is producing new problems, it requires new solutions. The common good of all nations requires some sort of world government which should come into being by universal consent.[49] This world government should be directed towards the preservation of human rights and universal peace.

Vatican II (1962–65) "Gaudium et Spes"
Though it reiterated much of the Papal teaching the pastoral letter, Constitution of the Church in the Modern World, came out in favour of a government's right to legitimate defence. However, it added one new feature, namely, the right of conscientious objection:

> Moreover it seems right that laws make humane provisions for the case of those who, for reasons of conscience, refuse to bear arms, provided however that they accept some other form of service to the human community.[50]

Therefore, the Council established, alongside the just war position, an option of Catholic pacifism. By supporting the moral argument for legitimate defence, it continues the debate of what is legitimate. Indeed the purpose of the just war theory has been an attempt to answer this question since the time of Augustine. The Council condemns total war and weapons that are indiscriminately aimed at the destruction of entire cities along with their population. A point made by the WCC in its Second Assembly,[51] August 1954. Whilst succinctly stating the moral dilemma posed by deterrents, the Vatican Council chooses not to make a final judgement. We are, therefore, left with the problem. However, it can be said that, in general, a decisive shift comes in the whole approach to war. This can be detected in "Pacem in Terris" and is now crystallised in more cogent categories of analysis. The Council argued that a whole "new attitude to war" is demanded. Obviously attitudes have been changed by this new kind of warfare.[52]

Paul VI (1963–78)

An outstanding apostle of peace, Paul VI introduced the Annual Day of Prayer for Peace throughout the Catholic Church. He was also the first Pope to address the United Nations.[53]

His plea in Bombay (December 1964) is noteworthy for calling on a nation...

> ... to contribute part of its expenditure for arms to a great world fund for the relief of the many problems of nutrition, clothing, shelter and medical care which affects so many peoples.[54]

This plea was later repeated in his encyclical "Populorum Progressio".[55] Only a world-wide collaboration, he says, of which the common fund would be a means and symbol, will succeed in establishing peaceful existence between peoples. The encyclical lays great emphasis on development in all its forms, speaks of the duty of human solidarity, distribution of wealth, the unity of the world and the problem of world hunger. It was in this encyclical that the famous phrase was introduced, namely, that development was the new name for peace.

Above all, Paul VI was convinced that peace had to be built upon a profound change of heart and mentality. More and more he points to what is at the heart of the crisis of contemporary human life; it is a crisis of hope in the face of a kind of progress that threatens to turn against its very authors. Here, he seems to imply that technology can become an evil structure:

> We live in an era of hope. It is, however, a hope in the kingdom of this earth, a hope in human self-sufficiency. And it is precisely in our day that this hope is undergoing a most serious crisis.

> Before the gaze of contemporary man, a grandiose and complex phenomenon emerges. First of all, prosperity itself, built-up by intelligent and painful human efforts, easily becomes a source of even greater evils. Progress itself, in some fields, creates enormous and terrible dangers for all humanity. The use which modern

man can make of the murderous forces which he has mastered no longer raises hope on the horizon, but heavy clouds of terror and folly.[56]

Once again, an appeal is made for an effective world authority.

John Paul II (1979–)

The present Pope brings his own distinctive style to the debate and condemns the arms race and the diversion of resources from hungry people. He emphasises the horror of nuclear and conventional warfare. At Coventry, 30 May 1982, he stated that modern warfare is totally unacceptable as a means of settling differences between nations:

> Wherever the strong exploit the weak: wherever the rich take advantage of the poor; wherever great powers seek to dominate and to impose ideologies, then the work of making peace is undone; there the cathedral of peace is again destroyed. Today, the scale and horror of modern warfare – whether nuclear or not – makes it totally unacceptable as a means of settling differences between nations. War should belong to the tragic past, to history; it should find no place on humanity's agenda for the future.[57]

However, John Paul seemed to modify his position later in regard to nuclear deterrence. For example, in his address to the United Nations Special Session on Disarmament, he says:

> In certain conditions "deterrents" based on balance, certainly not as an end in itself, but as a step on the way towards progressive disarmament, may be judged morally acceptable.[58]

The debate is not taken further and we are left with the problem of the possession of nuclear weapons as a deterrent. Vatican II was also ambivalent in this matter. It did not endorse the nuclear deterrent, nor did it condemn it. It simply acknowledged that: "Many regard this state of affairs as the most effective way by which peace of a sort can be maintained."[59]

CONCLUSION

It is evident that the Churches at the highest levels have tirelessly tried to teach and alert the worldwide Christian

conscience about war and peace. They have wrestled with the
agonizing problems that have increased during the nuclear
era with its threat to peace and the survival of the human
race.

In particular, the CCIA called for assistance to poor countries and reduction of arms as early as 1950–1. This appeal came
in the First Assembly Period of the WCC and seems to be the
first of its kind in official Church documents. The same point
was repeated by John XXIII in 1961 and later in 1963 in his
letter *Peace on Earth*. Indeed the diversion of valuable resources from the Third World to the arms race has now become a central theme in official Church documents.

Again, in the early 1950s, both the WCC and Pius XII were
referring to international inspection of armaments and international control of some form to co-ordinate the interaction of
sovereign states in an independent world. In the Second
Assembly, the CCIA appealed for unilateral abstention from
nuclear testing, noting at the same time the question of radiation and genetic effects even for the unborn.

The arms race was rejected from the beginning – the WCC,
Pius XII and John XXIII all indicated its madness and abuse.
Later John XXIII made explicit his feelings about it, especially
the scandal where the hungry millions were concerned, in both
"Mater et Magistra" and *Peace on Earth*.

Finally, the use of indiscriminate weapons and those
weapons aimed at population centres were noted as morally
unacceptable in the early 1960s by the Vatican Council and the
WCC. Even in July 1950, Pius XII had anguished about the
terrible potential of the new weapons to destroy, not only
towns, villages and cities, but also non-combatants because of
their powers of annihilation. The questions of international
authority, the sovereign State and armed conflict have also
been subjects of much reflection. As early as July 1968 the
WCC was calling for governments to forswear the first-use of
the nuclear weapon. The problem of the nation or sovereign
State is highlighted by the WCC on more than one occasion,
by the Popes and the Vatican Council; hence the local Churches had a very useful framework from which to start. As
Cardinal Bernardin, the chairman of the ad hoc Committee on
War and Peace of the NCCB said in his address to the bishops
in November 1981:

We do not start from scratch. As religious leaders in a nation which possesses an awesome arsenal of destructive powers, we are heirs of a body of moral teaching from the universal Church, and we ourselves have contributed to that teaching by our previous statements on war and peace.[60]

With these thoughts in mind, we can now proceed to examine the position of the NCCB and the Church of England on the nuclear problem. The framework of Church documentation has not produced one moral posture on this position but has resulted in a series of related positions. There has emerged a significant school of Catholic pacifism now supported by an authoritative statement of Catholic teaching. Others use the traditional or modern moral categories to form a judgement. The issues are difficult and the arguments are complicated. But all the Churches are striving to give a sincere Christian witness when challenged and threatened by one of the gravest problems of all time.

CHAPTER FOUR

The Response of the United States Catholic Bishops

FIRST STAGE

One of the principle insights and achievements of Vatican II was the emphasis it placed on the importance of the local Church and, consequently, on the national boards of bishops and how it relates to the Papacy and Episcopal Collegiality and the Christian traditions. The universal teaching already mentioned in the official documents has set the background for the teaching of the local Church.

In the United States the local Church addresses the question of peace and the arms race within the public debate of one of the super powers and, therefore, in a very real sense has a more complex character.

> This complementarity of the universal and local levels of Catholic social teaching fits the model outlined by Paul VI in his apostolic letter, "The Eightieth Year (1971)".[1]

Perhaps this idea was more neatly expressed by the same Pope in his letter "Evangelisation in the Modern World" when it emphasized that the Church *toto orbe diffusa* would become a mere abstraction if it did not have body and life precisely through the individual Churches: "Only continual attention to these two poles of the Church will enable us to perceive the richness of this relationship between the universal Church and the individual Churches."[2]

The relationship will inevitably have its tensions, which are already noticeable in the nuclear debate between the United States hierarchy and the national hierarchies of the nations in the Atlantic community. The potential fruitfulness of these tensions between the various hierarchies and indeed the Papacy will depend, to some extent, on the ability of each national episcopal conference, and the Pope, to understand and respond with trust to the initiatives of all the others.

The Bishops and the Nuclear Problem

The Committee on War and Peace formed by the National Conference of Catholic Bishops (NCCB) had its beginnings in a lengthy discussion of the moral and religious dimensions of war which occurred at the 1980 general meeting. After several proposals on the topic had been introduced, Bishop Head, Chairman of the Social Development and World Peace Committee, proposed that the NCCB leadership accept responsibility for responding to the proposals.

In line with this proposal the President, Archbishop Roach established an ad hoc committee to prepare a pastoral letter on the topic of war and peace. The letter was to take into consideration what the NCCB had done on the question of modern war, the arms race, conscientious objection and related issues, and it was then to use papal, conciliar and other theological resources to develop a new policy statement designed to respond particularly, but not exclusively, to the challenge of war and the need for a theology of peace in the nuclear age.

Archbishop Roach asked Cardinal Bernardin (Chicago) to chair the ad hoc committee and four other bishops were invited to join: Bishop Fulcher (Lafayette), Bishop Gumbleton (Detroit), Bishop O'Connor (Military Ordinariate) and Bishop Reilly (Norwich). The Conference of Major Superiors of Men and the Leadership Conference of Women Religious were invited to appoint representatives as consultants to the Committee. They were Rev Richard Warner and Sister Juliana Casey. Bruce Martin Russett, Professor of Political Science at Yale University, was engaged as the principal consultant for the letter. The staff of the committee were Bryan Hehir, of the United States Catholic Conference Office, and Edward Doherty, adviser for political military affairs in the same office. The First Draft of the Pastoral Letter was dated 11 June 1982. The Second Draft was published in October 1982 and was debated by the bishops 15 to 18 November 1982.[3]

One can sketch the public discussion that led up to this event by emphasising some of the more important events. Cardinal

Krol (Philadelphia) spoke before the United States Senate Committee on Foreign Affairs during their hearings on the ratification of SALT II in September 1979.[4] He made a statement on behalf of the United States Catholic bishops in favour of ratification of SALT II. Krol's testimony can be summarised in three steps:

1. It is immoral to use the strategic nuclear arsenals of the United States.

2. It is immoral to threaten to use them as part of the strategy of nuclear deterrence.

3. Mere possession of nuclear weapons can be tolerated as the lesser of two evils "while negotiations proceed".[5]

It generated the story of the year and was the beginning of one of the most significant political developments in America in recent years.

It was really a summary, though an authoritative one, of the various American Episcopal initiatives on this question. The public discussion since that statement was really an unfinished dialogue between the two groups of bishops – a large majority:

"Adhering tentatively to the position set forth by Krol in 1979," and expecting to issue an elaborate and clarifying statement of the moral arguments and moral effects for individuals of that position, and a small, but highly publicized group, who wish to lead the Church further in "a prophetic stance against the risks and immoral obscenity of nuclear deterrents".[6] In this latter number is Archbishop Hunthausen (Seattle) who, in a speech to the Pacific Northwest Synod of the Lutheran Church in the United States, had said in 1981: "Our willingness to destroy life everywhere on this earth for the sake of our security as Americans is the root of our problems."[7] He referred to the basing of Trident submarines in his territory as "the Auschwitz of Puget Sound" and that, together with MX and Cruise missiles, they are to be understood as a build-up to first strike capability. Therefore, he concluded taking up the Cross with Christ in the nuclear age meant unilateral disarmament. To the objection that this encourages the risk of war, he replied that it is "a more reasonable risk than constant nuclear escalation". He called for non-violent resistance and declared that a definite step towards disarmament would be:

> A sizeable number of people in the State of Washington, 5,000, 10,000, 500,000 people, refusing to pay 50 per cent of their taxes in non-violent resistance to nuclear murder and suicide. I think that would be a definite step towards disarmament. Our paralysed political process needs that catalyst of non-violent action based on faith. We have to refuse to give incense – in our day, tax dollars – to our nuclear idol. On 15 April we can vote for unilateral disarmament with our lives.[8]

Not only that, but Hunthausen actually made himself one of that number. The impact was electric. His statement was both praised and criticized. It was backed by 16 leaders of nine denominations in Washington State. Some people condemned it as naive, emasculating the nation's right to security and not compatible with just war thinking. Professor McCormick of the Kennedy Institute of Bioethics, believes that such reactions miss the point and purpose of Hunthausen's intervention:

> The bishop referred to the "polarized political process" and "despair" at the political analysis of the nuclear build-up. There is an independent and uncontrollable dynamic of escalation in the nuclear build-up of our time. It seems that nothing we think or do can stop such madness and that incapacity can lead to public apathy.[9]

It was against this pervasive feeling in the United States that Hunthausen's statement makes eminent good sense. Later, when interviewed by *Our Sunday Visitor* Hunthausen said that several bishops supported his statement "and that he was not saying anything different from the Holy Father ... or what the Second Vatican Council said on the arms race". However, he did go on to say that he was not advocating that people withhold taxes as a protest against the arms race: "My comment was more in the nature of wonderment. I was wondering what would happen in this country if many people did withhold taxes. I wondered what kind of change this would effect." He then insisted that unilateralism meant a "deep conversion and change of heart".

There is no way I can tell you that. There's no way I can paint that picture. But if, as a people, we were willing to come to that stance, this would signify to me a deep conversion on our part. We would be seeing ourselves and the world in a totally different way. We are not likely to unilaterally disarm unless we have a change of heart. That change of heart would bring all sorts of additional changes in the way we spend our money, how we help people, what we do with disease, hunger and the needs of the world. These are going begging now.[10]

Whatever way one examines this statement, one is forced to concede that it is courageous and symbolic and capable of disturbing apathy and raising ethical issues too long left to the politicians and the armaments industry. At any rate, according to a recent report, Hunthausen did withhold half his tax for 1982. In Britain he was followed by Canon Paul Oestreicher who withheld ". . . that proportion of tax owed to me by the Inland Revenue which roughly corresponds to the proportion of government spending on the British Nuclear Weapons Programme".[11] Tax resistance campaigns have developed in a number of countries and it is very likely that Hunthausen had a major influence on this form of conscientious objection.

It would be unjust not to mention bishops like Thomas Gumbleton, President of Pax Christi, who had been a prophetic and lonely voice for many years.[12] A few years ago Pax Christi attracted a few bishops only; now the number is over 50. There have been an abundance of Episcopal statements claiming the immorality of possessing nuclear weapons and one October 1981 statement was signed by no less than 29 bishops. Special mention too should be made of Bishop Matthiesen (Amarillo) who urged Catholic workers in a local nuclear weapons assembly plant to consider resigning on the grounds of conscience:

We urge individuals involved in the production and stockpiling of nuclear bombs to consider what they are doing, to resign from such activities and seek employment in peaceful pursuits.

He denounced the decision to produce and stockpile neutron warheads as "the latest in a series of tragic anti-life positions taken by our government".[13] On 10 September 1981, all twelve Catholic bishops of Texas joined Matthiesen:

We, his brother bishops of Texas share Bishop Matthiesen's concern and fully support his appeal to those involved in the manufacture of these weapons in every nation to consider the moral and ethical implications of what they are doing.[14]

There are many noteworthy statements made by different bishops but that of Archbishop Quinn (San Francisco) is worth quoting. It was 4 October 1981, the 800th anniversary of St Francis of Assisi, patron of San Francisco, when Quinn said: "A just nuclear war is a contradiction in terms." Having referred to the biological, environmental and genetic effects which could damage generations, he asked: "What good could possibly be proportionate to such uncontrollable suffering and mass destruction?"[15] Quinn called for prayer and education to heighten the awareness of the horrors which United States policies imply.

It is true that the majority of bishops would line up behind Krol's statement. Nevertheless, there is an ever-increasing number of mainstream religious leaders who in some ways are quite conservative, but are most prophetic on peace and disarmament. As one studies the various Episcopal statements, several characteristics emerge:

1. There is a straightforward moral condemnation of the use of nuclear weapons.

2. There is a rejection of the arms race.

3. There is a universal frustration at the insensitivity of the policy makers who are involved in a race to death and annihilation.

4. There is an intense desire to inform the consciences of people about the moral implications.

Perhaps one other point of interest could be added. Some contrasts are to be noted in the statements of Krol (who claimed to be speaking for the great majority of bishops) and the other bishops. Krol did not condemn mere possession of nuclear weapons. But, as has already been noted, 29 bishops do condemn such a position. If it is permissible to possess nuclear weapons, it cannot be immoral to make them. Yet Matthiesen and many other bishops request those working in nuclear plants to leave their positions for more peaceable pursuits.

Again, Krol does not believe unilateral disarmament is a moral demand but Hunthausen does – and with him all those who believe mere possession of nuclear weapons is immoral. This brings us to the interesting situation of the drafts for the Pastoral Letter which more or less reflect what we have just seen.

The Pastoral Letter
The First Draft was really built-up on the Hierarchy Statements on Arms in 1976.[16]

   a. A condemnation of first use of nuclear weapons or a threat of first use.

   b. A ban on deployment of such weapons against civilian populations, even in retaliation and even against military targets if massive civilian casualties would result.

   c. Experimental disarmament steps by the United States alone to see whether the Soviets would join in.

It consisted of 66 pages and was sent to 376 bishops asking for comment. It was dated 11 June 1982. The response was voluminous; the consultations that led up to it were extensive. Some peace people were, in any case, surprised that the Draft did not flatly rule out all use of nuclear weapons. They also objected to its assertion that: "It was marginally justifiable to possess nuclear weapons in a deterrence policy so long as disarmament talks were proceeding."[17] In July 1982, the Committee met to consider the comments and revised the Draft in the light of them.

The Draft was then revised and submitted for debate in a Plenary Session of the Episcopal Conference in 1982. According to *The Tablet*, the sub-committee under the chairmanship of Bernardin had held fourteen meetings consulting with military experts, politicians, ethicists, theologians and anti-war activists.[18]

These two "First Drafts" had been floated as trial balloons testing public opinion as well as Episcopal opinion. Their structure seems to follow the general lines of the official position of the United States bishops and reflects, in particular, Cardinal Krol's testimony before the Senate Committee. The vigorous Catholic debate was not limited to members of the

Church.[19] Indeed, it caused extraordinary reactions in the administration, and of course, added to the feverish discussion that was taking place among various groups. There is no doubt that this initiative by the Catholic bishops was one of the most important developments that has taken place in twentieth-century United States history, and the ground-swell generated against United States militarism and nuclear-dominated national security mentality was enormous.

So the White House launched a carefully worded defence of its nuclear policies. The case was presented by the National Security Adviser – and, incidentally, Catholic layman – William Clark. In an open letter to Cardinal Bernardin, Clark said that the White House agreed with the Pope and indeed much of what the bishops were saying, but that he and President Reagan were especially troubled that the Draft ignored American proposals on achieving steep reductions on nuclear arsenals or reducing conventional forces and a variety of measures reducing the risks of war. He also argued that it was perfectly moral for the United States to make certain that the deterrent forces remain sufficiently strong to assure effective deterrence. The goal was to prevent war and to preserve the values that are cherished in the United States.[20]

SECOND STAGE

The Second Draft Document

The Second Draft condemned the first use of nuclear weapons, endorsed a mutual freeze on development and deployment of new weapons, but stated that deterrence was morally permissible only if it leads to progressive disarmament. There was an overwhelming consensus amongst the bishops on the basic thrust of the document. However, there was a request for more discussion and reflection on the key issue of nuclear deterrence. In the First Draft it was held that in retaliation one could use nuclear weapons against military targets if massive civilian casualties were avoided. This seems to have been dropped in the Second Draft because the bishops considered that any nuclear confrontation would escalate into an all-out war, although the wording is not very sharp.[21] Consequently, the key statement of the Second Draft seems to be:

The moral judgement of this statement is that not only the use of strategic nuclear weapons but also the declared intent to use them involved in our deterrence policy are both wrong.[22]

It also rejected all targetting of civilian populations. But the question immediately presented itself about the possession of nuclear arms as a deterrent. The Draft expressed its dissatisfaction with the policy of deterrence and stressed the importance of reducing stock-piles, but it is my opinion, it appeared to be reluctant to go beyond John Paul's words to the United Nations in June 1982 where he said that deterrence cannot be accepted as an end in itself and that it must be a means towards progressive disarmament. This prompts the question: did the Episcopal Conference feel itself inhibited by the Papal Statement?

As we have already noted, the Second Draft Document was debated by the bishops in November 1982. They were seeking to develop a theology of peace and attempted to ground the task of peace-making solidly in the Biblical vision of the Kingdom of God. It specified the obstacles in the way of peace as understood theologically and in the social sciences. It identified the specific contributions a community of faith can make to the work of peace and relates these specific gifts to the wide work of peace pursued by other groups and institutions. The document underlined the message of hope and added that:

> For a community of faith the Risen Christ is the beginning and end of all things. For all things were created through Him and all things return to the Father through him.
>
> It is our belief in the Risen Christ which sustains us in confronting the awesome challenge of the nuclear arms race.[23]

Furthermore, the centre of its teaching on peace was the dignity of the human person:

> The human person is the clearest reflection of the presence of God in the world; all of the Churches working in pursuit of both justice and peace have desired to protect and promote the dignity of every person. For each person not only reflects God, but is the expression of God's creative work and the meaning of Christ's redemptive ministry.[24]

Finally, it challenged some of the fundamental assumptions and defence strategies of the administration and reminded the powers-that-be...

> ... that men of this generation should realise that they have to render an account of their war-like behaviour; the destiny of generations to come depends largely on the decisions they make today.[25]

The bishops acknowledged that the United States threat to use nuclear arms in response to a Soviet assault might prevent the outbreak of war, but, nevertheless concluded that the whole policy is unsatisfactory because it creates, and keeps in place, a balance of terror that all too easily could lead to a holocaust. They also commented on the cost of maintaining deterrents which takes money away from the progress of the poor:

> We see with clarity the political folly of a system which threatens mutual suicide; the psychological damage this does to ordinary people, especially the young, the economic distortion of priorities; billions readily spent for destructive instruments and pitched battles being waged daily in our legislatures, about a fraction of this amount for the homeless, the hungry and the helpless here and abroad.[26]

The question of the nation-State and its problems was also discussed:

> In a world of sovereign states, devoid of central authority and possessed of the knowledge to produce nuclear weapons, many choices were made, some of them clearly objectionable, others well intentioned with mixed results which brought the world to the present dangerous situation.[27]

The bishops called for a mutual freeze on development and deployment of nuclear weapons, which is opposed by the Administration and by many experts, and urged the Administration to strive for disarmament agreement with Russia. Additionally, this Second Draft rejected any first use of nuclear weapons and also rejected the threat or declared intent to use them. While not involving themselves in the technical debate on limited nuclear war, they asked a number of searching questions and were sceptical about the real meaning of "limited". The issue at stake was "the real as opposed to the theoretical possibility" of keeping such a war limited and within the stringent bounds of the requirements for a just war:

> To cross this divide is to enter a world where we have no experience of control, much evidence against its possibility, and no justification for submitting the human community to this risk.[28]

Deterrence was accepted as the lesser of two evils only if it leads to *progressive disarmament.*

> As long as there is hope of this occurring, Catholic moral teaching is willing, while negotiations proceed, to tolerate the position of nuclear weapons for deterrence as the lesser of two evils.[29]

The document then proceeded to quote from the address made by John Paul II, to the United Nations Second Special Session on Disarmament, in June 1982:

> In current conditions, deterrence, based on balance, certainly not as an end in itself, but as a step on the way towards a progressive disarmament, may still be judged morally acceptable. Nevertheless, in order to ensure peace, it is indispensable not to be satisfied with this minimum which is always susceptible to the real danger of explosion.[30]

The bishops' Second Draft was therefore based on two suppositions taken from John Paul II. The first was that deterrence cannot be accepted as an end in itself; and the second that deterrence must be a step towards progressive disarmament. This, as I have suggested, indicates that, at this stage, the Draft was not willing to go beyond the Papal position, though the bishops did apply this general Papal statement to their local position. As one writer has put it:

> The Pope has spoken in a broader framework; the bishops have taken his position as a point of departure and then proceeded to be more specific as is proper for the national hierarchy of the first nation to use nuclear arms, and one of the handful that can directly affect the outcome of the arms race.[31]

However, on a closer examination of the text it is possible, at first sight, to detect a stricter attitude on the bishops' part than that contained in the Papal Statement. The Draft regarded the nuclear deterrent as *"morally tolerable"* and if only it is seen as a step towards progressive disarmament. The Pope, on the other hand, regards the deterrent as, in some sense, *"morally acceptable"*. The Draft followed the wording of Cardinal Krol in holding that deterrence is an "evil" which may be tolerated in certain circumstances but can never be passively "accepted".

Finally, for the bishops, nuclear weapons presented a "new sin" because they threatened the "Sovereignty of God over His Universe". The Draft also condemned all targetting of civilians and rejected attacks on those targets whose destruction would devastate nearby populations.[32]

Some Criticisms
Germain Grisez, Professor of Christian Ethics at Emmitsburg, made a sharp attack on the nuclear deterrence position of the Second Draft in a circular to all members of the NCCB.[33] He asserted that the Second Draft admitted the nuclear deterrent includes the threat to attack civilian populations. The Draft quoted from the United States Military Posture Statement for FY 1983.[34] It spoke of willingness to strike "targets of value", which is military parlance for people and the things they care about. Grisez argued that since the bishops realised this, it was difficult to understand how such an evil could be tolerated as the "lesser". He pointed to the teaching of Jesus on intention and added that this "will to kill the innocent is always wrong". Moreover it is nonsense "to suggest that one may tolerate one's own immoral evil doing".

His second criticism contended that the quotation from the Pope in the Second Draft was not helpful. When the Pope addressed the Second Session of the UN he was speaking in the context of the arms race and disarmament; when he stated that deterrence was "acceptable" it could mean "some deterrence", but did not specifically refer to "nuclear deterrence" and much less to the present United States deterrent.[35] There is no evidence, he said, to show "that John Paul II knows (or believes) that the present US nuclear deterrent includes the threat to kill the innocent."[36]

While admitting the paradox of deterrence and the fact that

some would hold it actually prevents the use of nuclear
weapons, the bishops claimed that it was a case of the lesser of
two evils. Indeed, in the document they said that though the
deterrent posture of the United States "is from a moral point of
view" unsatisfactory, the use of "nuclear weapons by any of
the nuclear powers would be an even greater evil".[37]

According to Grisez, this simply would not do: it was
equivalent to saying that one could do evil that good may
come, which is alien to Christian morality as expressed by St
Paul (Rom 3 : 8). Whether "acceptable" or "toleration" were
used of the lesser evil, the fact was that they justify the deterrent on the grounds that it prevents a greater evil and that,
according to Grisez, is tantamount to "the end justifying the
means".

Finally, Grisez concluded his criticism by complaining that
the bishops dismissed the alternative of unilateral disarmament
in one sentence. The next Draft needed modification; indeed,
he thought, it should include a hypothetical proposition such
as:

> If the present nuclear deterrent is focused on non-combatants and
> its threat includes a choice to kill them if deterrence fails, then that
> deterrent is immoral and nothing can justify it.[38]

Perhaps Grisez was too hard on the Second Draft, but he had a
valid point about the need for clarification on the United States
deterrent policy; and this was indeed treated in the Third
Draft.

But for Grisez to criticise the NCCB on the question of the
"lesser of two evils" is quite another matter and one doubts the
validity of his argument. The principle of "not doing evil that
good may come" is violated when the evil is *intentional* and
follows as a *direct* effect. That is to say, it does not apply to
indirect and *tolerated* evil where no other course of action
is reasonably possible. This seems to be the situation with
which the bishops were dealing. All the same, it should be
added that the question of "means to ends" and the principle
of the "lesser of two evils" have been much debated in recent
years.

There is a detailed discussion on the implications of this
"principle" by Richard McCormick and Paul Ramsey.[39] Some

would say that the principle of the "lesser of two evils" applies only in the case of two alternatives, either of which is bound to happen if the other does not. An example of this is the ectopic pregnancy. Failure to act will cause the death of both. In this case one so arranges matters that the less damaging result is incurred – the survival of the mother. Nevertheless, in the nuclear case the issues are less clear. Abandoning the nuclear deterrent might make a Russian attack on the West more likely – it would not make it certain. Has Grisez a valid point here? Is another course of action reasonably possible? If the "lesser of two evils" can properly be invoked in this case, could it not be invoked in so many other cases that it became equivalent to saying one can do evil that good may come?

The fact that the Second Draft was debated before the full glare of television lights and under the gaze of the international press is a sign of our times. In another age, the meeting would have been held in seclusion or secrecy. It might have been concluded that division and disagreement would have scandalised people. Furthermore the document was not in any way couched in dogmatic categories. On the contrary, the text had been prepared by the sub-committee under the chairmanship of Bernardin, working with all the bishops and a wide range of priests, laity, theological and scientific experts. The Church was not imposing a final synthesis; rather, it was emerging as a community of faith in which vigorous and enlightened moral discourse took place. With the new impetus from Vatican II and Paul VI[40] a more active...

... role amongst the bishops has been noticed, especially in regard to social questions. Moreover, a substantial number of the bishops in the US have been appointed in the last decade and most of them are comfortable with the idea of collegiality.[41]

Many of them have been drawn from pastoral settings; frequently their concerns reflect their background:

They are as interested in social action as in doctrinal debate and Church administration. This development, coupled with the gradual awakening of the collective awareness in the American episcopacy provides a new willingness on its part to speak out on social issues that are of particular interest to Americans.[42]

It is unlikely that such a debate could have taken place in the 1950s. The bishops would never have agreed to deliver a joint pastoral letter on such a controversial subject. And so it is that the National Conference of Catholic Bishops has come of age and is maturing with a new-found confidence.

Nevertheless, as we have shown, the bishops are not without their critics, both within their flock and outside it. Even some Catholic journalists, made up of highly academic members as in *Catholicism in Crisis*, would prefer the bishops to stay out of the nuclear discussions. That lay people take issue with the bishops is not something unheard of in the United States. What is new is the harshness and stridency of their criticism which accuses the bishops of bringing political divisions into the Church. Clergy should stick to their "priestly roles (and dress) and stop patronising talk about the priesthood of the laity". Again, priests and bishops should not usurp lay roles and invade the temporal order. Bishops have: "No special authority in temporal matters, particularly of this type."[43] But no one seems to raise questions about the competence of journalists who publish editorials offering extensive analysis on the nuclear question. Are they really expert, in a technical sense, in every field they write about? They write on the basis of study and on their conversations and reflections with others. The same is true of the bishops who are quite within their rights in discussing the moral implications of peace, arms and the nuclear question. What they are trying to do is to focus on the teaching of the Gospel as they understand it and to apply that teaching to the various questions of today. It is true that these questions do have a political as well as a moral dimension, but this does not mean that the bishops should not reflect on them. As Professor Curran remarked:

The human act is broader than any of its particular aspects, such as the military or the political science aspect. For this reason I do see the competency of the ethicist and the Church in the realm of the prudential precisely because Christian and human values are at stake here.[44]

As Paul VI maintained, evangelisation has to teach the whole of life "about life in society, about international life, peace, justice and development – a message especially energetic today about

liberation".[45] To do otherwise would be to exclude the proc-
lamation of the Gospel from the great issues that challenge the
Christians of today. It would reduce the Gospel to some kind
of interiority unrelated to the contemporary world.

Nevertheless, the Reagan administration was particularly
annoyed with the bishops, not only for their stance on the
nuclear question and intervening in policy-making but also
because of their criticism of his militarism in Central America
generally, and El Salvador in particular. To him, the Church
was a dupe of Moscow and was failing in its duty to oppose
evil, especially Russian communism which is "the focus of evil
in the modern world".[46] It has been reported that after an
approach had been made to the bishops by William Clark,
and Secretary of State George Shultz, Secretary of Defense
Caspar Weinberger and Director of Arms Control and Disarmament Agency Eugene V. Rostow, an approach was then
made to the Pope.[47] I can find no solid evidence for this
suggestion.

Nonetheless the Draft itself seems to be infused with Papal
thinking; there was a meeting in Rome, 18 January 1983,
between some of the bishops representing their boards from
Europe and from the United States National Conference of
Catholic Bishops. It met under the chairmanship of Cardinal
Casaroli.[48] According to some reports, bishops from France,
West Germany and other European countries questioned their
United States colleagues on certain aspects of the Second Draft.
But the meeting was more in the nature of comparing positions, the moral implications and possibly a discussion on the
final draft of the United States bishops. Archbishop Roach,
reflecting on the Church-State issue, remarked that: "We may
never allow the separation of Church and State to be used to
separate the Church from society."[49]

Involvement with politics has always been part of the
Church's history. At times the involvement has been most
unhappy. Indeed its first involvement at the time of Constantine seems to have been a farewell to the pacifism which was
practised amongst the early Christians. One remembers the
cases of Richelieu, Wolsey, and Franco of Spain.

But concerns with the moral and social issues of politics, as
distinct from adherence to any particular party is a fundamentally different matter. People are beginning to under-

stand that the debate about mixing religion with politics is irrelevant in an interdependent, interconnected, unified world. A pietistic concept of God is as unreal and as inadequate as an activist one. The former is individual and introspective, the latter secular or purely humanitarian. Neither extreme does justice to man's true relationship with God and his fellows. The love of God and each other are inseparable. We are invited to love God totally in our fellow men. God in turn, cares for all of us and about every part of life in the world. It is because God made us soul and body, members of each other, that there is no escape from the fact that we are one community and have responsibility for each other. As Helder Camara says:

> Why cannot Christians once and for all establish the distinction between the political, which has to do with the common good, and political, which has to do with parties. To be political in the former sense is for them not merely a right but a duty laid down by the Gospel itself.[50]

This, of course, is in keeping with the message of Christ in Luke's Gospel, when he refers to his mission to the poor, the oppressed and the marginalised (Lk 4 : 18ff). Protecting human rights is a thoroughly Gospel task and this point will receive further reflection in Chapter 7.[51]

But even if one grants that the political dimension must be assessed by the values of the Gospel, was it really necessary for the bishops to be so specific about armaments? According to some critics, the bishops did not go far enough.[52] According to others, like Michael Novak and Quentin Quade and some of the staff of *Catholicism in Crisis*, the bishops' intervention in a nuclear problem was an "irritating brand of clericalism". However, the bishops, like other leaders, cannot have personal competence in all the highly diverse areas where they must give leadership. Like other national leaders, they have to consult the experts and know how to use them. If every national leader had to have personal competence in every international situation and in every discipline concerned in the highly specialised decisions of education, physics, social welfare and military science policy, all national leadership would be invalidated. In fact, the entire process of writing the pastoral can be characterised as a dialogue.

The preparation and consultation involved in the formation of the first two drafts was very extensive; the expertise consisted of former government officials, twelve moral theologian-ethicists, four scripture scholars, two conflict-resolution specialists, four Catholic peace organisations, retired military experts and physicians. The Administration's Caspar Weinberger, Lawrence Eagleberger (Under Secretary of State for Political Affairs), and Eugene Rostow were also consulted, as was former US Army general, and now ambassador, Edward Rowny. The documentation involved in the Second Draft consists of 83 footnotes.[53] So its consultation involves people from all political convictions and persuasions and the fruitfulness of this is evident in the scriptural and theological content of the pastoral. This wide-ranging discussion extended to a very broad community. Nevertheless, a member of the Justice and Peace Franciscan Office in Washington and Professor K. Himes of Washington Theological Union remarked that the spirit of dialogue "on matters where laity might be presumed to have some competence has been less than evident".[54]

This point is not immediately obvious considering the fact that a majority of the people consulted were, in fact, laity. Perhaps it would be of benefit if the protest against the Church voiced by people in *Catholicism in Crisis* and others should be, in some way, incorporated into the national policy of making and taking decisions. The national hierarchy must continue to consult the laity in discussions which affect the lives of all. But, in fairness, the American bishops have exercised their mandate well and indeed did seek broad involvement of the laity, both Catholic and Protestant, in the evaluation of their document.

Some Repercussions of the Second Draft
How far the average American Catholic would have been affected when the official pastoral letter was published is difficult to assess. The American Catholics form one-quarter of the population of the United States; and a Gallup Poll indicated that 82 per cent of them accepted the bishops' position while 13 per cent opposed it and 5 per cent were undecided.[55] Again, in the American Congress, the draft was criticised by 24 Catholic Congressmen (one-fifth of Catholic Congress members), 2 Democrats and 22 Republicans, on the grounds that the real

threat comes not from America's nuclear strategy but from Soviet ideology.[56] In New York, the American Catholic Committee, a body of lay Catholics set up in January 1983 and led by New York City former Labour Commissioner, James J. McFadden, accused the bishops of steering the Church away from traditional Catholic political attitudes.[57] If the pastoral letter had eventually moved to a total condemnation of nuclear deterrence, without qualification or condition, would the Catholic population have courageously faced the unpleasant consequences? – the rejection of manufacturing nuclear weapons; a refusal to pay tax; a refusal to take part in military service, to mention but a few. It should also be remembered that, according to some authorities, about 40 per cent of the American military are Catholic. The same logic would preclude Catholics from filling positions in the civilian chain of command for nuclear deterrence, ranging from President, Vice-President, Secretary of State for Defense, National Security Adviser to the President, Speaker of the House of Representatives, down even to government officials charged with articulating nuclear threats in times of crisis.[58]

To conclude this evaluation of the bishops' attitude in America, one must still ask the question as to why the sudden appearance of the NCCB is now so evident in the midst of the political scene, when political involvement in the past has been largely confined to the abortion issue and private education. How have they come to be so deeply involved in the vexed question on the nuclear debate? Some of the bishops are wondering themselves how on earth they got into this position. There can be no doubt that the United States bishops gained political sophistication and solidarity in their battle against abortion after the 1973 Supreme Court decision which gave more scope to legalised abortion. According to Francis Winter, some commentators...

... believe that it was the high profile taken by the bishops on the abortion issue that led them, somewhat to their own surprise, into the midst of the national debate about defence policies ... their conspicuous advocacy of the right to life of the unborn made it imperative for them to acknowledge that the same cherished values require an equally spirited campaign to reverse the momentum of nuclear escalation.[59]

Some critics feared that the Church, by remaining silent, would have given the impression of a moral myopia which recognised the threat to life only in the case of an endangered foetus. Another reason for their involvement is that the United States, above all nations, is burdened with the grave responsibility of the nuclear weapon and indeed was the first to use it. This is a heavy onus for a Christian country. It is interesting that the bishops who were noticeably conservative, compared with their European colleagues, during Vatican II, have now completely reversed this situation on the nuclear problem.

In making a distinction between the threat and use of the nuclear weapon on the one hand, and the retention of the deterrent on the other, it appears that the bishops have been seeking to do justice both to the claims of imperative restraint in the use of force and of national and international security. This, of course, has been a source of controversy but the distinction may be justified on the grounds that it deters Soviet aggression. While most people doubt the deterrent effect of a strategic system in the hands of a government renouncing the intention to use it, it seems to the bishops, to date, reasonable to believe that Soviet planners...

... would continue to stand in dread of the deterrent because they could not be sure of the genuine (as opposed to declaratory) policy of our government, and because the physical potentiality of the deterrent force would remain available for use if the government were to change its policy, reversing its earlier renunciation.[60]

It is interesting to note, in spite of this attitude, Eugene Rostow in a radio interview said:

I think the adoption by NATO of a no first-use policy would remove an element of uncertainty about our possible response to aggression. And I can see absolutely no advantage in taking such a pledge and many disadvantages, because after all, deterrence *is* uncertainty.[61]

Evidently, this comment would apply not only to the intention of a no first-use but also to the declared intent policy of never using it.

Finally, it could be said that the bishops have involved

themselves in a revolution – one of the most significant developments of our time, which has not only had repercussions on the Catholic community but on the body politic at large, as well as the Reagan Administration, directly affecting the whole NATO strategy. Initial reactions, at home and abroad, will continue to challenge the adequacy of their teaching and their "intrusion" into politics, despite the careful process of reflection and deliberation, and others will continue to accuse the bishops of compromising moral standards by tolerating the possession of nuclear weapons while stock-piles increase and the arms race continues, and forbidding the intention to use them. They will also be judged insensitive to the risks of Soviet aggression.

Yet if the pastoral letter had rejected the nuclear deterrent and rejected the manufacture and deployment of nuclear weapons, it would have gone further than any national hierarchy. To respond to all this, many would have to shed some of their intensely nationalistic ideas, which to a certain extent have been fostered in the past by the United States Catholic Church. While, therefore, it is courageous and refreshing for the bishops to speak out, which will undoubtedly help to stimulate discussion among Catholics and indeed the rest of the community, it was too much to expect wholesale Catholic opposition to nuclear deterrents. As a matter of fact, some of the members of the NCCB, such as Cooke (New York) recently deceased, and Hannan (New Orleans) preferred to emphasise the right of defence and the evils of Soviet communism, rather than the positive opposition to the nuclear deterrent. According to informed sources, the meeting in Rome, already referred to, was a reaction to the Second Draft by the Administration. According to one report the West German bishops were most critical of the American stance.[62]

Ethical Method
The method used by the bishops was a mutual and preparatory search for the truth. It was an invitation to their own people and indeed the whole political community to think long and hard on these complex questions of peace, nuclear arms and the dangers to survival, and to continue to bring the light of the Gospel to bear on the problems of our time.[63] The aim was not to solve all the problems but rather to raise certain values and

issues regarding the safety of the human race, the dignity of the human person and the survival of the planet.

The ethical criteria used in the draft were the traditional approach to the morality of an act. That is to say, the determinants are the *purpose*, the *means* or action, and the *circumstances*. The just war criteria are used as the test. This Second Draft explicitly stressed that "both the classical Christian position just outlined (the non-violent tradition and the just war position) are confronted with a unique challenge by nuclear warfare".[64] The distinction between direct and indirect killing is mentioned in many places, and illustrated by references to "the civilian population", "indiscriminate targetting" and "counter population warfare".[65] The principle of the "double effect" is also evident, especially in the section entitled "limited nuclear war" where reference is made to the side effects of "radiation" and "famine". The draft appealed explicitly to the principle of "proportion" and "discrimination" when considering the nuclear weapons, and decided that certain aspects of the Soviet and American strategies fail the test.[66] It rejected the "declared intent" to use nuclear weapons as morally unacceptable – all of which add up to the use of traditional moral categories.[67] All the same, it is a matter of fascination that two radical and progressive stances are underpinned by traditional moral categories.

The pastoral moved from the general to the specific. It considered peace in the modern world, peace and the Kingdom, the Kingdom and history, the moral choices for the Kingdom, war and peace in the modern world and religious leadership. Having reflected on such general questions, it proceeded to address the specific, such as the arms race, national sovereignty, the poor, the use of nuclear weapons, limited nuclear weapons, the threat of such use, escalation and nuclear deterrents.[68]

The bishops stated that they were clear on the necessity of saying "no" to the arms race and its effect on the poor, the young and ordinary people, but they admitted that:

We see with much less clarity how we translate a "no" to nuclear war into personal and public choices which can move us in a new direction towards national policy and an international system which more adequately reflects the values and vision of the Kingdom of God.[69]

THE THIRD STAGE

The Third Draft Document

The First Draft of the Pastoral Letter was dated 11 June 1982. A Second Draft from the ad hoc Committee on War and Peace was published in *Origins*, the Official National Catholic Documentary Service, on 28 October 1982. The Third Draft of the Pastoral Letter was sent out to the United States bishops before Easter 1983 and was released for publication on the 6 April 1983. It appeared in *Origins*.[71] It superseded the Second Draft and provided the basis for the discussion and debate at the Special Meeting of the United States bishops on 2 and 3 May 1983 in Chicago. This Third Draft includes much of the material of the Second Draft and has taken into account nearly 400 pages of comment. In response to the suggestions and criticisms made at the General Meeting of the bishops (November 1982) several sections were redeveloped, particularly the sections on scripture, deterrents, the just war tradition and non-violence. A 2,200 word precis has been added as well as a new discussion of the various levels of moral authority with which the bishops speak. In particular, it urges...

... mutual respect among individuals and groups in the Church as this letter is analysed and discussed.

Obviously, as bishops, we believe that such differences should be expressed within the framework of Catholic moral teaching. We need not only conviction and commitment in the Church, but also civility and charity.[72]

Another interesting addition is the reference to methods of interpretation:

Not all statements in this letter have the same moral authority. At times we state universally binding moral principles as well as formal Church teaching; and at times we make specific applications, observations and recommendations which allow for diversity of opinion on the part of those who assess the factual data of a situation differently than we do.[73]

The Draft, though modified, remained a sweeping critique of American nuclear deterrent strategy at the very time when President Reagan was caught up in a tense international struggle of the issue. It can be assumed that the contents have the approval of Pope John Paul II since the Draft was also debated in Rome in January 1983. The thrust of the document remains in its challenge to many central elements of American policy on relying on an arsenal of nuclear weapons. First-use nuclear weapons are categorically opposed but, whereas in the first two Drafts the bishops said they did not "perceive any situation" in which the initiation of nuclear war could be condoned, the Third Draft says: "We abhor the concept of initiating nuclear war on however restricted a scale."[74] The Second Draft called for a freeze or *halt* in the manufacture and deployment of nuclear weapons, whereas this Draft urged a *curb*.[75]

In fact, at the Chicago meeting of bishops on 2 and 3 May this was once again reversed and there was an overwhelming majority in favour of a *halt* rather than a *curb*. This immediately caused a vast challenge to the Reagan administration and, in particular, addressed the Catholic conscience.

In regard to deterrence, the bishops considered it a "sinful situation" that can only at best be tolerable:

1. To prevent the use of nuclear weapons.

2. Provided deterrence is based on balance not on a "quest for nuclear superiority".

3. Provided it is "a step on the way towards progressive disarmament".

This Draft gives a conditional acceptance of deterrence policy in concert with the evaluation provided by Pope John Paul II. "We have arrived at a strictly conditional moral acceptance of deterrence. We cannot consider it adequate as a long term basis for peace."[77] In an entirely new addition, the bishops recognise: "The responsibility the US has had, and continues to have, to protect allied nations from either a conventional or a nuclear attack."[78]

This reminder, one feels, was occasioned by the anxieties of the European bishops, who reportedly feared that our

American colleagues were moving towards support of isolationism.[79]

What the pastoral has to say about objectives of nuclear weapons is identical in all three drafts:

> Under no circumstances may nuclear weapons or instruments of mass slaughter be used for the purpose of destroying population centres or other predominantly civilian targets.[80]

The Third Draft specifies:

> It would be a perverted political policy or moral casuistry which tried to justify using a weapon which "indirectly" or "unintentionally" killed a million innocent people because they happened to live near a military significant target.[81]

The bishops regret that there is no international organisation with authority to mediate effectively or prevent conflict. More important than any other factor, in the writer's opinion, is the very expanded section on non-violence and ways of defending peace other than by force of arms.[82] About 3,000 words have been devoted to the history of non-violence in the Church from the early Fathers down to our time, referring to a variety of historic examples, including the movement to Indian Independence led by Gandhi. This Draft suggests that non-violence, rather than being rejected as "impractical or unrealistic" should be studied seriously. Here it is suggested, for instance that:

> Citizens should be trained in the techniques of peaceable non-compliance and non-co-operation as a means of hindering an invading force or a non-Democratic Government from imposing its will.[83]

It called on educational and research institutions:

> To take a lead in conducting peace studies: scientific studies on war, its nature, causes, means, objectives and risks have much to teach us on conditions for peace.[84]

One other fact should be mentioned which appeared in the Second Draft and recurs in the Third Draft. It is the explicit concern about the abortion problem in the United States. Speaking about dulling sensitivities, and the many faces of violence, the document states that if...

> ... innocent unborn are killed wantonly, how can we expect people to feel righteous revulsion at the act or threat or killing non-combatants in war? ... Nothing can justify direct attack on innocent human life in or out of warfare. Abortion is precisely such an attack.

> ... if the arms race is not reversed resources will not be available to human needs so evident in many parts of the globe and in our own country as well.

Sensibly, the bishops call attention to the need of making the transition from "defense industries ... to other forms of employment".[86] An interdependent world requires an understanding that key policy questions "today involve mutuality of interests". The truth is that the globe is inhabited by a single family "in which all have a right to the goods of the earth".

Finally, and in answer to the criticism about meddling in politics, the bishops insist that the question of war and peace has a "moral dimension". The fact that this question is also political "is no excuse for denying the Church's obligation to provide its members with the help they need in forming their consciences".[87]

Some Criticisms

Naturally there was disappointment because this Third Draft softened its attitude in regard to the production and deployment of nuclear weapons. Evidently there were various reasons for this, such as pressure from the Administration, from Catholics and particularly those who work in this area, not to mention those who emphasise the right of a country to defend itself. Moreover, it is very likely that the ad hoc Committee would be sensitive to the problem of conscience that could be caused by this stance. Nevertheless, as has been said above, the new section about curbing rather than halting was overwhelmingly rejected at the final debate, and this immediately caused consternation in the services where so many Catholics work.

The acceptance of the nuclear deterrent, even though "conditional", is disappointing for many. As we have already stated, it would seem that the bishops were reluctant to go further than the Pope. Daniel Berrigan is reported as calling the pastoral a "betrayal" because it endorsed most of President Reagan's arms policies.[88]

However, Archbishop Roach, the President of the NCCB and Cardinal Bernardin, Chairman of the NCCB ad hoc Committee on War and Peace, said the Third Draft "is significantly at variance with the current US policies especially in its advocacy of no first-use". Bishop Gumbleton, the pacifist Bishop of Detroit and member of the ad hoc Committee held that "in the long run the Third Draft becomes a stronger document". He said that it was part of a bishop's job to heed the views of others "with compassion, understanding and sensitivity". He felt the strength lies in the fact that because it has taken into account criticisms of early Drafts, it "had a better chance of being accepted, of being a challenge to those who may disagree with some of its more unspoken and critical passages".[89] It clearly underlined that current American nuclear strategy is morally wrong. On the other hand, it was interesting to note that the administration's reactions before the meeting of the bishops in May were substantially more favourable towards the Third Draft than its predecessor. Cardinal Bernardin declared that the objective of the pastoral was "to state a central moral imperative – that the arms race must be stopped and disarmament begun".

One should not elaborate the pastoral solely in the context of the present state of affairs in the United States. Rather the moral critique is directed not just to issues of the moment "but to issues with a long history in our national life".[90]

Still this Draft does indicate clearly that the bishops are patently uncomfortable with the basic concept of the deterrence position. In reference to Grisez, whose criticisms have already been mentioned, this Third Draft clearly states:

There are moral limits to deterrence policy as well as to policy regarding use. Specifically, it is not morally acceptable to intend to kill the innocent as part of a strategy of deterring nuclear war. The question of whether US policy involves an intention to strike civilian centres (directly targeting civilian populations) has been one of our factual concerns.[91]

The document cites a letter, dated 15 January 1983, to the NCCB from William Clark. It holds that the United States does "not target Soviet civilian populations as such" but the administration cannot issue policy statements "which might suggest to the Soviets that it would be to their advantage to establish privileged sanctuaries within heavily populated areas". This would induce the Soviets to place some of their war fighting capacity within urban sanctuaries. This policy of the United States, as stated by Clark, is confirmed by Secretary Weinberger in his report to Congress.[93] At any rate, while this military posture does uphold the immunity of non-combatants from direct attack, it does not address the problem that attacks on military targets could involve "indirect" ("unintended") massive civilian casualties. According to the Draft, there are 60 military targets within the city of Moscow alone and 40,000 of the same targets exist in the whole of the Soviet Union. In their consultations with the administration, the bishops learned that retaliation could be massive with catastrophic casualties. Even if attacks were limited to "military targets", the number of "deaths in a substantial exchange would be almost indistinguishable from what might occur if civilian centres had been deliberately and directly struck".[94]

This immediately infringes the principle of proportionality. Even with highly accurate weapons, because of escalation, large numbers of casualties would be involved. These points were of agonising concern to the bishops who limit deterrence to the "specific objective of preventing the use of nuclear weapons".[95] "Counter-strikes" are therefore not acceptable to the bishops. Consequently, any use of nuclear weapons which violates the principles of discrimination and proportionality "may not be attempted in a strategy of deterrence". This, of course, is clearly opposed to the military posture of the United States.

It is worth referring to an article written by Peter Hebblethwaite, an expert in Vatican affairs, about the highly publicised meeting in the Vatican on 18 and 19 January, when representatives of the American and European bishops discussed the moral question that had arisen from the Second Draft.[96] Hebblethwaite quotes from a report by Jan Schotte, Secretary of the PCJP. He also refers to a memorandum, dated 25 January 1983, from Archbishop Roach and Cardinal Bernardin.[97]

It is clear from the report that there were substantial disagreements. One radical objection came from the acting chairman, Cardinal Ratzinger, Prefect of the Sacred Congregation for the Doctrine of Faith, who acted as chairman during the meeting. He proposed, as a point for discussion, that a national bishops' conference does not have a *mandatum docendi*. This belongs, he contended, to individual bishops of the College of Bishops in union with the Pope. This was certainly an odd remark, apparently challenging the very competence of the NCCB to make any collective pastoral statement; and suggesting that a group of bishops are less likely to provide more effective teaching than one bishop. Ratzinger's objection could equally apply to cardinals and congregations! Since the Vatican II rediscovery of and emphasis on collegiality it would seem that bishops can exercise collectively their pastoral office in such a case as the United States context. Behind this lies a debate about the nature of a bishops' conference. Vatican II defined that:

> An episcopal conference is a kind of council of which the bishops of a given nation or territory jointly exercise their pastoral office by way of promoting the greater good which the Church offers all mankind, especially through forms and works of the Apostolate, which are fittingly adapted to the circumstances of the age.[98]

Another interesting point, made by Hebblethwaite, was that some participants felt that bishops should stick to open or shut cases, rather than contribute "elements that encourage debate". Ratzinger also indicated that the Draft discussed the moral options of non-violence and the just war on the same basis and that clarification was certainly needed. Later, other members claimed, according to Hebblethwaite, "that non-violence has never been seen in the Church as an alternative to the just war theory". They challenged the contention "that leading theologians in the first four centuries" opposed military service. In short, as the memorandum later said ...

> ... the concern was ... whether too much weight was given to the non-violent position in the light of traditional Catholic teaching on self-defence and how we understood these two moral choices on non-violence and just war as they apply to the policy of states.

The bishops declared that "they will study again the draft text where reference to the Church's tradition on war and peace is examined".

Interestingly enough, the result led to more space being given to the whole question of non-violence. In fact, the Third Draft spelt out even more clearly the support for non-violence in the early Christian Church by giving the names of the leading thinkers and, not only that, they also quoted liberally from them. Some of the names that were explicitly mentioned were Justin, Cyprian of Carthage, and Martin of Tours. Moreover, they dealt with every category of the just war theory in detail.

It was also suggested at the meeting that a clear line should be drawn between "statements of principle and practical choices based on prudential judgement". In the memorandum that followed, Roach and Bernardin declared that they would give more attention to the different levels of authority in the different parts of the pastoral. This they did, because the Third Draft explicitly distinguishes between principle and practice. They both found the tone of the meetings positive and the results were helpful to the work of the NCCB committee in their preparation of the Third Draft. Some writers expressed surprise that the Pope, himself, did not attend the meeting on a subject of supreme importance.[99]

Additionally, the memorandum declared that a follow-up meeting between the American representatives and the Pope did take place on 21 January 1983, but that the "topic of the pastoral letter was not discussed". However, Bernardin did have a private discussion with Casaroli, Ratzinger and the Pope at a later date.

Before concluding this section, a reference should be made to one of the failures of this pastoral letter. In my view, its biggest weakness follows from the use of scripture in the Second and Third Draft. While it is true that the biblical section of the Third Draft is an improvement over the corresponding sections of the first two Drafts, in that it demonstrates better the relationship between the Old and New Testaments, it still fails to integrate the biblical material with the central reasoning of the document. This point has also been taken up by Sandra Schneiders who also felt that the pastoral should have put greater emphasis on the preferential option for the poor in contrast to the American government's clear preferential option for military spending at the cost of unemployment, hunger and disease.[101]

It is a pity that, having used so much biblical material, a better attempt was not made to establish the real connection between scripture and the moral argument which followed. No attempt was made to remedy this defect in the final publication after the Chicago meeting.[102]

Some Repercussions of the Third Draft

The two dimensions, or moral options, regarding war are given detailed attention in the Third Draft. That is to say, much more space and analysis have been given to the just war ethic and the non-violent tradition. The document points out that while these options are distinct, they are interdependent methods of evaluating warfare: "They diverge on some specific conclusions but they share a common presumption against the use of force as a means of settling disputes."[103] Douglass has, perhaps, a point when he says that "the nuclear age is leading Christians to a pacifist position".[104] Many people have failed to notice that over recent years, in Britain and elsewhere as well as in America, a most important extra-parliamentary debate is taking place about a commitment to non-violent direct action.

Certainly this Draft has adopted a sympathetic and positive attitude to the value of non-violence. It gives an interesting description of its history by quoting from the Fathers like Justin who, in turn, quoted Isaiah about: "Turning swords into ploughshares."[105] Again, in the concluding paragraphs of the Draft, the bishops returned to the option of non-violence "which deserved much more study and consideration than they have thus far received". They quoted the examples of the Danes and the Norwegians in Nazi times. Organised popular defence instituted by governments received favourable mention, and also training citizens in techniques of peaceable non-compliance and non-co-operation:

These principles are thoroughly compatible with – and to some extent derived from – Christian teaching and must be part of any Christian theology of peace.[106]

With John Paul II, the bishops called upon educational and

research studies "to take the lead in conducting peace studies ..." To achieve this end, the bishops urged that funds equivalent to a designated percentage even one-tenth of 1 per cent of current budgetary allotments for military purposes, be set aside to support peace research.[107]

This is very encouraging, but it would be a mistake to conclude that Catholic opinions concerning war will automatically shift in any large way to this kind of thinking. Nevertheless, the shift is dramatic in a document of such importance, and this applies whatever opinion one holds about absolute or selective pacifism. No one in Catholic high places 30 years ago would have been willing to recognise pacifism or non-violence as an acceptable, much less equal, option for Catholics. Very few Catholic thinkers would have given serious thought to non-violence as a possible alternative to war. As Gordon Zahn wrote in 1980:

> If it can be said that the majority of our Catholic faithful are apathetic or indifferent to the moral dimensions of war and resistive to statements of ecclesiastical officials, which might try to change these attitudes, it was probably ever thus – at least since the introduction of the just war ethic.[108]

Even at this late hour, peace work and its support is still very much a "Cinderella" in the Catholic Church, even though there are Peace Days every year and justice and peace groups spring up in every country. At the same time, many of the Church's concerns are still very peripheral and indeed parochial, and justice and peace work does not get a high place in the Church's list of priorities.

Certainly the careful definitions and distinctions of the Third Draft are important and, to a certain extent, revolutionary, but it will be interesting to see what influence they will have on the body politic in America, and indeed on American Catholics who often pride themselves on their nationalistic loyalty, and so tend to believe that it is not for them to question their government's activities and policies, especially in wartime.

Maybe this gives us a clue regarding the official Church's rejection of pacifism until recently. The notion of resistance, disobedience, or conscientious objection gives the individual an autonomy that could be seen as a threat to the institutional Church itself and thereby a challenge to authority. This might be one of the explanations why pacifism has received more support in the Protestant traditions. The case for peace in our time will require much more effort and indeed resources if the teaching that dominated the earliest years of Christianity is to be promoted.

Ethical Method

In the Third Draft the method follows the criteria of its predecessor, but it expands the just war ethic. Not only that, but it pays detailed attention to each of the criteria which were mentioned in Chapter 2, with the addition of one extra which is called "Comparative Justice". Do the rights and values involved justify killing?

This Draft drops one reason previously offered by the Second Draft for the acceptance of deterrence. Deterrence was an evil situation that was "tolerated" because of the danger of unilateral disarmament which could involve a greater evil. There is no reference in this Draft to the "lesser of two evils" (Krol's argument before the Senate). Nor is there any trace of the word "toleration" which was criticised by Grisez and to which reference has already been made. The argument is confined to John Paul's statement on deterrence but, even here, it responds to the criticism of Grisez and others when it spells out what it believes the Pope meant by "deterrence".

> Having offered this analysis of the general concept of deterrence, the Holy Father introduces his considerations on disarmament, especially, but not only nuclear disarmament. Pope John Paul makes this statement about the morality of deterrence:

> "In current conditions, 'deterrence' based on balance, certainly not as an end in itself but as a step on the way towards progressive disarmament, may still be judged morally acceptable. Nonetheless, in order to ensure peace, it is indisputable not to be satisfied with this minimum, which is always susceptible to the real danger of explosion."[109]

Not all would agree with the United States bishops and the Pope on conditional deterrence. Many, for example, see it as an evil in itself which could not be justified for any reason.[110]

CONCLUSIONS

The Final Debate in Chicago

As we have already noted, during the final debate on 2 and 3 May 1983 the bishops explicitly altered the Draft to include "*halt*" to the further testing, production and deployment of nuclear weapons. In response to criticism from right-wing Catholics and also from the Reagan administration, the word "halt" (freeze) which had appeared in the First and Second Drafts was omitted in the Third Draft and the word "curb" was substituted. It was decided, however, at the final meeting, by an overwhelming majority (238 to 9) to replace the word "curb" with "halt". Thereby the bishops confounded those who expected the Third Draft to be a subdued document more in line with government thinking than earlier Drafts. The change of wording is significant because it gave an expression of support for the nuclear freeze campaign which had been endorsed by a number of congressmen and by voters in various state referenda.[111]

Finally, the preparation of this pastoral has been an interesting exercise in testing ideas, and engaging in consultation in a very serious and open effort to obtain deeper insights. This enables the busy Christian, caught up in the daily affairs of life, to have a sounding-board where the basic value question can be assessed and thought through in a supportive context. Freedom of enquiry and expression are essential elements in a pilgrim community in attempting to seek the truth. Mistakes must be tolerated, even within a body such as the NCCB. It is all part of a learning process and it is to be hoped that this sort of community decision will become a commonplace experience to reflect on social and moral issues that pertain to our international community.

In short, it is evident that the making of the Pastoral Letter relied heavily on the traditions of the whole Christian community in regard to war and peace. The bishops wished to explain and explore the resources of the moral-religious teaching and apply it to specific questions of today. The problem of deterrence, nevertheless, remains. The Reagan administration wishes to spend millions of dollars over the next few years on armaments. Increased expenditure on more sophisticated weapons can hardly be taken as evidence of serious commitment to progressive disarmament. Will the United States bishops then declare the possession of nuclear weapons as immoral, which would evidently follow from their posture on deterrents? How would this affect Church-State relations and attitudes within the Roman Catholic Church? These questions remain unanswered at the moment, but are sure to surface again in the future.

CHAPTER FIVE

The Response of the Church of England

REFLECTIONS ON WAR AND PEACE

The Archbishop of Canterbury had raised a radically trenchant protest against the momentum of the arms race in 1980. Speaking to the British Council of Churches on 24 November 1980, Archbishop Runcie offered a statement on the morality of nuclear deterrence which was outstanding for its precision and balanced judgement. He urged vigilance against the "hygienic vocabulary" of defence officials and specialists whose stock-in-trade covers over what he judges to be "lunatic" policies. With persuasive allusion to the creative power of the Word to heal the wounds of human nature, the archbishop urges a return to the well-spring of Christianity in order to animate a renewal of Western approaches to peace. He argues that it might be possible to have a just war "but there can be no such thing as mutual obliteration ... and the old distinctions about the just war, I find unconvincing in this climate ... We are capable of unbinding forces which lie at the heart of creation and destroying the whole planet."[1] Nevertheless, Runcie counsels against unilateral nuclear disarmament which might shatter the Atlantic Alliance but he urges the adoption by NATO nations of a "no first-use" nuclear weapons policy.

He then shrewdly cautions against expecting that financial savings in this regard would be transferred to more humanitarian purposes. He foresees that the money would be spent by the Alliance to improve its conventional forces in Europe.

The Working Party Document

The document which perhaps has had most influence on the nuclear debate in Britain, *The Church and The Bomb*, came as the result of the Working Party and later was discussed at the General Synod of the Church of England.[2] The Report takes its origin from a resolution of the General Synod of the Church of England. The Synod, meeting in London 1979, agreed to explore:

> How the theological debate relating to discipleship in this field (promoting and preserving peace) might be more effectively and purposefully conducted throughout the Church of England in the light of the witness and insights of the whole ecumenical movement.[3]

The Board for Social Responsibility had already produced a report on the subject of arms and disarmament which had been debated by the Synod. The Board now responded to the Synod's resolution by inviting certain members to serve on a Working Party:

1. To study the implications for Christian discipleship of the acceptance by the major military powers of a role for thermo-nuclear weapons in their strategy.

2. To consider the bearing of this on the adequacy of past Christian teaching and ethical analysis regarding the conduct of war.

3. To advise the Board on ways in which members of the Churches can be helped to participate more effectively in public debate on these issues.

4. From time to time to prepare for publication discussion papers on the matters under consideration.

The members were: the Bishop of Salisbury (Chairman), Sydney Bailey, John Elford, Paul Oestreicher, Barrie Paskins, and Brendan Soane (the Roman Catholic theologian). The Working Party met for the first time in July 1980. At a very early stage, they asked the Board to relieve them of the third and fourth items. They expressed a wish to consider other types of nuclear weapons as well as thermo-nuclear. Aspects of their task were discussed with various experts and the group as a whole worked on each draft chapter, while each member of the Working Party made himself responsible for drafting a particular chapter.

Structure of the Report

The Report divides into two parts. The first part consists of Chapters 1 to 6. It surveys the various aspects of the subject matter – technological, strategic and political. The matter is evaluated in the light of the common ethical tradition and the distinctively Christian theological presuppositions. The second part, Chapters 7 and 8, examines the possible options and forms conclusions.

The first part of the Report reminds us of the probable effects of nuclear war. It mentions the efforts of centuries to restrain recourse to war. But both international law and moral tradition of the West have judged that recourse to armed force is sometimes acceptable, "both have sought to contain war-making, by stating limits beyond which no law-abiding person or group should go in pursuit of justice".[4]

The Report proceeds to look at the law on war and the just war criteria. It sets out the criteria very simply, and by reflecting on them, makes its case against nuclear deterrence on the basis of the just war doctrine. The exposition contained in Chapter 5 of the Report could scarcely be bettered for clarity and insight into the real meaning of the tradition. Non-combatant immunity, the principle of proportionality and the principle of the double effect are carefully analysed before the Report examines the criteria of the just war in the nuclear age. The conclusion is that, while the first three conditions – lawful authority, just cause and last resort – could possibly be satisfied, the last three – reasonable hope of success, proportion and the immunity of non-combatants – could almost certainly never be fulfilled in a nuclear war. In regard to the principle of discrimination, the question of direct and indirect killing is introduced, but the Report notes that the use of nuclear weapons "amounts to wholesale and foreseen killing and injuring of non-combatants which cannot be described as discriminate".[5] Nor does the principle of the double effect offer relief as the deaths would not be accidental or incidental; they must be classed as direct killing of the innocent: "After all, it is the protection of the innocent which justifies going to war in the first place."[6] Nor is the action proportionate to the end in sight. For this reason, the use of nuclear weapons is not morally acceptable.

Reflecting on the principle of proportion, the Report con-

cludes that because the weapons would cause so much devastation they are "inherently unsuitable". Even small weapons
used against isolated military targets have to be examined in the
"total military strategy" apart altogether from the problem of
indiscriminate fall-out. Because of the likelihood of escalation,
even small weapons are disproportionate and unacceptable.

The chairman, the Bishop of Salisbury, clarified this point in
a letter to *The Times*:

> Our conclusion that nuclear weapons cannot be used in a way
> which respects the vital principle of non-combatants' immunity, is
> based on the fact that nuclear weapons release radiation, whatever
> the target, and this radiation is distributed in a way that cannot be
> accurately predicted. Radiation causes both somatic and genetic
> harm and the latter threatens future generations.[7]

Thus, the Report concluded that:

> The use of nuclear weapons cannot be justified. Such weapons
> cannot be used without harming non-combatants and could never
> be proportionate to the just cause and aim of the just war.[8]

Ethics of Nuclear Deterrence

This question revolves around the morality of possessing the
weapons for the purpose of deterrence. The argument in the
Report rejects the nuclear deterrent on the grounds that it is
immoral to *threaten* to do, under some future circumstances,
what it is immoral to do: "Such conditional intention implies
that one has consented in one's mind to act immorally".[9] Two
possible ways of side-stepping this conclusion are carefully
analysed in the Report. These ways are called the Bluff Theory
and the Stability Theory.

THE BLUFF THEORY   A distinction, according to some supporters, can be made between *the intention to use* and *the
intention to deter*. They contend that the latter is certainly
morally acceptable. But the Report states that this is a fantasy,
because for deterrence to be effective, the intention to use has
not only to be repeatedly stated, but also backed up by training
of personnel, targetting, maintenance and constant deployment of new weapon systems.[10] All the people concerned with

these activities would have to be kept out of the bluff secret, i.e., of the fact that the order to fire would never be given. This secret must effectively be confined to two or three top political leaders who, in a democratic society, might be replaced at any moment by people who did not share this view. In fact, practically everyone, both in the public sector and in the services, would have to be constantly indoctrinated with the belief that the use of nuclear weapons was in the last resort justified, while the bluff was nevertheless maintained. This, the Report says, could never be a national policy, nor could it work in practice.[11]

THE STABILITY THEORY This argument is based on the belief that nuclear deterrence keeps the peace. In fact, many Western governments, such as the Reagan administration and the Thatcher government have constantly presented this argument. In short, the intention is *not to use* nuclear weapons but to *prevent* the use. The Report refuses to accept this argument. Proliferation, increasing possibility of accident, the intention of pre-emptive strike and retaliation – all make it unsound and unconvincing.[12] In fact, one could question the presumption that nuclear weapons have helped to keep the peace over the years – a point taken up by Professor James O'Connell in the correspondence that followed the Report's publication. In short, the Report adds that paradoxes contained in the theory of deterrence can be distilled into . . .

. . . one fundamental form, around which the whole debate ultimately revolved; if the deterrent is to work, you have to convince the enemy that you are willing to use it; but if you have to use it, it has failed.[13]

The Report does indicate "another way" in the form of pacifism. For many Christians it is the only "acceptable solution to the problem of violence".[14] Defenders of the just war and pacifists are agreed on the need to search for means to reduce international tension; both regard war as evil, "they work together to bring about disarmament, which has for so long eluded humanity".[15] The Report mentions three forms of pacifism: pacifism of principle (which some argue is of the essence of Faith, while others claim it is rather a vocation);

prudential pacifism (which some claim represents the most prudent and, therefore, the most moral course); and selective pacifism (which does not reject war as such, but certain forms of it, e.g. the nuclear war). The Report claims that its conclusions are the same as those of the nuclear pacifist:

> That condoning or taking part in nuclear war, or any conflict which is likely to lead to nuclear war, is incompatible with the Christian Faith.[16]

In the last section, while dealing with options and conclusions, the Report positively recommends "unilateral measures at the start in the hope of getting multilateral reductions moving".[17] It contends that it is not hypocritical "to give up one's nuclear weapons and yet remain in an alliance where other members deploy theirs".[18] It also recognizes the other option, that of those who "wish their country to pull-out of nuclear weaponry" and prefer that "we should leave NATO and take up a neutralist role ... we do not ourselves see the necessity of it, and there are many reasons to the contrary".[19] It further recommends that Britain cancel the Trident missile at once and "phase out the Polaris missiles and submarines, including the work of Chevaline".[20]

Amongst other recommendations, the Report suggests that "existing disarmament negotiations should be vigorously prosecuted and backed to the hilt".[21] There should be support for the UN in its work of peace and "renewed and determined efforts should be made to secure a Comprehensive Test Ban Treaty".[22] Finally, it mentions the options of the Peace Tax Campaign which is striving to promote legislation "to enable a proportion of objectors' taxes to be paid into a fund earmarked for specific peace projects".[23]

The Report ends by stating that the cause of right cannot be upheld by fighting a nuclear war and poses a question which is at the heart of this thesis:

> Has not the technology of war now reached a point where, at any rate in major conflicts, it is no longer possible in the military profession to give one's life that others may live, but only that others may die?[24]

Some Repercussions

The point of immoral intention was taken up by Clifford Longley, the religious affairs correspondent for *The Times*.[25] It caused a vigorous and interesting correspondence. His claim was that there was an intrinsic moral flaw in the argument that the conditional intention to perform an immoral act is always itself immoral. Moreover, he quoted Paul Oestreicher as saying that: "It was not a morally sound argument." Not only that, but Longley indicated that the United States bishops themselves were challenged on using this kind of an argument in their draft pastoral "by representatives of the most sophisticated Roman Catholic hierarchies of France and West Germany ..." which took place at a top level meeting in the Vatican. However, Bishop Butler, the Auxiliary Roman Catholic Bishop of Westminster, attacked Clifford Longley's argument on the ground that it contained a logical fallacy in trying to negate the moral-intention proposition:

> For it is impossible to intend to respond to a situation which, you are certain, will never arise. No one can intend to do what he knows he will never have occasion to do. Hence, if deterrents were certain to succeed permanently, it could continue as a policy, although there could be no intention of translating it into an act. Unfortunately, such certainty, as is generally admitted, is not attainable.[26]

Oestreicher replied that the argument in the Report did follow the traditional lines and, in fact: "I fully agreed with the conclusion."[27] Rushton of Oxford, in the same correspondence, hastened to add that what the United States bishops were saying was that practising nuclear deterrence could lead to the real risk of one day having to use weapons which had been targetted on another nation. The actual use: "would be a great crime against humanity, and there can be no adequate reason for risking such an action." The risk is inseparable from the practice of deterrence. This then, he says, is the moral argument at its simplest. It contains no logical fallacy; it is simply that such use cannot be justified, nor could such use be intended.

Longley further added that the Working Party used traditional moral categories and followed an "absolutist position" which was contrary to the Anglican moral tradition. He claimed that Oestreicher admitted that had he been responsible for that particular chapter, he would not have produced this argument at all;[28] to this Oestreicher replied by saying that he fully agreed with the conclusion contained in the Report and "were I to argue the case from my own tradition, I would reach the same conclusion".[29] In other words, he would accept the conclusion for different reasons.

Another member of the Working Party, Brendan Soane, hastened to point out that the Report did outline...

> ... an alternative non-absolutist point of view on pages 100 and 101 of the Report... As we say on page 145, there are clearly a number of positions for which a respectable moral case could be made. Although we recognise the weight of the argument in favour of nuclear deterrence, we do not think it sufficient to outweigh the imperative not to use nuclear weapons.[30]

Paul Johnson argued that the principles of Christian theology are against unilateral disarmament and nuclear deterrence is the only moral course.[31] Indeed, the same argument was also put by the Jesuit, Father Langan,[32] who reasoned that unilateral disarmament "constitutes a drastic limitation in a nation's right to self-defence and may well prepare the way for a surrender of national self-determination".[33]

Michael Howard, one of Britain's leading experts in military strategy, asserted that the Working Party's Report failed to discuss a central aspect of the moral issue; the United States and her European allies decided to rely on nuclear deterrence in 1953 "for the defence of Western Europe for one simple reason; it was cheap", it gives "a bigger bang for the buck". It is the initiation of the use of these weapons that causes so many of us profound concern, and we have "acquiesced in a decision to maintain a standard of living far higher than that of our adversaries, rather than providing resources for a convincing defence by non-nuclear means of the territories of Western Europe".[34] Howard saw this as a profoundly moral question.

Walter Stein accused the Bishop of London of making contradictory statements: "He recognises the utterly appalling prospect of the use of nuclear weapons, yet pronounces their possession and their use morally acceptable."[35] *The Times* leader, in a criticism of the Report believed it had really got it wrong...

> ... the primary intention is not to kill the enemy, except in extreme circumstances, but to keep the peace. Does the immorality of something which will only happen in extreme circumstances, outweigh the morality of what is being achieved day by day?[36]

Repeatedly, it has been said that the possession of nuclear weapons has been a factor in keeping peace in Europe over 30 years. Indeed, William Rees Mogg, former editor of *The Times* produced a very clear and objective analysis of this situation.[37] Professor James O'Connell, however, reminded us that there are other important considerations. Whilst it seems reasonable, he said, to allow that such weapons, with their destructive powers, may have contributed to restraining the countries of the two great alliances in Europe from attacking one another, nevertheless countries such as Britain and Germany have found good reasons for all sorts of co-operation. Peace was consolidated as countries discovered that their interests converged. The factors that went into the making of the Common Market have been deeper and more pervasive than military considerations.[38]

If nuclear weapons have been a factor in peace-keeping, many other more powerful factors have also been at work. The British case is different because, it can be argued, by possessing a threat against a super power, it thereby possesses a threat to itself. O'Connell also argues that the retention of nuclear weapons within an already over-armed alliance poses further questions about the dangers of such policies, such as the concealment of public policy by the government (Chevaline for example), the diversion of money and skills from economic growth, and the growing bitterness of the politics of a divided nation.

Finally, as I have indicated, some writers felt that the Report was rather inconsistent because it held that no nuclear war could be just, yet was quite willing to shelter within the defence of NATO. It was for this reason that Conor Cruise O'Brien claimed that the Report was "having it both ways"[39] because it recommended Britain should have no nuclear weapons on its own soil but remain under the umbrella of NATO.

Deterrents – Ethical Evaluation and Practical Options

All contributors to the debate agree in their attempt to prevent nuclear war. The disagreement arises about methods. One school of thought claims that the prevention of nuclear war can only be maintained by the possession of the nuclear deterrent; the contrary is maintained by others. Paradoxically, the unique moral problem posed by the nuclear strike is, therefore, not so much the use of nuclear weapons but the threat to use them which is, according to some, equivalent to an evil intention.[40] This was the point discussed by Krol before the United States Senate and taken up by the NCCB and by the Working Party in the Report. Many thinkers distinguish immediately between the intention *to use* and the intention *to deter*.[41] The former is seen by some as being immoral because a formed decision to do evil carries the same degree of culpability as the execution of the evil act. So the advocates of this theory claim that possession of nuclear weapons is based on an immoral intention.

However, the opponents of this school of thought reject that reasoning on the basis that the intention is really *not to use* but to *prevent the use* of nuclear weapons. Put in another way, it is deterrence of recourse to nuclear war rather than the intention to use nuclear weapons that is implied in *possession*. Possession, therefore, is peace-keeping. However, it has been pointed out that in history the attempt to maintain the balance of power has never succeeded. At most, it has postponed major wars and encouraged minor ones. Therefore, according to some thinkers, the policy of deterrence is bound to fail. Add to this other factors such as proliferation, miscalculation, the madness of fanaticism of leaders, and escalation, and the position of a deterrence policy will be seen to be palpably false.[42]

It is difficult to ascertain how the argument can, in fact, be settled in the abstract as there are theologians, politicians and academics on both sides.[43]

So it would seem clear that the real test is what happens in practice. Does the policy in question actually make this world a safer place? Does it increase the likelihood of nuclear war? To pursue a policy that increases the possibility of nuclear war is to *intend* this outcome. But to pursue policies which can be reasonably projected to make nuclear war less likely is to *intend* the avoidance of war. Consequently, the moral judgement on the intention behind the deterrent cannot be separated from an evaluation of the reasonably predictable outcome of the policy choices. In a word; will this concrete strategy lead us towards or away from nuclear confrontation? In reality one has to examine specific defence postures which, in turn, should involve effective arms reduction negotiations rather than the ever-increasing arms race. This also means that the policies of the government in question must be constantly under review. Pacifists, nuclear pacifists and just war theorists can all contribute to a consensus on this point which will be of significance in the evaluation of deterrent policies.

Some could reasonably argue that because the Soviet Union has declared a no first-use of nuclear weapons and ratified the SALT Treaty, both items which the United States has failed to match, indicates clearly the direction of the United States Administration.[44] Indeed, the United States has a considerable way to go before it will convince the international community about peace and disarmament. Moreover, the fact that the United States is giving cheap grain to the Soviet Union, thereby allowing more money to be spent by the Soviets on armaments, indicates the inconsistencies of the United States Administration's policy. Jean Kirkpatrick, former United States Ambassador to the United Nations, made this point vividly:

> To appreciate the full absurdity of this nightmare, we have to understand that we are paying our subsidy twice over; first, by extending credits to enable Russia to build their weapons; and second, by then having to match the newly developed Soviet arsenal with accelerated weapons – development of our own.[45]

On the other hand, Rees Mogg argued that though Andropov also called for the prohibition of chemical weapons,[46] the Soviets were nonetheless using them in Afghanistan.[47] But Bruce Kent, Chairman of CND, replied that the evidence for such claims is simply not there...

> ... when the United Nations, rather than the United States, says it is, I shall take a different view. Meanwhile, I commend to Mr Rees Mogg *The Yellow Rainmakers*[48] which investigates the claims about the use by the Soviets of chemical weapons and rejects them as based on shoddy evidence and wild speculation.[49]

He went on, that the United States had failed to give a *no first-use* undertaking, and that the Western military commitment to tactical nuclear weapons is no safe way to guarantee peace.

On reflection it is becoming increasingly clear that the condition on which the moral acceptance of the deterrent is based is gradually diminishing as time goes by. Pressure will inevitably be on the United States bishops and the Pope to renounce the nuclear deterrent as morally unacceptable because it appears that the policy of the American government is towards an arms build-up and an ever-increasing nuclear strike. Furthermore, no allowance is made for miscalculation, madness or accident. The nuclear deterrent which is supposed to ensure security has built into it the very danger that threatens the human race. The scientist, Owen Chamberlain said that:

> If 108 Pershing II missiles are placed in Germany they could take out Soviet missiles in their silos with only 6 minutes warning. The United States' warning systems have already suffered 107 computer malfunctions that signalled an enemy attack. In one such case it took fully 6 minutes before it was determined that it was merely a computer error.
>
> If, for example, the Soviets, whose computers are believed to be less advanced than NATO's, suffered the same kind of computer error after the Pershing II had been installed, they might be forced to make a decision in less than 6 minutes to launch their nuclear missiles, thus destroying large parts of Europe and the United States, in retaliation against an imagined NATO attack.[50]

For the Working Party, on the other hand, nuclear deterrence is morally unacceptable.[51] Unilateral disarmament, therefore, should have been recommended on this basis. Yet oddly enough, the Report gives the reason for unilateralism as the "hope of getting multilateral reductions moving", not because of the moral unacceptability of the deterrent. Moreover, if the nuclear deterrent is, as the Report says, unacceptable morally, it is difficult to see how the use of the nuclear umbrella of NATO can be justified. There does indeed seem to be an inconsistency here. It could be claimed that the United States bishops were equally inconsistent because they condemned all use of nuclear weapons, yet allowed the deterrent which implies their possible use. This point is developed by Winter, who seems to hold that the stance is justified on the principle of the double effect. The good effect is peace-keeping, the evil effect (the capacity of the deterrent for destruction) is tolerated. Additionally, this evil effect is not morally but only physically evil, since moral evil cannot reside in "a physical potency but only in a choice".[52]

Allowing for these problems, the fact remains that it was a considerable achievement that both the Synod and the Pastoral Letter rejected the first-use strategy, even though both accepted the nuclear deterrent. Can it not be spelled out that, given the proximity of a nuclear disaster, the total rejection of the use of nuclear weapons (first-use or otherwise) may be the most fitting stance for the Christian who takes a higher and wider view of reality? Faith will always involve an element of risk and here the risk is worth taking. Reliance on weapons of absolute destructive power is an offence against Faith, rejects trust in God and threatens the annihilation of His Creation. It is the pretence of the sovereign State to absolute power embodied in these weapons which gives such an impression of irrationality and atheism. Meanwhile, the urgent task of the Church is to keep the moral issues before the eyes of the public by focusing on the issues of massive killings (direct and indirect), peace, the arms race, world poverty and war.

It is, however, likely that the debate regarding possession of nuclear weapons for deterrence, as distinct from their use, will continue as theologians and Churches strive agonisingly to discover God's will in a dangerous world. The recent argument which has caused a lively and interesting literature still centres on possession, intention and the notion of threat, and whether they can be separated. It would of course, be unrealistic to see the American Episcopal Document or the debate of the Synod as the final word on the subject. Serious scholars disagree, and there are arguments supporting both sides. While the moral legitimacy of national defence is still accepted by many, nevertheless the problem of even limited nuclear war remains because of the almost unavoidable danger of escalation. Perhaps the best summing up of the position is that of Professor McCormick:

We have been able to arrive at only the following clarities:

1. The possession of nuclear weapons is, at best, morally ambiguous and, therefore, at best tolerable. It may not even be that.

2. Such possession is tolerable only for the present and under certain circumstances.

3. These conditions are: a firm resolve never to use nuclear weapons and a firm resolve to work immediately to assure their abolition, in law and in fact.

4. While unilateral disarmament may not be a clear moral mandate, unilateral steps towards multilateral disarmament certainly are.[53]

THE PUBLIC DEBATE

A Reaction by the Board for Social Responsibility

In January 1983, the Board for Social Responsibility prepared a document which claimed to give a considered response by the Board on the nuclear issues and to reflect on central matters raised in the Working Party Report. It did not comment on all aspects discussed in the document *The Church and The Bomb*.[54]

There was both support for and anxiety about the central arguments in the Working Party's Report and its conclusions. The Board pointed out that some members of the Working Party admitted that, as their discussions proceeded, they became more unanimous about their conclusions. The Board referred to the Working Party's attitude to the just war and concedes that if nuclear weapons are fundamentally flawed they cannot be rescued by any appeal to international attitudes: "Ideological positions and wickedness by any nation can never provide justification for the use of such weapons."[55] However, some held that under the just war concept a nuclear war was morally possible because the three principles of double effect, discrimination and proportion were neither absolute in the sense of permitting no exceptions nor tenable in some of the senses in which the Report used them.

Some members of the Board thought that the Report paid insufficient attention to the problem of power; its use of moral argument was weak when set against the stern realities of power in a fallen world. The intention of those who wielded power had to be assessed, and this could shift the argument in favour of multilateral approaches rather than unilateral decisions.

The Board believed that the seriousness of the threat posed to our world by the possession of nuclear weapons must be accepted without question. It wished to reinforce the Board's sense of urgency especially in regard to our work and prayers for peace. However, in this process of making and keeping peace, we have to be realistic; and whilst in no way exonerating Western attitudes, some members had deep reservations about Soviet policy and intentions. Some also held that there is a moral inconsistency in the suggestion of ridding Britain of nuclear weapons while continuing membership of NATO which is based on a nuclear defence policy. The question of increased military expenditure was also relevant: "It also has to be noted that reductions in nuclear weapons might involve an increase in commitments to conventional weapons and in the size of the defence budget."[56] The Board criticised the Report for its scriptural treatment – it shows "an incompleteness in its theological treatment. In particular it may seem to miss that sense of hard realism which the Bible exhibits with regard to human action in a fallen world."[57]

As was indicated above, while praising the Board for its clarification on the criteria of the just war, a number of Board members did not agree that the Board's application "of the just war principles was sufficient to justify condemnation of the nuclear deterrent".[58] Accordingly, the principles did not necessarily lead to the difficult decision of foregoing the protection of the nuclear deterrent. If nuclear missiles are targetted on military objectives, and if the inevitable killing of some civilians is unintended, then, in the view of some members, the principle of the double effect is not violated. Again, the principle of discrimination which protects the immunity of non-combatants is not absolute, and so it cannot rule out the very possession of nuclear weapons as immoral. The third principle, that of proportion, could not be used to weigh one set of values against another: e.g. the suppression of human rights by totalitarian tyranny with an expansionist intention, against the appalling destructive power of modern nuclear warfare. Again, the principle of proportion does not seem to rule out the choice of a great good achieved at the risk of a great evil, "when the

alternative is almost wholly evil".[59] In short, the principles of
the just war were not necessarily incompatible with all forms of
nuclear deterrence.

Again, some claimed that any nation possessing nuclear
weapons must be prepared to use them, while others believed
that the principles of the just war are less relevant to nuclear
weapons than to conventional weapons: "The question of
deterrents is not a question about war, but about the risks of
war, and these are not the same."[60] In conclusion, the Board
was divided in its reaction to the diverse policy options regarding the British deterrent and its relationship with the NATO
policy, but it was united...

... in believing that on such difficult moral issues, Christians may
responsibly differ in their conclusions and this should encourage
us to open debate as we continue to seek the mind of the Spirit of
God for these vital areas of moral decision making.[61]

The General Synod of the Church of England

The debate took place on 10 February 1983. Two documents
were debated, the Report (The Working Party's *The Church
and The Bomb*) and the Report (GS.542) with the same title.
(As we have stated, the latter was produced by the Board for
Social Responsibility.)

In the course of the debate, the Archbishop of Canterbury
regretted that the recommendations contained in the Report
and further amplified by the Bishop of Salisbury's amendment,
were not coherent or convincing, nor did he believe that the
suggested unilateralism would lead to multilateral
disarmament.[62] He worried about the moral inconsistency in
seeking to remain in the alliance and drew attention to the
Brandt Commission's Report about the explosive consequences of denying justice in the Third World.[63] Graham
Leonard, the Bishop of London, believed that the Report failed
to guide because: "It elevates its opinion that the possession
and use of nuclear weapons is morally wrong to such a position
as to over-ride all other moral considerations."[64] He referred
to the threat of the communist world domination which, he
claimed, the Report had baldly rejected.[65] However, he was
unfair to the Report when he asserted that no consideration
was given as to how far the just war principles should be

expressed in the light of modern weapons, biological and chemical as well as nuclear;[66] the Report does precisely this when
it argues that the just war principles do not depend on the
question of particular types of weapons, but are derived by
reflection on how human beings should treat each other in an
unjust and violent war: "It is hard to see how they can become
out of date."[67] No matter how the principles are re-expressed,
the Report claims, immunity of non-combatants and the principle of proportion are more than ever endangered. Bishop
Baker proposed an amendment that the Church should dis-
sociate itself from nuclear weaponry. Again, this was opposed
by the Bishop of London. Baker's amendment contained a
number of factors such as ending the Polaris strategic system,
discontinuing all nuclear weapons wholly or mainly of British
manufacture, negotiating Britain's withdrawal from the man-
ning of nuclear weapons manufactured by others and ending
present or future deployment of nuclear weapons on British
soil. The amendment was put and lost, 100 voting for and 338
against. Immediately, the Bishop of Birmingham begged to
move an amendment. Two of the main points were...

> ... that even a small-scale *first-use* of nuclear weapons could never
> be morally justified in view of the high risk that this would lead to
> full-scale nuclear warfare; and that there is a moral obligation on all
> countries (including the members of NATO) publicly to forswear
> the first-use of nuclear weapons in any form.[68]

Once again, the Bishop of London opposed these two points.
He stated that, while he agreed with the other paragraphs, he
had grave difficulty about these two points. He claimed that
NATO had already said it would not use nuclear weapons as
first-use, except in response to an attack. Nevertheless, the
amendment was put and the chairman ordered a division of the
whole Synod; the result was: "Ayes, 275; Noes, 222. The
amendment was therefore carried."[69]

The motion as amended was put and carried. 387 voting for,
49 voting against, and 29 abstaining, in the following form:

That this Synod recognising –

(a) the urgency of the task of making and preserving peace; and (b)
the extreme seriousness of the threat made to the world by the

contemporary nuclear weapons and the dangers in the present international situation: and (c) that it is not the task of the Church to determine defence strategy but rather to give a moral lead to the nation:

(i) affirms that it is the duty of Her Majesty's Government and her allies to maintain adequate forces to guard against nuclear black-mail and to deter nuclear and non-nuclear aggressors;

(ii) asserts that the tactics and strategies of this country and her NATO allies should be seen to be unmistakably defensive in respect of the countries of the Warsaw Pact;

(iii) judges than even a small-scale first use of nuclear weapons could never be morally justified in view of the high risk that this would lead to full-scale nuclear warfare.

(iv) believes that there is a moral obligation on all countries (in-cluding the members of NATO) publicly to forswear the first-use of nuclear weapons in any form;

(v) bearing in mind that many in Europe live in fear of nuclear catastrophe and that nuclear parity is not essential to deterrence, calls on Her Majesty's Government to take immediate steps in conjunction with her allies to further the principles embodied in this motion so as to reduce progressively NATO's dependence on nuclear weapons and to decrease nuclear arsenals throughout the world.[70]

CONCLUSION

The Working Party Report was one major input into a wide public debate to which other churches in Britain also contri-buted. The Pastoral Letter of the NCCB was publicly debated at all stages and thrice revised before being issued in its final form.

The Pastoral Letter, the Synod and the Working Party Re-port all draw from their traditions, that is to say, from WCC, Papal and Conciliar documents. The NCCB and the Synod base their case on the dignity of the human person, made in the Image of God.[71] Both the NCCB and the Church of England Synod forswear the first-use of nuclear weapons, which is a considerable contribution by both Churches. The NCCB cal-led for a halt (freeze) to the manufacture and deployment of all nuclear weapons. However, the effect is considerably lessened because they linked the freeze to a bi-lateral agreement: "In the same spirit we urge negotiations to halt . . ."[72] The Report does not explicitly discuss the freeze as such. Nevertheless, something of the same idea appeared in its recommendations, where it speaks of "renewed and determined efforts to secure a comprehensive Test Ban Treaty".[73] As the chairman of the Working Party, the Bishop of Salisbury, John Baker, pointed out, "such a treaty is very closely akin to a freeze because without the testing of weapons and weapon systems, it is impossible to deploy new ones".[74] However, nothing like this appeared in the motion passed by the General Synod. Both the Synod and the NCCB permit nuclear deterrents, though the latter only conditionally ("a step towards progressive disarmament"). Here the Working Party went further than any organisation or body in recommending unilateralism. Nevertheless, it somewhat blurred the issue by its inconsistency where NATO was concerned. It is interesting to note that all referred to the just war criteria and to traditional moral categories in arriving at such progressive conclusions. The message from all three sources, the Report, the United States bishops, and the Synod, is therefore essentially the same "nuclear weapons must go".[75]

We may make three final points. First, Cardinal Ratzinger, in an interview with *Der Spiegel*, said that the United States bishops were courageous and that he saw their Pastoral Letter as "a rational application of the Sermon on the Mount".[76] Secondly, Archbishop John Quinn (San Francisco) pointed out that Catholic military personnel should disobey orders rather than launch a nuclear attack against populated targets, and this would apply even if the order came from the president of the United States. He also added that soldiers had the right to disobey orders, even in war-time, if those orders were immoral – a right established beyond doubt at Nuremberg.[77]

Thirdly, one should comment on the Bishop of London's claim that "NATO has already said it will not use nuclear weapons as first-use, except in response to an attack".[78] This is very close to a contradiction in terms. The NATO policy envisages the possibility of the use of nuclear weapons, rather than accept conquest, when faced with superior conventional forces.[79] In fact, NATO has no declaration or policy of no first-use. It keeps its options open and refers to "flexible response".

CHAPTER SIX

The Response of a Local Church – Field Research

A PARISH AND PEACE REFLECTIONS

Both the United States Pastoral Letter and the Working Party Report call on the Churches to do more to promote and practise peace. The Pastoral indeed urges every diocese and parish to implement...

> ... balanced and objective programmes to help people at all age levels to understand better the issues of war and peace. Development and implementation of such programmes must receive a high priority during the next several years.[1]

The Working Party likewise advises that the Churches need to purge out "dehumanizing prejudices" from within their own fellowship "to pray, preach and practise peace".

In this chapter, I propose to reflect on my own field work regarding peace education and to grapple with the question of how to change people's minds and hearts in regard to war and peace. It must be emphasised that the research was a joint effort – a collective witness which is carried out in the main by the laity. Mistakes were naturally made and it is hoped we learned from them. Nor do I delude myself that this venture was an easy undertaking. It does, however, give some outline of the way attitudes can change in the local community. The field work does explore projects in which the local community can contribute to peace, justice and human rights. It shows too, that there are untapped resources in these areas and that I have released but a few of them. After all, it was in the area of the local community that local relations succeeded in the past.[2] Local Churches have much more potential than is imagined and so far it has not been developed, especially in this most important work of justice and peace.

Background

To many people, world affairs seem awesome in their scale, confusing in their complexity and demanding a considerable effort for comprehension. Closely connected with the complex nature of global issues is the widespread feeling that the effort to understand global affairs is not worthwhile – that no individual effort could exercise noticeable influence over such policies. Few realise that foreign affairs, particularly in today's world, have a direct and important bearing on each individual life. Insofar as the ordinary citizen is willing to expend any time or effort in these matters, it is topics such as wages, prices, taxes and employment that attract attention. Once again, self-interest plays the key role, and in such options the local Church and its members do not seem to be essentially different from people at large.

In this chapter I have made an attempt to describe my own research at local level over a period of nearly 20 years where the objective was to relate moral convictions to concrete situations. In the belief that involvement is one of the best means of education, projects were introduced into the worship and action of the parish so that an introspective and pietistic religion could be changed into one that included horizontal as well as vertical aspects, and thereby be more sensitive and open to the international community. It was underlined that all these aspects formed one Christianity. Voices were raised at first because it was thought that we were confusing the sacred and the profane by involving ourselves in political situations and projects which had controversial dimensions. It was argued that here again the secular should not be mixed with religion and worship. Therefore, it had to be repeated over and over again that these areas should not be placed in separate compartments; that religion, worship, mission and politics cannot be polarised. They are all parts of the Christian totality. If our worship is to be authentic, therefore, these aspects had to be combined.[3] Again, the work for peace and justice was not to be seen as an optional extra. Rather, as we shall see later in this chapter, all such commitment was to be incorporated in the parish work. It was to be God-centred and in the service of

Christ and his people. In short the horizontal was balanced with the vertical. Bearing these points in mind, and also that mission involves peace, justice, community and all aspects of life, I try here to describe the search for peace through mission and Eucharistic worship. There was also a serious attempt to develop the concept of global compassion. At about the same time useful peace studies were being conducted by the Canadian Peace Research Institute showing the important impact of compassion on various attitudes and traits, especially on justice and peace, war and aggression.[4]

Parish
The parish should be the place where Christian conscience is formed and where, in consequence, a collective witness is given. In its peace work it should create events as well as respond to them. The object should be to initiate new situations, structures and thought forms about the way we see the world and its people. These ideas were incorporated in the work of our parish for peace and justice, so that peace work is not seen as occasional, but rather as a regular, sustained and often specialised effort which is an essential part of the continuing work of the parish – in a word, it was to be an organic and essential commitment, linked intrinsically with Eucharistic liturgy.

The members of the parish of Our Lady of the Wayside in the Birmingham suburb of Shirley, about 1,600 in number, were not very different from the ordinary citizens in the locality. They were vaguely aware of the Third World and its problems and the nuclear challenge to peace and survival. It was not surprising then to find some who believed, as already stated, that we should be concerned primarily with removing the parish debt, which at that time was £50,000, with its high interest rate. So charity began at home and, in this particular case, should remain at home. This is another way of saying that preservation and concern start with self. In any case, it was felt that economically and otherwise it would be imprudent to take on further commitments. It was argued that many politicians in some poor countries were gravely incompetent and had their priorities wrong. They had spent their time buying armaments rather than feeding their people. However, every effort was made in seminars and discussions to open up the subject of peace, race, development, environmental studies and stewardship. Like many other questions, people were inclined to polarise "home" and "abroad", religion and politics, personal and social morality, and the Church universal and the Church local, whereas in fact all these are different aspects of the same reality. Others, whilst subscribing to one set of values, automatically excluded the other. Nowhere was this more obvious than in the confusion that existed about religion and politics, and subsequently about Christian attitudes and responsibilities in the subjects of justice, peace and human rights. Above all, the biggest challenge touched again on one of the most agonising problems of our time, which has been mentioned already in this work, namely, how to switch from a whole set of loyalties which deal exclusively with the nation-State to a new set which accepts the fact that we are primarily a planetary society and one single community. I felt it was imperative to couple with this effort the vocation of all Christians who should be concerned about people everywhere in the spirit of the Good Samaritan. Moreover, Church people who were insular and parochial in their attitudes were in danger of becoming parasites, that is to say, adopting a life style that lived off the world but denied responsibility for it.

New Beginnings and Designs

Fortunately, all the people in the parish were from the beginning involved in designing the new Church. The result was a plan which emphasised water as a symbol of life and growth. A feature of the Baptistry is the moving water, not only as a symbol of spiritual rebirth but as a reminder of the necessity of pure water to sustain life on earth. Water is a matter of life and death, spiritually and physically. Every day more than 20,000 people die of diseases transmitted from impure water. Likewise, a survey of eight developing countries showed that 90 per cent of infant mortality was traceable to unsafe water and related to insanitary conditions; in addition to fatal diseases, there are deficiencies which can be traced to water problems and which sap the strength of man, woman and child. It is estimated that more than 300 million people are unfit to work due to physical problems that can be traced to foul water.[5]

The fountain and moving water in the Baptistry and the plants growing within the building and the bronze sculpture of the Risen Christ were but simple efforts to stimulate thought about international problems and to remind people that life, liberation and redemption came from the Risen Christ who is the point of cohesion of all creation. This figure of the Risen Christ dominates the whole building, and so is constantly a reminder to the parish that redemption not only includes healing of the soul and liberation from sin, but also liberation from oppression, illiteracy, poverty and disease. In hindsight it can be freely admitted that the building had its faults, caused largely by inexperience. It was soon obvious that the seating was cumbersome and impractical. It has also been said, and with good reason, that the external walls and windows of the Day-Chapel gave the impression of a fortress, thus negating the very point of "openness" that we were endeavouring to establish. All this illustrates that we were involved in a learning process in which mistakes naturally occurred.

The Eucharist

Before proceeding to describe some of the different projects the parish undertook it is essential to state that the whole research work was anchored on the celebration of the Eucharist where bread is broken and the life of Christ freely shared. Tissa Balasuriya has reminded us that the Eucharist has an extraordinary potential for "personal and global transformation".[6]

Every week, about 200 million people meet all over the world in Christian communities which is probably the largest global assembly for any shared purpose. Yet the influence of these assemblies, in my opinion, has not had the effect on justice and peace that might be expected.[7] In fact, the Eucharist should be the means of generating more social and international concern. But probably due to the great divide between religion and life, the Eucharist has become vertically orientated and only gradually are attempts being made to correct this attitude. Gutierrez writes that without a real commitment against exploitation, alienation and indeed injustice, the Eucharist becomes an empty action.[8] Perhaps this overstates the case but it serves to make the point that the Eucharist instituted for man requires respect for others in Christ and hence the promotion of human rights.[9] It should be a vital force for Christian liberation because it is the celebration of spiritual and political liberation rooted in the Jewish Passover. Instead its liberating force has been weakened by privatization or domestication. In the early 1960s I tried to make the Eucharist central in Christian life where friend and enemy, while differing in many issues, are unified on equal terms at the Eucharistic Table.[10]

The Eucharist is the best place to express in concrete terms, the ideas of peace and justice. If God shares with man, men should share with each other. I was deeply conscious of the different political and indeed religious attitudes in the congregation where big political questions were involved – this was especially noticeable in the differing attitudes about communism, as for example in Eastern Europe, and in South America and elsewhere, and also the different attitudes to Russian and South African oppression. Frequently, those who were anti-communist and anti-Russian were most tolerant where apartheid was concerned. Not infrequently this attitude was reversed. Needless to say, all consciences should be respected at the Eucharistic Table. Perhaps De Clercq put it accurately when he wrote:

> I think the political struggle must be openly and explicitly involved in the liturgy. At the same time, Christian Unity must be seen as a unity of believers, that is, of people who are involved in conflict and are yet trying to express their conviction that unity can eventually be obtained as the result of this conflict.[11]

Or as J. G. Davies has written: "Just as the cross was a sign of reconciliation, and at the same time, a sign of conflict, so the Eucharist can have, and indeed does have, this dual character."[12] And because of what we hold in common, the differences and opposing interests can be resolved.

The identification with Christ means, in a certain sense, the removal of all barriers. The Eucharist repeats the death and resurrection of Jesus and gives insight into the real state of man and the world as well as the true character of liberation. If the Church, as defined by Vatican II, is to share in the world's history by solidarity with the whole of mankind, then the liturgy of the Eucharist must be instrumental in effecting this vision. This vision entails both the liturgy and action of the Church. Failure in action means that our liturgy becomes alienated, ritualized and domesticated. It is perhaps a measure of our "domestication" and "ritualization" of the Eucharist in the West that we can celebrate it without...

... being confronted by the glaring scandal of world hunger for which, with our diet of meat, we are in part responsible.[13]

Indeed, it is difficult to see how we can celebrate the Eucharist authentically unless it is a celebration which involves a firm commitment, in practice, to the poor and marginalised, because in the Eucharist we should be celebrating freedom. Failure to realise this means that the congregation becomes a group of people performing a privatized ceremony concerned only with parochial events, with scarcely any recognition of responsibility for the world. Consequently, it does not share in Christ's global work.

So it was that the Eucharist celebrated on Sundays became an essential feature in the educative process of the parish for peace, justice and human rights and helped people to learn that work for peace and justice was not an optional extra – something that happened during Christian-Aid Week or One-World Week and was then left aside until the following year. Rather it was a permanent search and challenge, an ongoing process, which was but highlighted by these annual and other events. Again, as J. G. Davies says, an introverted worship...

... performed by the covenant people is, therefore, a contradiction of their office, a rejection of their commission and a failure to participate in the Missio Dei. It makes nonsense of the whole idea of covenant and priesthood.[14]

This means that only a form of worship which is outward-looking and related to the world can be regarded as an authentic act of Christian worship. If it is not worldly, in this sense, then Christians are not exercising their baptismal priesthood. Constant reflection and teaching on these factors as well as other aspects of Eucharist theology had to play a major part in the formative and difficult years of preparation. Moreover since every social action has a provisional character, because the struggle continues till the eschatological has been attained in future blessedness, the effort has to be continually sustained and reviewed.

A PARISH AND PEACE WORK

Project India

After four years of preaching, liturgy and discussion, the first project, which was known as Project India, was introduced. It was explained at the Eucharistic assembly and every effort was made to avoid all attitudes of "hand-outs" or charity because, in fact, the objective of this project was to eliminate such thinking. It was stressed that in the case of world hunger, we were not so much dealing with aid and charity but rather justice and human rights, because God made the world for all and, therefore, everyone has the right to food, health and literacy. The Brandt Report also takes the argument about world poverty out of this context, reminding us that it is not a matter of charity but of justice. Indeed, in Britain today welfare benefits, financed by taxation, are seen as the basic rights of everyone in need. This, too, is a matter of justice and not charity. In other words, we have travelled a long way from "the hand-out" idea of Victorian times. If the human family or international community means anything at all, then it must be accepted that what applies here on a national level is equally true on the international scale. Therefore, the project should be a *sustained effort*. In short, we wished the project would become a partnership which would encourage self-reliance so that the people concerned would be helped to help themselves to live as befits human beings. So we eventually linked up with the Salvation Army in Calcutta who, through Major Gardiner, operated a food run whereby starving people were given at least one good meal a day. There were nine Indian helpers working in the project. Several thousand people – Hindus, Sikhs and Christians – were served daily, and education was provided for about 300 schoolchildren. Many people were too sick or weak to collect their food from the jeep, so the food was taken to them to prevent them dying of starvation. When these people were rehabilitated an effort was made to find work for them; then others took their place, and so the work continued. In trying to offer free education to the children we were learning that it is one thing to keep people alive, but another thing to prepare them for living. We also noticed that medication was sorely needed. In the meantime, the parishioners were asked to introduce weekly self-denial, or what was called weekly mortification, so that they could, over and above their normal contributions, give their savings towards this project weekly and thereby link their mortification with the desperate needs of others. It entailed going without a luxury or a meal sometime during the week, preferably on a Friday, and then joining their offering with the Eucharistic celebration on Sunday. The contributions, which are placed at the entrance of the Church as people enter for Mass, have reached the surprising total of £300 weekly, and since 1967 £200,000 in cash alone has been sent to promote this work in Calcutta.

But something more important was happening. It will be remembered that reference has already been made in Chapter One to alms and offerings in the Scriptures. Paul saw contributions and collections as a means of expressing our concern for each other. It was an aspect of self-giving which we share with Christ.

> The identity of life between Christ and his members, which characterizes the Koinonia, means that the giving of money is an expression of his own self-giving.[15]

Consequently, people united their offerings with the giving of Christ and identified with their fellow human beings in Calcutta. For giving to others is giving to Christ, who gave Himself for us. In this way the vertical and the horizontal, worship and mission, were bound together. The project was most vividly emphasized in a liturgical vestment depicting Christ (the Fish) with the hungry people of all nations stretching their hands towards Him for bread. Above all, people were, for the first time, acquiring a global attitude.

In 1980, CINI (Child in Need Institute) became part of the Calcutta Project. An Indian paediatrician, Dr Chaudhuri, teaches mothers baby-care and explains the facts about nutrition. CINI treats ill children who suffer from calorie-protein malnutrition. In the intensive care wards, babies are admitted with life-threatening diseases such as diarrhoea, meningitis and chest problems. But the key to mother and child health is prevention. Therefore, a home feeding supplementation programme has been planned which is based on cheap and local grown products. Mothers are informed about the preparation of this supplement so that the food is prepared at home and fed to the children three times daily. Health workers are also trained to take the message of health into local villages. Tuberculosis is still a common disease in India. When it affects the bread-winner, starvation often follows.

Besides health-care there is a poultry unit, a fish farm and vegetable cultivation. All this inspired new interest in the poor and marginalised, so that further questions were raised as to how we could expand the work locally and internationally. How could local politicians be educated in these needs? How could the electorate itself be educated since the majority of MPs reflect the minds of the electorate? Here above all we felt that the parish could be the pioneer: discussion groups, ecumenical meetings, places of education and especially personal involvement with overseas projects could play an important part in forming the mind of our people and subsequently the community. Again, the people of the Third World could learn that poverty is not mystically pre-ordained and unchangeable but something that could be removed from the face of the earth. After all, the situation in the West was not very different in the nineteenth century; changes were brought about here in Britain because people were persuaded that poverty, slavery and child labour were not their eternal lot.

One of the most effective ways of stimulating thought was the reading of the feedback letters which we received from Major Gardiner and Dr Chaudhuri in Calcutta, and which were most descriptive and dramatic at times. These were read at Mass every two months to the people and gradually changed people's way of thinking. We also made use of the Sunday weekly bulletins by which we dispensed information about our plans for future development of the project. It was becoming more evident that people's attitudes were undergoing a substantial change. Prayers at the Eucharist became more alive, more politically conscious and more globally aware. Moreover, because of constant requests, it was decided to reflect on the possibility of providing medical help, especially for the predominant needs in the Third World as well as Calcutta.

The Medical Project
After some time we realised that people in the Third World were not only enslaved by hunger but experienced considerable suffering from diseases that could be treated by ordinary

basic medicines. These medicines were often wasted and discarded here in the West. We decided to do a big survey on the doctors in the area, asking them questions as to what they did with their medical samples and if they would be prepared to stretch their healing hand to the poor and deprived in other parts of the world. The response was quite extraordinary. The big problem was how to deal with all the medical samples that were sent to us by the doctors. So eventually a small group in the parish had to devise a scheme by which these medicines could be classified, sorted and priced for Custom purposes, packed and eventually exported by ship or air to Calcutta. Moreover, as the project developed we found that not only were the doctors interested but manufacturers with discontinued lines and superseded medicines were also keen on giving to us rather than destroying them. Wholesale suppliers and hospitals also found that they had surplus or superseded medicine which frequently took up much shelf-space in their storage rooms. On the other hand we were deeply aware of the fact that we should not send medicines indiscriminately. That is to say, a briefing sheet had to be sent to Calcutta, and eventually to other places, whereby doctors out there clearly stated their needs. Therefore, no medicines were sent that were not useful. So successful was this project that many other small missionary units and dispensaries learned about it and now we are shipping to about 14 countries annually. The total annual value is about £300,000. The combined human rights work from June 1982 to June 1983 extended to one dozen countries in the Third World. Special medicines were sent to Mother Teresa's Home in Calcutta at the request of the nuns in charge, financial help given to an exiled Peruvian family in Birmingham, two pigs purchased for the wife of a prisoner of conscience in the Philippines and food sent to a prisoner of conscience in Russia. To date over £6,000,000 worth of top quality medicines and equipment has been exported to countries in Asia, Central and South America and throughout Africa. The religion or culture of the group is not taken into account. "Need not Creed" is the motto. This entails, of course, specialized training for some of our people, but it is interesting to add that in spite of the fact that two teams, each with over a dozen people, work two nights a week from 7 o'clock to 10 o'clock, there is a waiting list for vacancies on the teams.

Here again we are concerned with long-term preventive medicine as well as curative. The tendency to polarise manifests itself when, in fact, both aspects are complementary. However, we are also inclined to favour requests that have para-medical personnel training in their programmes. It is more beneficial to train volunteers in the developing countries, who have come up from the local communities on a crash course of two years medical training, than to spend money on a sophisticated hospital which caters for a small percentage of the population. The World Health Organisation acknowledges that this is the most efficient way of bringing basic health-care to the majority of humankind. The result of pilot schemes have been particularly impressive. Trained auxiliaries are bringing medical assistance to rural areas where most people live.

The influence of the project has been extensive, not only in the Third World but also here in England. It stimulates interest in human rights, peace and justice amongst doctors, hospitals, companies and indeed politicians who naturally want more information about the implications of the work. One other aspect is worth mentioning. When specialised medicine is requested which is not in our possession, we are helped by the Joint Mission Hospital Equipment Board, an ecumenical venture, which allows us to purchase medicine at one-third of the cost price.[16]

The Political Prisoners Project
The object of the Project India was to emphasise the right to eat and the importance of sustained commitment by regular identification with the needy. The aim of the Medical Project was to concentrate on self-help, literacy and extensive para-medical units and preventive as well as curative medicines. Once again it was a question of people having a right not only to life and to eat, but also a right to health and literacy. Finally, the aim of the Political Prisoners Project was to demonstrate that human rights, whether they are economic or political, are indivisible and universal. Therefore, one cannot be selective where human rights are concerned or where different countries are involved. Infringement of human rights anywhere was the concern of people everywhere. However, it is extraordinary, even at United Nations level, that there is so often a conflict between

the sovereignty of a nation-State and the question of human rights. For example, most nations are inclined to plead in their own defence that a given infringement is an internal question even where crimes against humanity are perpetrated.

As a reminder that the projects here in the parish were situated in the Eucharist, four banners were permanently displayed in the church which could easily be seen by all the people while they worshipped. They exhibit the main objectives of the projects. They depict freedom from hunger, freedom from disease, freedom from illiteracy and finally freedom of conscience. A special Eucharistic vestment was designed for the Political Prisoners Project. It was purple with the candle of hope surrounded by barbed wire and used on special occasions like Lent, Human Rights Day, and Prisoner of Conscience Week. This project was linked very closely to Amnesty International shortly after the latter was founded. In those days, people, and especially Church people, were considered to be acting dangerously if they were identified with such a "political" organisation. The parish or group was in danger of being accused of "politicking". Nevertheless we felt that identification with Amnesty was useful due to the belief that human rights were a moral question and very much within the competence of the Church and its mandate. Amnesty provided an effective way of working for the voiceless and forgotten prisoner of conscience. The project is a record of human tragedy because in its extensive files, it traces the agony, loneliness and torture of many people of many countries. It demonstrates clearly what happens when human beings are treated as sub-human or cast on the scrapheap as second-class citizens.

Early in the 1960s we were sending thousands of Christmas cards to prisoners of conscience all over the world. One particular Christmas, 9,000 cards went to prisoners in 24 different countries. The card has a picture of the crucifixion, reproduced from that etched in the brickwork of our Church, and surrounded with barbed wire. The caption on the card reads: "He too was a prisoner of conscience."

Every month we petition for a prisoner of conscience. A short history of the case is placed in the weekly parish bulletin, which is available at Sunday Mass. The names and addresses of leaders of the country in question, or prison governor, are provided. The whole congregation has the opportunity of participating. The result is that hundreds of cards are sent appealing for justice in accordance with the Universal Declaration of Human Rights. The card expresses concern; the motivation is justice and charity. People are advised not to adopt an aggressive standpoint when writing to Heads of State. Sometimes a prisoner is released. At times he makes contact with us afterwards. This is an occasion of great joy.

More extensive casework, of course, is done through our Human Rights Group. Part of its effort is on behalf of adopted prisoners of conscience; the information is received from Amnesty International. The work is not only for prisoners of conscience, but also the dependents who frequently have no financial support. The group also works for other minority groups and is involved in various human rights campaigns. We have worked for prisoners of conscience in Spain, Morocco, India, Paraguay and Chile and for Jews in Russia and Arab countries.

One other important change took place – prayers of intercession became more realistic. Such prayers were never meant to be an escape from our responsibility. We do not discharge our obligations by applying a poultice of cliches to the gaping wounds of humanity. Bidding prayers, therefore, during the Eucharist are better related to mission and to the suffering and the deprived who were part of our commitment. In short, people began to take part in mission through these prayers of intercession and to understand that prayer and political action are "two sides of the same coin".

The Bushmen Project (Wholeness and Holiness)
In the next chapter we will be concerned with the fragmentation fostered by religion. Instead of encouraging an integrated approach to man and the universe, religion has often allowed itself to be manipulated by groups, sects and nations which has resulted in conflict rather than harmony.

Religion, in the true sense, should encourage wholeness/holiness: i.e. a holistic view of man and his environment. It precludes sectarianism of any kind and fosters an ability to live together in a plural society, respecting other traditions and cultures. In an attempt to achieve this, the projects at my own parish, have, as will be seen, a multi-dimensional approach. That is to say not only are they concerned with the whole man, his health, his life, his development and education, but also they are concerned with those cultures which have been trapped by technological and political development of the twentieth century. This was very much in mind when I led an investigative team on behalf of the Archdiocese of Birmingham in the analysis of its investment policies with multi-nationals like Rio-Tinto Zinc, because of the impact that company had on Aboriginal people of South Africa. This was also our concern when our parish adopted the Kung San Foundation that is directly involved with assisting the Bushmen.

For over 22,000 years, the Bushmen have inhabited the Namibian and Kalahari Deserts and roamed freely in small bands, living like all our ancestors as hunter-gatherers. In 1960, the South African government established the first Bushmanland Administration Post at Tsumkwe. Within 20 years the Kung San's way of life had collapsed.

Without any economy of their own, many Bushmen joined the army for the money. This has created severe economic inequalities. In addition, the collapse of the traditional way of life has resulted in profound social problems, including apathy, alcoholism and murder. The objective now is to establish cattle posts and new development in agriculture, teaching them a settled way of life. This has a vivid impact from an educational aspect on the thinking in our parish and of stimulating a holistic approach to mankind. To date, £6,000 has been made available for this project.

CONCLUSION

The description of the field work has, of necessity, been confined to the major projects which, I hope, demonstrate possible ways of educating people by involvement in the search for peace and justice. Furthermore, because of space limitations, more has been said about the work than the liturgy. This is in no way to under-value the latter, which was an essential part of the whole programme. Indeed these faltering steps to be open to others were actually safeguarded and inspired by the Eucharist. The work is done in the name of Christ. It is united to God through worship and is an attempt to help people to be more human and more open to the world which is the object of God's love. Above all, people did realise that the family of God is worth serving and loving, and that in that service is security, peace and safety. In other words, self-preservation is given a new direction. "He that loseth his life for my sake will find it" (Jn 12 : 15; Lk 9 : 24f). People find they are safe in God's presence and service.

For the sake of world peace and for the freedom and development of all people, new thinking and greater effort are now ugently required on a world basis. I believe, from the evidence above, that attitudes and values can be changed at local level. It is true that unlimited demands are made on one's time and effort and mistakes are part of the process. However, it is worthwhile and though the value abroad is limited, the work at home is quite unlimited in its effects because the parish becomes a microcosm of development and justice which has corresponding influence on the rest of the local community. To give aid to small groups and villages in the Third World communities, together with support and help for prisoners of conscience and their dependents, who are often penniless, is very important. Nevertheless, the religious and educative factors are even greater because by worship and mission, introversion is counteracted and the people join with God in His work in His world.

PART III

The Technology of Death and the Search For Peace— An Overview

CHAPTER SEVEN

Can Man Live with the Technology of Death?

A NEW PROBLEM

How can man live with the technology of death? As I have demonstrated, especially in Part I, this is one of the great questions of our time and essentially related to the search for peace and justice in the human community. At the Synod, the Archbishop of York, Dr S. Blanch, clearly stated that man might try to dismantle the nuclear weapon but he cannot disinvent it.[1] Never before has humanity faced such a challenge to its survival. The two super powers have an overkill nuclear capacity capable of killing the human race many times over. It is probable that many more countries, in the not too distant future, will possess nuclear weapons of mass destruction. The military-industrial link-up contributes to the madness of the ongoing arms race. Like the problem of conflict, the nuclear weapon cannot be excluded but it can be contained. However, this will demand a deep change of heart in the community itself. It will also need a better appreciation of the gift of peace and the creation of new structures which contain man's aggression and also help in peace-making.

THE VISION OF PEACE

Peace is a difficult concept to define. It is a state of mind as well as a political order. It is a process more than a condition and includes a coherent system of justice. It is yearned for by mankind, religious and secular; it is the ancient vision of the Gospel; its names are Pax, Shalom, Eirene. The quest for peace has obsessed the greatest minds. It is a searching with an eschatological dimension or character. At the centre of Christian teaching on peace is the dignity of the human person who reflects God and is the expression of his creative work and the meaning of Christ's redemptive ministry. The wider civil community does not share this belief, but, since the vision of peace concerns the welfare of humanity, all nations and individuals are involved. The NCCB and the Working Party of the Church of England discussed both the religious vision of peace amongst peoples and nations and the problem associated with this vision in a world of sovereign states devoid of any central authority and "divided by ideology, geography and competing claims".[2]

The biblical concept of peace is eschatological. According to Isaiah, it will be in the final stage that men will live together in peace "and they shall beat their swords into ploughshares" (Is 2 : 2f). The establishment of peace in the full sense will coincide with the realisation of the Messianic Kingdom at the end of time. Therefore, peace which can only be achieved fully in the Kingdom of God is an ongoing process in this world. It is a continuing work which can only be precariously maintained. Building peace is the work of all of us and especially of the Church as a community of faith with a God-given mandate. Since it is both universal and local, it is the most effective agent to undertake this task. No other organisation is in this unique position. And so it should join with all people of goodwill and work for peace in the political context and in union with secular institutions, helping people to see more clearly what *is* in their interest.

The people of the Old Testament yearned for peace and, in the midst of their unfulfilled longing, they clung to the hope in the promise of an eschatological time when in the fullness of salvation "peace and justice would embrace and all creation would be secure from harm".[3] Peace in the Old Testament also denotes wholeness, mutual responsibility, justice, reconciliation and hope. In Jesus, peace and reconciliation become visible and He gives that hope to his disciples (Jn 20 : 19). They are called to be ministers of reconciliation who would make the peace of God visible through the love and unity within their own community (2 Cor 5 : 19f). Indeed, the New Testament dealt with conflict by sitting down at the Eucharistic table together, for the Eucharist is the place where peace and freedom are celebrated and conflict is contained and resolved

because Christ is present.[4] But peace on earth will, nevertheless, always be a challenge because of sin in man's heart.
Christians are called to live the tension between the vision of
the reign of God and its concrete realisation in history. As the
United States bishops said, this tension is often described in
terms of "already but not yet", that is we actually live in the
grace of the Kingdom but it is not yet the completed Kingdom,
and so a constant search for peace is required in this world of
sin and conflict.[5] In this "already but not yet" state, Christians
have to be aware that peace is possible but never assured. The
possibility has to be protected and developed and it is a work of
supreme importance for all of us, especially Christians, in the
face of obstacles and attacks upon it. It has to be remembered
that peace, even in the Old Testament, is something substantially more than the absence of war (Mic 4 : 3ff). Again there is
also a duty to promote peace, development and justice, as the
New Testament tells us (Mk 9 : 50; Rom 14 : 19; 2 Cor 5 : 18).
Institutions which are commensurate with this work in a fallen
world are necessary. Without such institutions "God's gift will
have no effective channel".[6] This, in fact, signifies that the
search for peace is not only a matter for religion but also for
politics. A task like this requires social structures and involvement which will promote justice and human rights because
without them there will be no true peace. And so the message
of peace has a social reference where justice and human rights
find their full relevance. All of us are called to be ministers of
peace (2 Cor 5 : 17f).

THE CONCEPT OF PEACE

A Religious and Political Issue

It is now realised that questions like war and peace, posed by
new situations such as the nuclear age, are indeed authentically
religious questions and of vital concern for the Christian.
Social conflict, violence, justice and poverty, war and revolution are subjects for theological analysis.[7] Moreover, there is a
growing realisation that the Church does, in fact, exist to
promote peace, justice and human rights. By service and reconciliation, it can make a very large contribution to the search for
peace. As Barth says, the Church ceases to be the Church if it
shirks the political problems of our time.[8] All this requires a

completely new attitude towards the relationship of religion with politics and a deeper sensitivity to the human problems of this world.

The idea that religion was a private affair began in the nineteenth century and, amongst other reasons, was perhaps a reaction to the close identification between the State and Church in the past. It has been with us ever since. Quite recently, there was deep outrage by some groups in the community here in Britain over Bruce Kent's association with CND. Some politicians were angry that a priest should meddle in such matters. Religion was a "private affair" between the individual and God and pertains not to this world but to the next. "Priests should stick to the spiritual matters and avoid worldly affairs."[9] All the arguments for the Christian involvement in politics have been excellently analysed by J. G. Davies. It is sufficient here to refer to some of his main points in passing.[10] Politics, far from being a distraction from the spiritual, is the medium through which we love our neighbour and promote justice, peace and human rights. People are political because their daily position is set within a web of social structures.[11] Unless we take the Incarnation seriously we cannot begin to see the proper relationship between politics and religion.[12] When Christ entered human history he became totally one of us. Therefore, like the Incarnate Word, all Christians should be involved in all aspects of life, including the political, the sacred and the secular, for Christ came to: "Preach the good news to the poor, to proclaim liberty to captives and free the oppressed" (Lk 4 : 16f). Concern for poverty, liberty and oppression indicates a deep religious and political involvement in human affairs. As scripture teaches, being one with our neighbour materially is a fact of economics (1 Jn 3 : 17f; Jas 2 : 2f).

Of course, such attitudes can cause a painful revolution in our thinking and our way of life. But if the Church is a sign of salvation, then it must be the vehicle of secular as well as religious deliverance, otherwise its message is bogus – an opium for the people. Christian practice, therefore, may not be restricted to the private and non-political sphere.[13]

One must admit that, over the last century and even today, many of the mainline Churches and, to a certain extent the new Churches that have sprung up, are more concerned with purely

ecclesiastical and private affairs than with the great moral and
political questions of our time. This applies particularly to
some faiths which are still inclined to orient themselves to the
local Church and are content with theological provincialism,
though the World Council of Churches has made a splendid
effort to offset these tendencies.[14] The Catholic parish can also
become extremely insular. Yet Helder Camara, in an address in
Munich in 1972, clearly emphasised the Christian responsibility by saying that to be political is not merely a right but a duty
laid on the Christian by the Gospel itself.[15]

From the beginning, the biblical message of "religious deliverance" was simply not separable from the area of temporal
deliverance. The new paschal mystery could not be divorced
from its context in the Exodus deliverance. From being a
particular event, it has come to express the permanent pattern
of God's action on his people. God frees his people from
oppression and gives them a land where they can be properly
fed.[16] So also the Church, the people of God, is not just a
collection of individuals but a worshipping community, the
Easter people, who should be concerned with temporal as well
as spiritual deliverance. Both are aspects of the same reality.
More than others, Christians should be able to present the
Gospel vision of one world and one family called to share with
each other the things of our planet. They should be identified
with the poor, the outcast and the marginalised. The Church,
above all, should be a living sign of the brotherhood and
equality of all people in the sight of God and in its search for
peace. No department of human life is outside its scope because Incarnation theology and religion must concern themselves with the secular as well as the sacred, the material as well
as the spiritual – in a word, the whole man everywhere.[17] That
is not to deny that commitment to Jesus is a personal matter,
but since people exist in a social reality, the concern for others
cannot be excluded. The implications of this attitude are quite
clear. It implies promoting peace, justice and human rights,
opposing exploitation and racial discrimination, respecting the
biosphere; these are responsibilities that fall on us as stewards
of creation and also as our brother's keeper.[18]

All these areas and many more are intensely political and
people, especially Christian people, are directly implicated
because they are body and soul, partly spiritual and partly

physical. Yet since God has made man Lord of Creation, man should act as a responsible agent: "It is precisely in this function as a ruler that he is God's Image."[19]

As we saw in the last chapter, the individual Christian has to be encouraged to think globally and to avoid polarisation of the universal and the local and, above all, to be concerned not only with conserving peace but also with the biosphere because both are interconnected.[20] Strangely, Christian people and nations have not taught respect and responsibility for the works of Creation. Max Nicholson in his book, *The Environmental Revolution*, writes with anger of Christian nations that attack bird migration, like France and Italy; referring to this point, *The Tablet* aptly remarks that we need to regain the spirit of St Francis of Assisi.[21] After his account of the feeding of the multitude, St John's Gospel quotes Jesus as instructing the Aposles "... to pick up the pieces left over so that nothing gets wasted" (Jn 6 : 12). And speaking of ecology, Davies says:

> To save nature from destruction, it is necesary to engage in political and economic activity, both at the national and international level – there is no other way.[22]

Consequently, if prayers are to be more than a word game or an escape from our responsibility, they must be backed-up by appropriate action. It is little short of frivolous to ask God to give bread to the hungry, or peace to the world, unless people are prepared to do something about these needs.[23] It can be argued that the Liturgy often becomes a word game and the Eucharist, which is one of the most political statements of our time, can be emptied of its meaning. Peace, justice, reconciliation and liberty – which, as we have shown, are essentials of the Gospel message – should find an expression in our Christian commitment and liturgies (Is 58; Lk 4 : 18ff). If, therefore, the new attitude to war and peace and indeed human rights, which the World Council of Churches and Conciliar documents contemplate, is to find a central place in our liturgy and action, a much greater awareness will be demanded in Christian communities. Is it too much to hope that a percentage of the Churches resources will be directed towards research, education and peace work at local as well as international level? The United States Catholic bishops recommended in their Pastoral that funds be made available for educational and research institutions conducting peace studies.

> To achieve this, we urge that funds equivalent to a designated percentage (even one-tenth of one per cent) of current budgetary allotments for military purposes be set aside to support peace research.[24]

It is hoped that the Church will do likewise.

Eschatological Aspects and Christology

In the Synod debate, Archbishop Blanch made a further interesting contribution. The Church, he said, ought to be seen to be concerned with the theological and not just with the moral and political issues of peace. The ancient world was haunted by the fear of universal disaster as real as our nuclear threat. What was distinctive about the Christian attitude to the end of the world was that it was associated "with joy and not just fear", hence the utterances of Christ Himself that are written in the New Testament.[25] The prophets of the Old Testament were deeply involved in the moral issues and political decisions of their day. They did, however, have much to say about a transcendent God who presided over the destiny of the world. Our world will have to live with a fear of nuclear disaster, either as a consequence of military action or of miscalculation or accident. The secret of nuclear power is with us forever. So while we do everything in our power to contain it, we cannot exclude it. From now on every generation will have to live with the possibility that it could be the last generation on earth. The Church has to enable mankind, he says, to cope with the fear as well as the threat. According to him, the return of the Son of man is not determined by governments. The decision regarding the end of the world is not man's but God's, even though the sovereign-State and others might attempt to abrogate or usurp that power. The Son of man, therefore, he says, is the Lord of Creation – the alpha and the omega. The Christological approach to help humanity to live with this fear of death by hope is an aspect of the concept of peace. The archbishop reminded the Synod that we can temper man's fear and enable him to "lift-up" his head when redemption draws near (Lk 21 : 27f). Indeed, whenever death faces an individual Christian, belief in the Risen Lord assures that life is changed not ended. The sadness of death gives way to the bright hope of immortality. This distinctive Christian position is most relevant in a nuclear age. So the Church, whilst striving to promote peace with justice, can also offer this hopeful vision which points to a universe which is in the merciful providence of God. Or, as Maurice Latey wrote: " 'Fiat justitia et ruant coeli' (Let justice be done though the Heavens fall)."[26] Once again, the here and the hereafter, the present and the future, the sacred and the secular should not be polarized.

Belief in the Lordship of Jesus Christ, which is above all other loyalties, like country, political party or personal commitment, was Barth's theme. Equally, in this new kind of society, created by modern technology, man's responsibility and accountability must be underlined. A restatement of Christian values is required which emphasises the priority of peace, justice and love whereby the brotherhood of man, which means the international community, becomes a reality and humankind is saved not only from sin but also from the unjust structures caused by it. Overall we need a greater awareness of our interdependence and unity as people, one single interdependent community under the headship of Christ, children of the Father, who have been given charge of the resources of the planet. This is not to exclude local loyalties as country, family or community, but rather to subordinate them to the highest loyalty of all which is God and the human family. In this quest for peace and survival, not only can all Christians be ecumenically concerned, but also all the members of the human family, in which secular and sacred institutions can join hands. We all face the greatest challenge in history, namely the search for peace and survival of God's planet.

Having said all this, the once-and-for-allness of nuclear weapons is a matter of considerable moment for religion. In spite of what Archbishop Blanch has said, it can be argued that the end of the world can now be decided by governments: the decision could be man's not God's. The outcome depends on human input. The divine act of love and creation can be thwarted by human abuse. There is now a movement amongst some thinkers to stress human responsibility to the world.[27] Human beings are accountable for their actions to God and especially to themselves. God is present in this moment of nuclear danger and crisis and while He influences people by his grace, he does not make the choice. There is now a huge responsibilty in the hands of mankind and, according to some, "bombs" are in the control of the powerful and the aggressors whereas God is with the weak.[28] In recent thinking this is represented by a "Christology from below" school of thought, which tends to say that in history God is God as a human being who cannot help being a figure of compassion and suffering. The God revealed in Christ is the God of the present moment. He is revealed in the world in weakness and dependence and, like the poor nations, which are powerless, so God-revealed-in-Christ does not, in a very real sense, make the final choice about the world. He has left that final decision to mankind, and especially to the powerful. The God revealed in history in weakness, the God who chooses the poor and speaks to us through them, has left the future of the human race to us. Moreover, human rights, nuclear arms and world hunger are all a matter of the powerful of this earth lording it over the powerless. In the powerless God awaits our decision.

PEACE AND RELIGION – PROBLEM AND PROMISE

There is a gradual accumulation of evidence about the kinds of personal characteristics that tend to be associated with some attitudes. Nationalism is associated with certain patterns of religious ideology where God is seen as a power figure and there is an emphasis on ritualism and the authoritarian factors of the in-group.[29] With these characteristics, other attitudes are frequently found such as conservatism, belligerence, intolerance, racialism or prejudice and ethnocentrism. There are, of course, many variables, depending on time and circumstances and a variety of other factors within a social context. But, in general, one could say that the cluster of characteristics present a coherent overall picture.

Levinson in the United States refers to a 1951 study of the IN Scale.[30] As in many similar studies, various political and religious groupings were found to differ in their average degree of nationalism. The Republicans had a significantly higher (more nationalistic) IN Scale than the Democrats. With regard to religious groupings, the Catholics had a higher IN Scale than the Protestants. The Protestants had a higher IN Scale than the Jews, and all were higher than those with no affiliation. In the case of religious attendance, those who attended services weekly had a higher IN Scale than those who attended occasionally, and both groups had a higher IN Scale than the non-attenders.

Findings of this sort have been obtained in a number of surveys which used various types of samples and scales.[31] Moreover, the studies reported in these works are mainly centred in the United States though the work done by researchers (as reported in the *Peace Research Reviews*) has a wider basis because more countries and varieties of people are involved. Nevertheless, it would be more useful and very interesting if the work could be extended to more people, with special reference to the poor, the uneducated, the powerless amongst different nationalities, ages and classes. Since most of the works that have been listed are Western-orientated, and since even religion reflects the thinking of the body politic, it is not surprising to find capitalistic tendencies in the Churches and religious groupings. Consequently, such findings must be taken with caution.

Levinson's research in *The Journal of Conflict Resolution* draws the (at first sight) strange conclusion that Republicans are more nationalistic than Democrats and Roman Catholics are more nationalistic than Protestants,[32] but fails to account for the fact that Roman Catholics in America generally tend to be Democrats. Furthermore, Professor Allport of Harvard remarks that: "Religion is a highly personal matter; it has quite different meanings in different lives."[33] He says, elsewhere, an institutionalized religious outlook and an interiorised religious outlook have opposite effects on the personality. Belonging to a Church because it is safe, powerful and a superior in-group is likely to be the mark of an authoritarian character and to increase prejudices, ethnocentrism, belligerence etc. On the other hand, belonging to a Church because its basic creed of brotherhood expresses the ideals one sincerely believes in, is associated with tolerance, peace and other such virtues. According to Allport, the role of religion is paradoxical. Religion sometimes becomes the focus of prejudice because it stands for more than faith – it is the pivot of a cultural tradition of a group. However sublime the origins of religion may be, it can become secularised by taking over cultural functions. Islam is more than a religion. It is a well-knit cluster of related cultures. Christianity can become so locked with Western civilisation and structures that it is difficult to keep in mind its original message. Sects of Christianity have become so tied into sub-cultural and national groups (like Paisleyism in Northern Ireland) that religious divisions march hand in hand with ethnic and national divisions.

But, while granting all this, there seems to be a sharp contradiction between the actual practice of religion and the message of love and peace, both in Christianity and other religions. It is an interesting point that whenever religion was represented in its pure form, without force or colonialist trappings, it thrived not only immediately but long afterwards. In fact, great cultures and civilisation have sprung from this kind of missioning. For example, the coming of St Augustine to England, which was assisted by the Irish monks, Columba and Aidan and others, and the post-Patrician monks in Ireland, caused a seedbed of great culture and civilisation. The Irish monks spread the Christian faith across Europe and the Benedictines made an extraordinary contribution to faith and learning in Western Christendom. Even today there are traces of this faith and culture.[34] On the other hand, the Portuguese and Spaniards brought the faith to South America where it was identified with militarism and colonialism and little culture resulted. Today we are witnessing there a theology of liberation and a liberation of theology so as to dismantle the status quo and establish justice and development in that great continent.

Ferguson acknowledges this paradox in religion and describes a tension existing between the two "pulls":

> One is the tendency of religion to social conformity, the tendency to be different in societies and to change with the times. The Zoroastrianism of the military monarchs of Persia is not identical with the Zoroastrianism of the peaceable Parsee of India. The established Christianity of the 19th century in Britain or America seems remote from the 1st century Christianity in Palestine...[35]

Ferguson proceeds to claim that if the pull were all towards social conformity, cynicism might justifiably be the order of the day. But it is a tension with a pull in the other direction that is towards non-conformity and criticism of the existing institutions. The results of these two opposing "pulls" have been paradoxical. As Ferguson says, two great religions, Christianity and Buddhism, have been most clearly pacifist in their origins and essence. Yet both have been deeply involved with militarism from a fairly early stage in history. So religion is always challenged to resist the pressures of society and respond to the call of prophecy so necessary in modern times.

In a most illuminating study,[36] Richard Friedli analyses the doubt about the contribution of religion to peace, and examines the correlation between militarism and Christianity.[37] Various theories were advanced in an attempt to explain this contradiction between the love preached by the Christian Churches and the effect of that preaching in everyday life.[38] Indeed it is surprising that religions, and indeed the Christian Churches, which emphasise agape and love of neighbour, can be so aggressive and bellicose in practice. The preference for violent means of solving conflict, according to Russel, is essentially bound up with the Christian message itself; even the message of Jesus emphasises a conditional love. According to Russel, an analysis of the context of the Koran or of the preaching of Jesus can show that their respective messages could easily be made to support the above described mentality of institutional and authoritarian orthodoxy, and it is only against a background of self-criticism and an awareness of negative factors within religions, together with an open objective presentation of the love that pertains to God and our neighbour, with all its implications, that a positive contribution by religion can be made in the search for peace.

THE DYNAMICS OF PEACE MAKING

Self-Preservation

Friedli refers to the self-preservation drive in the individual and indeed in the whole group which seeks to retain intact the experiences and tradition of its community.[39] It will be remembered that this point about self-preservation was very much borne out by the writer's own research in justice and human rights as was demonstrated in the last chapter. So often in discussions, people insisted that "Charity begins at Home" and that one's first final loyalty was to one's own country, locality or group. As we have seen, even when the first project was introduced in our parish it was seen, at the outset by some people, as a case of charity to inferiors.[40] The idea of aid for meeting the problems of hunger, disease and illiteracy, in the Third World especially, was seen in terms of charity rather than justice. This thinking was institutionalised in the "Poor Law" in Britain where aid and charity were identified. So even today, for the vast majority, aid and charity are still associated. Hence it has to be emphasised that this is a case not of charity to inferiors, but justice amongst equals or, as the Brandt Report puts it, it is a matter of human rights.[41] Moreover, it was something of a surprise for some to realise that with a rapidly contracting village-world this planet is *home* and that self-security in this age can only come from peace and safety for the human family as a *whole*. Indeed the skill of the Brandt Report was the emphasis it placed on this very factor, namely, that the rich must share with the poor if they are to retain their wealth. If there is not a radical change in the world's economic system, the very survival of the human race is at risk. However, it is of paramount importance that people see clearly that their pre-servation is now bound-up with the security of the international community as well as the safety of the planet. Therefore, it is helpful that the work of peace is promoted within this context, namely that peace for the world, i.e. the human family, means peace and security for the individual. As has been stated this kind of thinking needs a global approach and an understanding that "my neighbour" is everyone.

The public is not always convinced by reason. Frequently it is moved by personal motives. In a television debate Bruce Kent of CND, argued that possession of nuclear arms was always immoral and, therefore, that Britain should give them up. Keith Ward, of Kings' College, London, opposed this motion. Surprisingly, the jury found in favour of Kent, even though he defended an absolutist position. But the reasons the members of the jury gave for their decision were all personal or self-orientated.[42]

The conclusion, once again, seems to be that self-preservation is the most telling argument for all; namely, that people have to be shown that working for human rights and justice is ultimately in their own interest as well as that of the international community. Or, as Brandt put it, the rich cannot prosper without the progress of the poor. In other words, international peace and personal survival must be shown to be

ultimately connected with the individual. Even where religion
is concerned, its failure to promote peace can frequently be
traced to the instincts of fear and self-preservation which take
on various distorted forms. The big challenge in modern times
is to direct these basic instincts to peace and unity by a better
understanding of what self-preservation and security really
entail and, that by realising these natural instincts are, in
reality, deeply religious ones which can include the love
of God and neighbour as well as the ordinate love of one-
self.

Yet frequently, as we have seen, there seems to be a gap
between the theory and practice. In politics as well as in
religion, difficulty is experienced in relating security and preservation to global safety and international stability.

A sample of 3,144 Japanese high-school students, compared
with 260 American students, were more internationally tolerant, more politically sophisticated, more orientated towards
peace, more keen on the United Nations, less nationalistic and
less racially prejudiced. But 52 to 63 per cent of both groups
believed that international co-operation was more important
than national sovereignty. However, only 25 per cent of both
groups were ready to surrender national allegiance to world
government.[43] A cluster of reasons lays behind this attitude,
such as insecurity and self-preservation, fear of the outsider,
the uncertainty about the foreigner, ignorance, preoccupation
with the absoluteness of truth and its opposition to error –
"error has no rights". Again, insecurity is aggravated by the
fear of war, the bogeyman of Communism and political propaganda, which all add to the self-preservation drive and the
need to be on the defensive, or to take refuge behind masks of
power and authority.

The rest of these characteristics increase according as the
vertical or institutional religion is emphasised and the horizontal is neglected. In fact, the aim should be to present and
practise a more adequate concept of the Gospel message. A
true relationship with God enhances the horizontal as well as
the vertical which includes the social and the political in a deep
concern for peace, justice and human rights. Somehow or other
the big challenge for all people, and especially for Christians, is
the need to understand that the international community is
really God's family which He loves infinitely and has re-

deemed totally, and that everyone in that community is my neighbour. For the salvation that Christ brought was not just about the individual soul but about the salvation of the world itself which relates to peace, justice and reconciliation. That is to say, Christianity is not only concerned with the liberation from sin but also about liberation from the effects of sin. Likewise, it is not sufficient to claim that religion is about the next world where all will be rectified. The world to come must not be polarised from this world; this world and the next are really aspects of the same reality and one leads to the other in the historical series. So the sacred and the secular are interconnected just as all people are interdependent. Love of God and neighbour implies a responsibility for this world and the people in it. This should be manifested in the attitudes of Christians and other religious adherents. It will entail a struggle to create a responsible society, where social justice is sought and the biosphere is respected. In a word, it means that man lives as a steward of creation and is true to his calling as a person made in the image of God Himself. But it is necessary to repeat that this responsibility can only be effectively realised through the mediation of political structures.[44] Politics are the means through which we flesh out the love of our neighbour through justice and social commitment.

All this calls for a massive educational effort in the Liturgy, in preaching and in action so as to change the lopsided posture that is adopted even by religious people. In any case it *is* possible to make a much greater contribution to peace and unity. This quest for justice is now on a world scale and the Church can help to promote directly this movement because the Church is universal as well as local and has got unique facilities. No philosophy, no religion, has emphasised the unity of the human race and the dignity of each individual so much as Christianity. Now it is called to practise what it preaches and to help to make the idea of universal justice and peace a reality. It is the special vocation of the universal Church to promote the more local and limited experiments that have taken place in justice within the nation to the new international level. The Church is ideally equipped for this task because it is the only organisation which is both local and universal. Moreover, it has two thousand years of history and motivation and can raise questions that politicians would not dare to voice. Politicians depend on elections whereas the Church has its authority and mandate from God. It has a network which is probably the best in the world in that it connects universally all the local communication points such as parishes, institutions, colleges, universities and convents, to say nothing about societies throughout the world. For example, when my own parish worked on a prisoner of conscience in Taiwan for Amnesty International, it was able to ask the Apostolic Delegate in London to make contact with the Taiwan Ambassador in Rome – the only Ambassador that Taiwan had in Europe. This was accomplished by the fact that the Church was universal and local. The Apostolic Delegate referred the matter to Cardinal Villot, the Papal Secretary of State, who in turn made representation to the Taiwan Ambassador.[45]

Christianity, therefore, is challenged in this new kind of society, to lead people away from purely introspective loyalties and nationalistic thinking, to an international attitude which entails the love and service of all people who in reality are physically and morally neighbours. The nation-State cannot be the highest loyalty for the followers of Christ. In fact, the nation is no more than a group, different only in degree from nomads, tribes and city states. The world still retains nearly all these phases amongst different cultures. This is not to claim that local and planetary loyalties are mutually exclusive. After all community is an essential part in the development of people. The tribe is a collection of people, so is the nation and ultimately the larger family of mankind. They are different ways in which people are grouped. There is nothing wrong about loyalties to these groups or places of origin. But patriotism becomes perverted when it is vainglorious, setting itself above other cultures, people and countries. The human community is greater than any of its parts and the well-being of the nation has to be compatible with that of the international community. In other words, nations and states can no longer see themselves as self-contained and self-sufficient. All this demands a radical change of emphasis in evangelisation which has not always communicated a sense of Christian responsibility in global terms. This new kind of thrust and concern not only opens Christians to the universal dimension of their beliefs but even offers to each member of the world community the best recipe for security and self-preservation. Here the secular and religious ethic have an opportunity of working together for peace.

Again, if self-interest and self-preservation have been major factors for some in the past because of an introverted religion, these motives can now be extended to the more noble commitment of peace-making based on the unity and interdependence of the world community. Nor is self-preservation, properly understood, opposed to the virtue of charity. True love of self is a presupposition of love for others and responds to the glory of God: "Thou shalt love thy neighbour as thyself" (Mt 22 : 39). This indicates that the virtue of love is a three-fold love: God, neighbour and myself. Love of self involves the procuring of the necessary means of livelihood, security and health. There is a tendency to polarise the love of neighbour and the love of self, just as there has been, as we have shown, in the case of the love of God and the love of neighbour. Nevertheless, self-love and self-preservation can fall properly under the virtue of charity. As Thomas Aquinas says:

> God being the principle of all good, that which a man loves in himself is the divine good communicated to him and he loves his neighbour by reason of fellowship in that good.[46]

Speaking of self-love, Tillich contends that it might be more helpful for clarification to speak of "self-affirmation", "self-ishness" or "self-acceptance" according to the context.[47] But he grants at the end of his interesting analysis that "man cannot solve any of his great problems if he does not see them in the light of his own being and being itself".[48]

In a nuclear age, promoting peace and justice in the international community is effecting the love of one's neighbour and thereby underpinning self-preservation and personal security. In the security of all is the security of each. This is not only theologically sound; it is also political sanity. Since the love of God includes love of neighbour as well as the ordinate love of self, self-preservation in this sense is prevented from becoming introspective and self-centred as has happened in the past, even in a religious context when the horizontal and vertical are improperly related. Indeed by this benevolent love, love of self is rightly promoted. Perhaps this is similar to the claim of Tillich that...

... the agape quality of love cuts into the libido, eros and philia qualities of love and elevates them beyond the ambiguities of their self-centredness.[49]

World Order and Planetary Unity

The various dangers threatening the social and physical fabric of the planet all point to the need of a world order which would regulate the diversities of divisions of the present fragmented international system. There is, therefore, the need of a new conception of political authority which supersedes nationalism and sovereignty. Various models have been put forward. Some experts believe in the desirability of a two-pronged strategy which aims at the development of a universal culture while, at the same time, hastens the demise of the modern nation-State. This would entail mobilizing intellectual, religious, philosophical, scientific, ethical and other resources to advance the realisation that all people are one international community – one universal civilisation. But, according to Cammileri, while some form of international organisation is necessary its parameters ought to be clearly specified and integrated into a much richer and more complex process of decision-making, centred on political and economic entities that are closer in size to the small town than to the large industrial state.[50] In any case, as citizens of the world, all people have a responsibility to try to make sense of this planetary unity which is now, for the first time, technically possible. Furthermore, many of the big questions of today like pollution, trade, human rights, world resources, environment and peace itself can only be treated effectively at an international level. For example, the scale of industrial development has far outstripped the scale of political development. The multinational company, like an octopus, has spread throughout the world in its subsidiaries. It can only be controlled by an international code. Again, Sweden's anti-pollution measures are powerless against acid rain from British factories. But for Britain, to allow Sweden to take action against the offending factories, would necessarily imply some surrender of national sovereignty. Thus international approaches and attitudes are becoming more necessary, not only from a religious but also a secular point of view. At the most down-to-earth level of self-interest, it is the realization of the world's continuous and interconnected systems of air, land

and water, as well as the interdependence of nations and people that can foster loyalty and commitment to global unity. In fact, already in some of the supra-national institutions, such as Strasbourg, the European Economic Community and the United Nations, there are sketches which give definite guide-lines or pointers. More than ever, the words of John Donne are true:

No man is an island, entire of itself.
Any man's death diminishes me, because I am involved
In mankind; and therefore never send to know for whom the bell tolls:
It tolls for thee.

Can we make this leap? It has been shown that peace promotion is much more than the abolition of nuclear weaponry, and that peace is linked with social and human liberation. One of the greatest destabilizing factors is the need of liberation and development for the majority of the international community, known as the Third World. Once more, education, communication and the Church can make significant contributions in this area, especially by underlining the importance of development and disarmament.

The Power of Education

As has been demonstrated, the Church, in particular, should strive to implement its belief in the unity of God's family. Furthermore, *all* people, whatever their beliefs, are challenged to work together for peace and survival. But this demands a massive education programme. Nevertheless, with modern means of communication, information and travel, awareness has been increased; this vast array of communication can be harnessed to create a more peaceful world. For example, Gallup Polls in the *Peace Research Reviews* show the power of education and information on foreign affairs because support for the United Nations was considerably increased by these efforts.[51] Recent studies indicate that during the Korean War, Catholics were only slightly less inclined than Protestants to express reservations about war and "like other Americans, they became increasingly dissatisfied and inclined to support a negotiated settlement ... in the early 1950s".[52]

During the Vietnam War, Catholics were more inclined to

support the war than Protestants and Jews. But their attitudes changed with events and so did those of the United States Catholic bishops, which shows that information and education can significantly change public opinion.

Lately in Britain there has been a revival of adult political education and a parallel quickening of interest in education for international understanding.[53] Above all, there is a vast untapped potential in the Church throughout the world which could lead people to become more faithful to the priority of love of God and neighbour and to make a massive contribution to peace, justice and human rights in the world community.

Throughout history, people have made the change from family to clan, from clan to city-state, to the nation-State. It was accomplished without our forms of technical progress. Therefore, it seems reasonable to conclude that with our means of communication and technology, people can be educated to perceive what is in their own interest so that world order and planetary unity, in spite of our cultural diversity, can become more acceptable. There is no room for fragmentation in a nuclear age where, in spite of man's progress, he is more vulnerable than ever – not simply because of the crisis of nuclear weaponry that threatens everyone, but also because of the grave disparities that exist, and especially because of the strange logic of the arms race. It should not be an impossible task, with our vast array of technical achievements, to teach people that the international community has priority over the competitive nationalism of the sovereign state. To put it in the most basic and acceptable terms, it is a matter of self-interest and self-preservation because the security of the human race means the security of each individual.

Non-Violent Means of Peace-Keeping

Before concluding, one should reflect on the alternative to war and other means of defence which do not depend on annihilation. This point received extended treatment from the United States bishops.[54] They argued that non-violent means of resistance deserve more study and consideration than they have received in the past. Moreover, non-violence is not the way of the weak. The Danes who would not turn Jews over to Nazis and the Norwegians who would not teach Nazi propaganda in schools are inspiring examples of non-violence. This method also offers a common ground for those who support pacifism and the just war theory. Nuclear war makes everyone realise that no one can win and all may die. Gordon Zahn believes that "total war has brought a rebirth of absolute pacifism".[55] He refers to Franz Jägerstatter and indicates that he was more advanced in his thinking than many of his peers. Zahn concludes that the modern challenge to a Christian is a return to the thinking of the early Church with a possibility of a second stage of martyrdom.[56]

This is also supported by Schillebeeckx[57] and recently by Rex Ambler in a very interesting paper about the nuclear problem.[58] Non-violent popular defence can mean the loss of lives but the consequences of the nuclear alternative are too terrible to contemplate. Resistance may not always succeed. Gandhi's success in India is one thing, but the resistance to Russian ruthlessness in Afghanistan is quite another. There is also the difficulty of organisation. It demands the united will of the people, patience and sacrifice, even to the extent of dying rather than killing, or as Ambler puts it "being ready to accept the consequences of not being protected".[59]

However, it is well to recall the power of the population of Iran, even though the Shah possessed one of the most sophisticated and efficient armies of modern times as well as a vicious police force. Prescinding from the objectives of the uprising, one can underline this revolt to indicate what a country's population can achieve when faced with a powerful military capacity.

The Report of the Alternative Defence Commission, *Defence without the Bomb*,[60] makes a detailed study of defence by civil resistance and indeed a minority of the Commission favoured moving to a system of exclusively non-violent defence, while recognising that the process would take time.[61] Most of the Commission, however, thought that a non-nuclear military capability was essential for defence[62] and for the foreseeable future it would remain the predominant element.[63] Reasons for this conclusion are put forward, but it was agreed that civil resistance could have a significant and perhaps "in time a major role",[64] and could provide a fall-back strategy if an occupation occurred.[65] The Commission recognised the possibility of nuclear blackmail which has influenced many to support nuclear deterrence. It is pointed out that this issue, in

any case, faces 95 per cent of the world's countries which are
still non-nuclear.

The military posture which is generally favoured by the
Commission is one of "defensive deterrence". This means
having the capacity to inflict heavy losses on an invading force,
but at most only a limited capacity to mount offensive operations in the opponent's territory. Renouncing nuclear weapons
is itself a major step in this direction; it could be extended by,
for instance, emphasising territorial defence, by limiting the
number of tanks, and by eliminating long-range bombers.
How far Britain or Western Europe should go in this direction
is a matter for further debate.[66] It should be said that the
Report explicitly excludes chemical and biological warfare
from its definition of conventional weapons. This would be a
posture which could not be interpreted as a serious threat to
other countries. However, as the Commission unanimously
states, a nuclear disarmed Britain could not accept NATO's
current nuclear based strategy; it debated at length...

> ... whether it would be better for Britain to stay in NATO and
> seek to influence its policy in a non-nuclear direction or leave the
> Alliance altogether.[67]

It will be remembered that the Report of the Church of England also recommended unilateral nuclear disarmament for
Britain but accepted the NATO nuclear umbrella. The
rationale of the Commission on rejecting nuclear weapons for
Britain is clearly stated in the Report and the case for alternative defence policies is well argued.[68] I believe, however, that
civil resistance has a significant contribution to make to defence in the British and European context. But while this could
be accomplished with a non-nuclear and military capacity
(they are not mutually exclusive) even the possession of conventional military capacity presents big problems. The armament industry in the West is heavily dependent on arms ex-
ports. As the Commission asserts:

> In European countries, especially where the home market is re-
> stricted, arms exports are necessary to make possible longer pro-
> duction runs; even Sweden has not altogether escaped from this
> situation.[69]

Therefore, would defence, even with conventional weapons, avoid this problem? If a conventional capacity is retained, would it not have to be updated and improved periodically? These questions are difficult to answer in a technological age.

The United States bishops in their Pastoral Letter also faced this problem by raising the question about the cost of conventional weapons in the absence of the nuclear deterrent.[70] They agreed they could "not settle the technical debate about policy and budgets" but hoped that a significant reduction in the "number of conventional arms and weaponry would go hand in hand with diminishing reliance on nuclear deterrence".[71]

Conventional weapons can also become indiscriminate in conduct and disproportionate to any valid purpose. Additionally one does not wish to encourage the arms race which expends vast resources annually on instruments of defence. Therefore, any programme that is directed at abolishing nuclear weapons is not likely to succeed unless it includes measurements to reduce tensions and conventional weapons. It must be stressed that not only is nuclear war to be prevented but also war itself.[72] Reason and experience tell us that a continuing upward spiral even in conventional arms, instead of maintaining peace, provokes war.

The organisational requirements for civil defence need much more reflection. Possibly a mobilisation of people similar to conscription, but without its drawbacks, would be a practical way of training for civil resistance. Unlike conscription, people would be trained in non-violent means of defence, whereas in conscription they are trained to kill others. Conscription has been carefully examined in *Defence without the Bomb* but this pertains to defence *with* conventional weapons.[73] Finally, for Christians, civil resistance is a practical option. It couples self-defence with the providence of God and is much more in keeping with the stance of the early Christians. If it demands a very high cost, even martyrdom, then so be it. It also has the advantage of being prophetic and clear-cut and is more in keeping with the spirit of the Beatitudes.

SUMMARY

While peace-making in a nuclear age is important, it does not solve the other great problems like world hunger and disease.

The unity and interdependence of the world means that some of the major problems like disarmament, development, environment and human rights require a global approach – this will be in the interest of all. The nuclear age is a matter of considerable moment for religion. Religion cannot be divorced from politics because faith is incarnate and historical. The Church must be concerned with man's temporal as well as spiritual affairs. Its contribution to peace should be based on a critical self-assessment with particular reference to the objective truth of the Gospel. This, in practice, demands that the horizontal has the same importance as the vertical. The universal Church has a prophetic role in co-operating with all men of goodwill in working and educating for peace, irrespective of colour and creed. Civil resistance may have a major role to play in future defence policies.

While preaching that "swords should be converted into ploughshares and spears to pruning forks", the Church has a vital part to play in helping people to live with the technology of death by proclaiming the hope of the Risen Lord. It is surely its task to emphasise mutuality of interest in an interdependent world, because the security of the whole human race is the security of each individual in it.

The time has now come for Christians to demonstrate by their attitudes, the priority of the international community over the nation-State, because of their commitment to the brotherhood of man and the unity of the human family. All communicators, religious and secular, have a responsibility to educate people about the importance of this attitude in a world where unity is a technical reality.

It is appropriate to end this section with the words from Deuteronomy (Deut 11 : 26):

I set before you life or death,
a blessing or a curse.
Choose life then, so that you and your descendants
May live in the love of Yahweh, your God ...

Conclusion

An Entirely New Situation

The problem is then, we are faced with an entirely new situation. Einstein once said that the nuclear bomb has changed everything except our thinking. The contention of this book has been to show that, while people might argue about civil resistance or defence with conventional weapons, nuclear war at any rate is unthinkable. Therefore, *in the short term*, as the National Conference of Catholic Bishops said, and the Working Party of the Church of England indicated, a halt is necessary to the production, testing and deployment of nuclear weaponry. This should be linked with positive steps towards progressive nuclear disarmament.

In the long term, since nuclear war is a new problem, it demands *a new* attitude to war and peace which, in turn, requires a change in mind and in heart. The nuclear problem cannot be handled within the just war categories. On the other hand, the majority of people is unwilling to accept absolute pacifism. Consequently, a common ground is necessary whereby religious people and all men of goodwill can unite more effectively to prevent the destruction of the planet and global holocaust. This approach can be acceptable to both the pacifist and the non-pacifist and is based firmly on the principle of self-preservation. In a nuclear age no one can win a war. Everyone stands to lose. It is in the interest of all to promote the unity and interdependence of the planet and to avoid war at all cost. This applies whether we are secular or Christian, believer or unbeliever. Needless to say, the Christian has a further contribution to make because of his belief in the Fatherhood of God and the brotherhood of man where nuclear fratricide is morally unacceptable. But everyone can agree on the basic factor that the supreme reality of our time is our indivisibility as an international community and our common vulnerability because of the technology of death. Nations and people act out of self-interest; self-preservation is one of the fundamental human instincts and the basis for good politics. In this area the Christian ethic of brotherhood and the secular ethic of *unity of people* can give us that sense of community, of belonging and living together in safety and security, without which no human society can, in this nuclear age, survive and prosper. Our links of blood and history, our sense of shared culture and achievement as people, our traditions, our faith are all precious and enrich the world with a variety of scale and function. But up to now, we have lacked the wider rationale of unity, under all the variations, which is now technically possible and absolutely necessary if we are to survive. As I stated in my introduction, if this vision of unity, underpinned by the instinct of self-preservation can become part of the common insight of the international community, then we may find beyond our inevitable pluralisms, just enough unity to build a more human and peaceful world.

It has to be repeated in this conclusion, that *the Church*, which is in the unique position of being local and universal, can play a much more positive part in its contribution to peace and justice. Indeed, it has a responsibility to do so. Like the United Nations, the Church, but with its own mandate, should remind nations and people that they are one community. Furthermore, the Church has the vocation to humanise and sanctify all nations. It must, therefore, think "world" and act globally. This opportunity and responsibility can form an essential part of the liturgy and mission of the Church which are powerful channels of education and formation.

Finally, *education* has an immense contribution to make in the commitment to planetary solidarity and peace. Schools, colleges, universities and the mass media can do more to make people aware that we are one people and this single planet is our home. Much greater emphasis can be placed on the priority of the global community over the nation-State. That is to say that people are more important than the way they are organised, and the tribe, the city state or the nation-State are only part of the one great whole – the global community. These structures of education have an enormous responsibility in helping people to change from loyalties that are merely nation centred to loyalties that have as their centre a planetary society. Important as peace-making is, in a nuclear age, it does not solve other major problems such as the disparities between the industrialised countries and the developing world. Millions continue to live in absolute poverty. Again the interdependence of the world gives rise to a set of interrelated questions, such as the environment, trade, resources, disarmament and human rights which can only be handled by an international approach. This is caused by the fact that an interdependent world requires that key questions today involve mutuality of interest. The need to prevent nuclear war is crucial but, even if this is achieved, there is much more to be done which will be a challenge to our idea of human community, our political will to support it and our educational structures to communicate it.

We can, therefore, live with the technology of death by acquiring *a new attitude to war and peace* and seeing mankind, not as a collection of nations all stressing their own nationalism, but as a single community with a unity of many countries and peoples, retaining their diversity that enriches that community, but whose unity is prior to any diversity. In such a world the practices and institutions which are familiar in our domestic societies can become, by suitable modifications, the basis of planetary unity. The sketch of such a system already exists in some of our national institutions. That people can experience such transformations is not in doubt. From family to clan, from clan to nation, from nation to federation – such changes have occurred without eliminating earlier loyalties. Today we can, with God's grace, and the vast array of communication and technology, hope to survive, in all our diversity, in spite of the technology of death, provided we can achieve this ultimate loyalty to this single planet carrying this *one* humanity to which we all belong. Realisation of this fact is the most down-to-earth level of self-interest and preservation and teaches that work for justice and peace-promotion are for the security of all.

In a word, while perfect peace is unattainable in this life, we can subscribe to the goal of creating an international community in which the use of violence is as rare and unnecessary as within our own structured domestic system. It must be admitted that this will have serious difficulties and complexities which involve a challenge and also the laborious task of learning languages, not simply as a means of communication, but as a means of understanding the mentalité of peoples that are culturally different. Some would question the possibility of this undertaking and there is no doubt that it will be exceedingly difficult. But given all the advantages, technical and otherwise, that are available in our times and also the motivation of self-interest, as well as the belief that the essential unity of humanity can be realised, then it seems highly probable that a structure can be organised by which global violence can be contained. For the Christian, Christ's eschatological teaching can give renewed hope; and by presenting a balanced view of man in his totality, with his vocation here and promise in the hereafter, it can enable man to live with the technology of death. The time has therefore come, in the quest for peace, to place less emphasis on swords and more on ploughshares. Each individual has a contribution to make. Indeed, many of the world's great movements of thought and action have flowed from the work of a single person. It is true, of course, that few will have the greatness to bend history itself, but each person can work to change a small portion of events and in the total of all these acts will be written the history of the future.

Notes

CHAPTER ONE: *Direct and Indirect Killing*

1. *Euthanasia and Clinical Practice*. The Linacre Centre, London, 1982, p. 37ff.
2. Plato, *The Last Days of Socrates*. Penguin Books, Harmondsworth, 1982, p. 104ff.
3. Plato, *The Laws*. Penguin Books, Harmondsworth, 1970, p. 376ff.
4. Stamm, J.J. and Andrew, M.E. *The Ten Commandments in Recent Research*. SCM Press, London, 1967, pp. 98–9.
5. Stamm's view has been discussed in more recent scholarship and a useful reflection on the word "Rāsah" is contained in *Exodus* by Childs, B.S., SCM, London, 1974, pp. 419–21. A thorough investigation of the verb "Rāsah" is contained in *Hebrew and English Lexicon of the Old Testament* by Brown, F., Driver, S.R., Briggs, C.A., Clarendon Press, Oxford, 1977, pp. 953–4; also "Exodus" by Hyatt, J.P., in *New Century Bible Commentary*. Marshall, Morgan & Scott, London, 1980, p. 214; and Eerdmans, Grand Rapids (Mich.).
6. Maimonides, *Mishneh Torah, Yad Hazakah, Roze'ah* 2 : 7.
7. Caro, J., *Shulhan Arukh, Yoreh De'ah*. 339, 1 + gloss.
8. Jacobitz, I., "Euthanasia" in *Encyclopaedia Judiaca*. Vol. 6, p. 979.
9. *Euthanasia and Clinical Practice*. p. 38 (footnote).
10. *Universal Declaration of Human Rights*. United Nations Office of Information, New York, 1976, Article 3.
11. Mt 5 : 21; Mt 15 : 19; Mt 19 : 18; Mk 7 : 21; Mk 10 : 19; Lk 18 : 20; Rom 1 : 29; 1 Pet 4 : 15; Jas 2 : 11 ff; Rev 9 : 21; Rev 21 : 8; Rev 22 : 15.
12. Rom 13 : 8–10; Gal 5 : 13ff.
    McDonagh, E., *Invitation and Response*. Gill & McMillan, Dublin, 1972, p. 145.
    Rom 13 : 4.
13. *Invitation and Response*, p. 145.
    Mk 12 : 13–17; Rom 13 : 1–7.

14. Bainton, R.H., *Christian Attitudes towards War and Peace.* Hodder & Stoughton, London, 1963. p. 57ff.

15. Noonan, John T., *The Morality of Abortion.* Harvard University Press, Cambridge (Mass.), 1970, pp. 7–14.

16. Jn 10 : 11; Jn 15 : 13; Rom 5 : 7.
Augustine, Sermon. 304, 1–4 on the martyrdom of St Laurence quoted by the Divine Office. Collins, London, 1974, p. 178.
Ambrose, Book 1. Chapter 2, 5, 7–9 on the martyrdom of St Agnes, Collins, London, 1974, p. 90.

17. *Christian Attitudes towards War and Peace*, p. 57ff.

18. Ambrose, *De Officiis Ministrorum.* Book 1; PL 16, 74–78, 81–86.
Augustine, Ep. 47 5; PL 33, 186–187.

19. Basil, Ep. 188; 13; PG 32, 682.

20. Ramsey, Paul, *War and the Christian Conscience* – How shall modern war be conducted justly? Duke University Press, Durham (N.C.), 1961, pp. 15–9 and p. 37.
The Just War: Force and Political Responsibility. Charles Scribner's Sons, New York, 1968, pp. 150–2.

21. *The Just War*, p. 142ff.

22. Curran, Charles E., *Politics, Medicine and Christian Ethics.* A dialogue with Paul Ramsey. Fortress Press, Philadelphia (Penn.), 1972, p. 76.

23. *War and the Christian Conscience*, pp. 15–39.

24. Aquinas, T., *Summa Theol.* 11–11, 64, 7.

25. Bonhoeffer, Deitrich, *Ethics.* Collins Fontana, London, 1970, p. 159.

26. Davis, H., *Moral and Pastoral Theology*, Vol. 2. Sheed & Ward, London, 1943, p. 153.

27. Barth, K., *Church Dogmatics.* T. & T. Clarke, Edinburgh, 1958, 111/4, 432, 437, 450ff.

28. *Invitation and Response*, p. 147.

29. *Summa Theol.* 11–11, 79, 3. Linacre Papers No. 2. London, 1978, p. 5.

30. *The Church and The Bomb* — Nuclear Weapons and Christian Conscience. The Report of a Working Party under the chairmanship of the Bishop of Salisbury. Hodder & Stoughton, London, 1982, p. 90.

31. *The Church and The Bomb*, p. 91.

32. Marshall, John, *Ethics of Medical Practice.* Darton, Longman & Todd, London, 1960, p. 109.

33. Kelly, G., *Medico–Moral Problems.* Burns, Oats & Washbourne, London, 1955, pp. 24–33.

34. Grisez, G., *Abortion: The Myths, The Realities and the Arguments.* Corpus Books, Washington (D.C.), 1970, p. 333.

Quoted in *How Brave a New World*. McCormick, Richard, SCM Press, London, 1981, p. 423.

35. *Acta Apostolicae Sedis* (AAS). 30 (1897–98) 703–04.
36. Bouscaren, T.L., *Ethics of Ectopic Operations*. Bruce Publishing, Milwaukee (Mich.), 1944, pp. 3–64.
37. Häring, B., *Medical Ethics*. St Paul's Publications, Slough, 1972, p. 109.
38. *Summa Theol.* 11–11 Quest. 64. Article 7.
39. *Politics, Medicine and Christian Ethics*, p. 123.
40. Lehmkuhl, *Theologia Moralis*. Vol. 1, N. 1010.
41. Connery, J., *Abortion: The Development of the Roman Catholic Perspective*. Loyola University Press, Chicago (Mich.), 1977, pp. 301–3.
42. McCormick, R. and Ramsey, P. (eds.), *Doing Evil to Achieve Good*: Moral Choice in Conflict Situations. Loyola University Press, Chicago (Mich.), 1978, p. 69ff.
43. Hollenbach, David, "Nuclear Weapons and Nuclear War" in *Theological Studies*. December, 1982. Vol. 43. No. 4, pp. 594–5.
44. O'Mahony, Patrick, *Multinationals and Human Rights*. Mayhew-McCrimmon, Essex, 1980, p. 9.
45. Pope John XXIII, "Mater et Magistra". Quoted in *New Aspects of the Social Question*. Catholic Truth Society, London, 1963.
46. Cranson, Maurice, *What are Human Rights?* Bodley Head, London, 1973, p. 81.
47. Falconer, Alan (ed.), "Theological Reflection on Human Rights" in *Understanding Human Rights*. Irish School of Ecumenics, Dublin, 1978, p. 205.
48. Ward, Barbara, "Peace Through Justice" in *The Tablet*, January, 1973, p. 51.
49. World Bank, Washington (D.C.), *World Development Report*. The International Bank for Reconstruction and Development, 1978, p. 1, 7 and 65.
50. "The North–South Divide".
51. UNCTAD 3, *Make or Break for Development* – A Report of the World Development Movement. London, 1972.
52. *Real Aid*: A Strategy for Britain. The Independent Group on British Aid. London, 1982, p. 16.
53. *Partners in Development* – Report of the Pearson Commission on International Development. Pall Mall Press, London, 1969, p. 172.
54. *Real Aid*, p. 24.
55. Overseas Development Institute, London. Briefing Paper No. 1. July 1982.
56. *North–South: A Programme for Survival*. Pan World Affairs, London, 1980, p. 16.

57. Deut 25 : 17–22; Lev 19 : 33; Lev 19 : 9; Ps 112 : 9; Ps 82 : 2–4.
58. Is 1 : 17; Is 5 : 8; Is 10 : 1–2; Is 58 : 6–11.
59. *The Tablet*, April, 1980, p. 334.
60. Camara, Helder, *Structures of Injustice*. The International Commission for Justice and Peace, London, 1972, p. 7.
61. *The Times*, 13 November, 1982, p. 10.
62. McNamara, Robert S. *Address to the Board of Governors at Nairobi*, 24 September 1973. International Bank for Reconstruction and Development, Washington, 1973, p. 29.
63. Aiken, W. M. and La Follette, Hugh (eds.), *World Hunger and Moral Obligation*. Prentice Hall, Englewood Cliffs (N.J.), 1977.
64. *North–South: A Programme for Survival*, p. 20.
    O'Mahony, Patrick, *Brandt: The Christian Connection*. Catholic Truth Society, London, 1982, p. 2ff.
65. Hardin, G., "Lifeboat Ethics – The case against helping the Poor" in *World Hunger and Moral Obligation*, p. 11ff.
66. Fletcher, J., "Give if it helps but not if it hurts" in *World Hunger and Moral Obligation*, p. 104ff.
67. *Partners in Development*, p. 55ff.
68. *North–South: A Programme for Survival*, p. 105.
69. In *World Hunger and Moral Obligation*. Rachels, H., "Vegetarianism and other weight problems", p. 180; Singer, P., "Famine, Affluence and Morality", p. 22ff; Narveson, J., "Morality and Starvation", p. 9ff.
70. Slote, M.A. "The Morality of Wealth" in *World Hunger and Moral Obligation*, p. 124.
71. In *World Hunger and Moral Obligation*. Aiken, W., "The Right to be saved from Starvation", p. 85ff; O'Neill, O., "Life Boat Earth", p. 148ff.
72. *World Hunger and Moral Obligation*, p. 157.
73. O'Mahony, Patrick, *Multinationals and Human Rights*. Mayhew-McCrimmon, Essex, 1980, p. 517.
    O'Mahony, Patrick, *Investment: a blessing or a curse?* Mayhew-McCrimmon, Essex, 1979, p. 15ff.
    O'Mahony, Patrick, *Money: The Christian Dilemma*. Catholic Truth Society, London, 1981.
74. Aiken, W. "The Right to be saved from Starvation" in *World Hunger and Moral Obligation*, p. 101.
75. *World Hunger and Moral Obligation*, p. 101.
76. Abbott, W.M. (ed.), *The Documents of Vatican II*. Geoffrey Chapman, London, 1966, p. 279.
77. Fitzgerald, Garratt, *Unequal Partners*. United Nations, New York, 1979, p. 70.
78. World Health Organisation. From the preamble to the Con-

stitution of the World Health Organisation. Adopted by the International Health Conference held in New York from 19 June to 22 July 1946 and signed on 22 July 1946 by the representatives of 61 States. Reprinted, with permission of the publisher, from *The First Ten Years of the World Health Organisation*, WHO, 1958.

79. *North–South: A Programme for Survival*, p. 14.
80. *T.V. Times*, 3 to 9 October 1981.
81. *North–South: A Programme for Survival*, p. 103.
    Brandt: The Christian Connection, p. 7.
82. McCormick, A., *Population Explosion*. Harper Colophon Books, New York, San Francisco and London, 1973, p. 56ff.
83. *Summa Theol.* 1–11 Q. 6. Art, 3. It could be argued on the principle of Aquinas "Potest et Debet Agere" that the North is guilty of manslaughter by collectively neglecting the hungry millions.
    cf. also Jas 4 : 17.
84. *North–South: A Programme for Survival*, p. 13.
85. *Ibid.*, p. 14.
86. *Bombs for Breakfast*. COPAT, 1978, p. 24.
87. *North–South: A Programme for Survival*, p. 14.
88. Sanger, Clyde. "Disarmament and Development in the 80s" in *Safe and Sound*. Zed Press, London, 1982, p. 18.
89. *Ibid.*, p. 19.
90. Sevard, Ruth Leger, *World Military and Social Expenses*, World Priorities, Virginia, 1982, pp. 5 and 15.
91. Thompson, Robert (ed.), *War in Peace*. Orbis Publishing, London, 1981, p. 280.
92. *Disarmament and Development*. United Nations, New York, 1972, p. 2.
93. Schell, Jonathan. *The Fate of the Earth*, Pan Books, London, 1982.
94. *Guardian*, 22 November 1982, p. 9.
95. O'Mahony, Patrick, *The Fantasy of Human Rights*. Mayhew-McCrimmon, Essex, 1978, p. 18.
    Maritain, Jacques, *Man and the State*. Hollis & Carter, London, 1954, p. 173ff.
96. *The Fate of the Earth*, p. 180.
97. *Ibid.*, p. 190.
98. *North–South: A Programme for Survival*, p. 284.
99. Pope Paul VI, Address to the United Nations General Assembly, 4 October 1965, Catholic Truth Society, p. 9.
100. *Guardian*, 16 November 1982, p. 9.
101. Duchacek, T., *Nations and Men*. Dryden Press, Illinois, 1975, p. 56.

Synder, Louis L., *The Meaning of Nationalism*. Rutgers University Press, New Jersey, 1954, p. 52.
102. Howard, Michael, *War and the Liberal Conscience*. Temple Smith, London, 1978, p. 133.
103. *Structures of Injustice*, p. 40.
104. Buhlmann, W., *The Chosen Peoples*. St Paul's Press, 1982, p. 42. Acts X 34–38.
105. Davies, J.G., *Worship and Mission*. SCM Press, London, 1966, p. 23ff.
106. *Peace and Disarmament* – Documents of the World Council of Churches. Presented by the Commission of the Churches on International Affairs (CCIA), Geneva, 1982, pp. 11–12 and 95–6.
107. Commission of the Churches on International Affairs Report.
108. *Ibid.*, p. 96.
109. *The Church and The Bomb*, p. 81.

CHAPTER TWO: *Pacifism and the Just War*

1. McFadden, W., *A Theological Evaluation of Nuclear Pacifism as held by Selected Christian Thinkers*. Unpublished Thesis: Boston University School of Theology, 1966.
2. Roszak, Theodore, "The Dilemma of the Just War" in *Nation*. 14 April 1963, p. 328.
3. *A Theological Evaluation of Nuclear Pacifism as held by Selected Christian Thinkers*, p. 162.
4. *Ibid.*, p. 46.
5. Zahn, G., *War, Conscience and Dissent*. Chapman, London, 1967, pp. 36–42.
6. Ramsey, P., *The Just War: Force and Political Responsibility*. Charles Scribner's Sons, New York, 1968, p. 164.
7. Lammers, Stephen, *The Just War Tradition – An examination of some modern claims to that Tradition*. Unpublished Thesis: Brown University, 1971, p. 146. Lammers does indicate that some just war thinkers admit a greater variety of positions where an attack on non-combatants is not envisaged. Probably it could be said that nuclear pacifists rule out all nuclear wars where just war thinkers simply say what cannot be done in nuclear war. For example, Father Langan, S.J., justifies a limited nuclear war on just war principles. (Langan, J., *Theological Studies*. September 1982, No. 3, p. 455.)
8. Aquinas, T., *Summa Theol.* 11–11 Q40, A.1 "Is it always a sin to fight?" This title by Thomas Aquinas seems to place the presumption in favour of non-violence.

9. Johnson, James, T., "On Keeping Faith: The use of History for Religious Ethics" in *Journal of Religious Ethics*. 7, 1979, pp. 112–13. Johnson, an expert on just war thinking, has here shown that this belief of universal pacifism is true in Patristic and Medieval writers. Indeed down through the centuries, the theme of Christian non-violence and pacifism has echoed and re-echoed, sometimes more strongly, and sometimes more faintly according to the period, but the majority view since Constantine has favoured the just war theory.

10. Second Draft of the United States Catholic Bishops ad hoc Committee on War and Peace, published by *Origins*, the Official National Documentary Service, 28 October 1982. Vol. 12, No. 20, pp. 305–28 and debated by the bishops during the Annual Meeting 15 to 18 November 1982. (Hereafter called the Second Draft.)

11. Bainton, R. *Christian Attitudes towards War and Peace*. Abingdon Press, New York, 1960. Chapter 4, 5 and 10.
Yoder, J., *The Politics of Jesus*. Eerdmans, Grand Rapids (Mich.), 1972.
Merton, T., *Faith and Violence: Christian Teaching and Christian Practice*. Notre Dame University, Notre Dame, 1968.
War, Conscience and Dissent, pp. 36–42.
Douglass, J., *The Non-Violent Cross: A Theology of Revolution and Peace*. Chapman, London, 1968.

12. Ramsey, P., *War and The Christian Conscience*. Duke University Press, Durham (N.C.), 1961, p. xv.
Ruede, E., *The Morality of War*. S.T.D. Thesis, Rome, 1970, p. 22.

13. *War and The Christian Conscience*. pp. xv–xvi.

14. *Ibid.*

15. *The Morality of War*, p. 22.

16. Shannan, Thomas, A., *What are they saying about Peace and War?* Paulist Press, New York, Ramsey, 1983, p. 842.

17. *Ibid.*, p. 842ff.

18. *Ibid.*, p. 12.

19. *War and The Christian Conscience*, p. xvi.

20. Abbott, William, "Pastoral Constitution of the Church in the Modern World" in *Documents of Vatican II*. Chapman, London, 1966, pp. 78–9.
Pope John Paul II, Address at Drogheda. *Origins* 9, 1979, p. 272 ff. However, both Vatican II and John Paul II reiterate the right to self-defence.

21. *Second Draft*, 1 c, p. 311.

22. *The Non-Violent Cross: A Theology of Revolution*, p. 175.

23. Hehir, J.B. *The Church and the Arms Race*. Document pre-

pared by the Commission for International Justice and Peace,
England and Wales. Catholic Information Office, Abbots
Langley, 1982.

24. *Ibid.*, p. 176.

25. Hollenbach, David, "Nuclear Weapons and Nuclear War" in
Theological Studies. Vol. 43, No. 4, 1982, pp. 589–99.

26. A prima-facie obligation is a moral duty, binding in conscience.
"It is to be distinguished from an absolute obligation, however,
for it may conflict with other equally important and binding
obligations. For example, I have an obligation to keep promises
I have made. If, however, taking time to stop and assist a person
injured ... were to cause me to leave unfulfilled a promise to
meet a friend ... the more important obligation shall take
precedence." *Ibid.*, p. 582.
"We have a prima-facie obligation not to harm or kill other
human beings." *Ibid.*
Childress, J., "Just War Criteria" in Shannon, Thomas, A. (ed.),
War or Peace? The Search for New Answers. Orbis Books,
Maryknoll, 1980, pp. 40–58.

27. Johnson, James T. *Ideology, Reason and the Limitation of War*.
Princeton University Press, Princeton, N.J. 1981.
Childress, J.F. "Just War Criteria" *War or Peace? The Search
for New Answers*, pp. 40–58.

28. "On Keeping Faith: The use of History for Religious Ethics in
Journal of Religious Ethics. 7, 1979, pp. 112–3.

29. *Third Draft*, in *Origins*, April, 1983, Vol. 12, No. 44, Section 3,
p. 706.

30. Ep. ad Marcellinum (138) 11, 9.

31. Ep. Bonifacium, 189. VI.

32. *Ibid.*

33. Surveys by the United States bishops of the history and theol-
ogy of the just war tradition included:
Russell, F.H., *The Just War in the Middle Ages*, New York,
1975.
War and the Christian Conscience.
Ramsey, P., *Just War: Force and Political Responsibility*, New
York, 1968.
Johnson, J.T., *Ideology, Reason and the Limitation of War*.
Princeton, 1981.
Walters, Leroy, *Five Classic Just War Theories*.
*A Study in the thought of Thomas Aquinas, Vitoria, Surez,
Gentili and Grotius*. Unpublished Ph.D. Thesis: Yale, 1971. cf.
Third Draft, p. 706.
One could also add another useful work:
O'Connor, D.T., *War in a Moral Perspective: A Critical*

Appraisal of the views of Paul Ramsey. Unpublished Ph.D:
Claremont Graduate School, 1972.

34. *Summa Theol.* 11–11, Q.40.
    Summa Theol. 11–11, Q.64. a6.
35. Ruston, R., *Nuclear Deterrence – Right or Wrong?* Catholic
    Information Service, Abbots Langley, 1981, p. 14.
36. Abbott, William, *Documents of Vatican II*.
37. Francisco De Vitoria, *De Jure Belli*, 467, 60.
    Francisco Suarez, *De Legibus*. ac de Deo Legislatore, Chapter
    13, Sect. 1, para. 7.
    Both quoted in *What are they saying about Peace and War?* p.
    126.
38. *Second Draft*, 11, p. 12.
39. O'Brien, W.V. "Just War Doctrine in a Nuclear Context" in
    Theological Studies. June, 1983, Vol. 44, No. 2, p. 197.
40. *Second Draft*, p. 312. The bishops are unaware of the very fine
    work of Professor J.G. Davies, *Christians, Politics and Violent
    Revolution*. SCM Press, London, 1976.
41. "Pastoral Constitution of the Church in the Modern World" in
    Documents of Vatican II, para 79–80.
42. The distinction between combatants and non-combatants
    varies in different historic circumstances. It may, at times, be
    difficult to make the distinction but one thing can be said with
    certainty; it is that there is a clear distinction between soldiers,
    on the one hand, and innocent children, hospital patients, nurs-
    ing mothers, the mentally and physically handicapped, and the
    elderly etc., on the other.
43. *Nuclear Deterrence – Right or Wrong?*, p. 18.
    The Morality of War, p. 98.
44. According to many thinkers, especially in the Catholic tradi-
    tion, even the intention to do so is wrong. This is backed up by
    Christ's teaching recorded in Mt 5 : 27–28 and Mk 7 : 21–23
    where Jesus speaks of sinning, even in the mind. This point of
    intention will receive detailed treatment again when we are
    discussing the NCCB and the C. of E. attitudes in the next
    chapter.
    cf. Curran, C, *Politics, Medicine and Christian Ethics*. A dia-
    logue with Paul Ramsey. Fortress Press, Philadelphia (Penn.),
    1972, p. 93.
45. *De Jure Belli*, 446/33 Quoted in *Nuclear Deterrence – Right or
    Wrong?*, p. 4.
46. Brown, David, *Choices – Ethics and the Christian*. Blackwell,
    Oxford, 1983, p. 148.
47. Langan, J. "The American Hierarchy & Nuclear Weapons" in
    Theological Studies, September 1982, No. 3, p. 455.

48. *Second Draft*, C2, p. 312. *The Church and The Bomb* — Report of a Working Party under the chairmanship of the Bishop of Salisbury. Hodder & Stoughton, London, 1982, p. 96 ff.

CHAPTER THREE: *The Ecumenical Response*

1. *Theological Studies*. March 1982, Vol. 43, No. 1, p. 113.
2. *Time*. 9 August 1982, p. 39.
3. *Peace and Disarmament* CCIA and PCJP Geneva and Vatican City, October 1982.
   Another work of great importance is *Nulcear Disarmament*: key statements of Popes, Bishops, Councils and Churches. Heyer, Robert (ed.), Paulist Press, New York, 1982.
4. *Peace and Disarmament*, p. vii.
5. Van Asbeck, F.M., "The Church and the Disorder of International Society" in *The Church and International Disorder*. Vol. 4 of the Amsterdam series on *Man's Disorder and God's Design*. Harper & Bros., New York, 1948, p. 63.
6. McFadden, W., *A Theological Evaluation of Nuclear Pacifism as held by Selected Christian Thinkers*. Unpublished Ph.D. Thesis: Boston University School of Theology, 1966, p. 162.
7. *Peace and Disarmament*, p. 15.
8. *Ibid.*, p. 2.
9. CCIA *Annual Report* 1950/51, p. 27. Quoted in *Peace and Disarmament*, p. 2.
10. *Peace and Disarmament*, p. 2.
11. *Ibid.*, p. 21.
12. *Ibid.*, p. 22.
13. *Ibid.*
14. *Ibid.*
15. *Ibid.*, p. 3.
16. *Ibid.*, p. 31.
17. *Ibid.*
18. *Ibid.*, pp. 5 and 37.
19. *Ibid.*, p. 37.
20. *Ibid.*, p. 6.
21. *Peace and Disarmament*, p. 38.
22. Pope John XXIII "Mater et Magistra". Catholic Truth Society, 1963, para 198.
23. *Peace and Disarmament*, p. 8.
24. *Ibid.*, p. 61.
25. *Ibid.*, p. 10.
26. Address by Dr Philip Potter. Secretary of the World Council of Churches, to the United Nations First Special Session on Dis-

armament, June 1978. Cited in *Peace and Disarmament*, p. 88.
27. *Ibid.*, p. 88, para 2 and 4.
28. Hehir, J.B., *The Church and the Arms Race*. The second of a series of studies on peace, defence and disarmament prepared by the Justice and Peace Commission of England and Wales. Catholic Information Services, Abbots Langley, p. 7.
Childress, James F., "Just War Theories" in *Theological Studies*. September 1978, Vol. 39, No. 3, p. 427.
29. Murray, J.C. "Remarks on the Moral Problems of War" in *Theological Studies*. 1959, 20, pp. 40–61.
30. "Summi Maeroris" 19 July 1950 cited in *Peace and Disarmament*, pp. 123–4.
31. "Remarks on the Moral Problems of War" in *Theological Studies*. 1959, 20, p. 51 (footnote).
32. "The Holy See on Disarmament and Peace". Cited in *Peace and Disarmament*, p. 109.
33. Christmas Message, December 1956. Cited in *Peace and Disarmament*, p. 138.
34. Pope John XXIII, "Pacem in Terris". Catholic Truth Society, 1980, para 136.
35. Paul VI, "Populorum Progressio". Catholic Truth Society, 1967, para 78.
36. Christmas Message, December 1954. Cited in *Peace and Disarmament*, p. 134.
37. Address to the VIII World Medical Congress.
38. Christmas Message, December 1959. Cited in *Peace and Disarmament*, p. 144.
39. "Mater et Magistra". New Light on Social Problems. Catholic Truth Society, 1961, p. 52.
40. *Ibid.*
41. "Pacem in Terris", para 136 ff.
42. *Ibid.*, para 11.
43. *Ibid.*, para 121.
44. *Ibid.*, para 93, 126 and 172.
45. *Ibid.*, para 109.
46. *The Church and the Arms Race*, p. 7.
47. "Pacem in Terris", para 128.
48. *Ibid.*
49. *Ibid.*, para 136.
50. Abbott, W.M. (ed.), *Documents of Vatican II*. Geoffrey Chapman, London 1966, p. 292.
51. *Peace and Disarmament*, p. 5 also cf. p. 8.
52. *The Church and the Arms Race*, p. 7.
53. Paul VI, *Appeal for Peace to U.N.* Catholic Truth Society, 4 October 1965.

54. *L'Osservatore Romano*, 5 December 1964, p. 1.
55. "Populorum Progressio", p. 51.
56. Christmas Message, December 1968. Cited in *Peace and Disarmament*, p. 172.
57. *The Pope in Britain*, St Paul's Press, 1982, p. 9.
58. *L'Osservatore Romano*, 21 June 1982.
59. Abbott, W.M. (ed.), "Pastoral Constitution of the Church in the Modern World" (Gaudium et Spes) *Documents of Vatican II* Geoffrey Chapman, London, 1966, p. 81.
60. Report on War and Peace, US Bishops Annual Meeting, Washington (D.C.), 16–19 November 1981. Cited in *Nuclear Disarmament*, p. 176.

CHAPTER FOUR   *The Response of the United States Catholic Bishops*

1. Heyer, Robert (ed.), *Nuclear Disarmament*. Paulist Press, New York/Ramsey, 1982, pp. 10–11.
   "The Eightieth Year" in *This is Action*. The Justice and Peace Commission, London, 1972, para 49.
2. Paul VI, *Evangelisation in the Modern World*. Catholic Truth Society, London, para 62 (not dated).
3. The Second Draft of the Bishops ad hoc Committee on War and Peace was published in *Origins*, the official National Catholic Documentary Service, 28 October 1982. Vol. 12, No. 20, pp. 305–28 and was debated by the bishops during the annual meeting 15–18 November. Hereafter called the *Second Draft*.
4. US Congress Senate, Committee of Foreign Relations. The *SALT II* Treaty Hearing on ex, 96–1 96th Congress. 1 September 1979, Part 4, pp. 116–30.
5. McCormick, pR., "Notes on Moral Theology" in *Theological Studies*. Vol. 43, 1982, No. 1, p. 117.
   Nuclear Disarmament, p. 100. (Cardinal John Krol, Bishop of Philadelphia, Testimony on behalf of the USCC before the Senate Foreign Relations Committee, 6 September 1979.)
6. Winter, F.X., "Nuclear Deterrence Morality" in *Theological Studies*. September 1982. No. 3, p. 429.
7. *Nuclear Disarmament*, p. 131 ff. Address at the Pacific Northwest Synod of the Lutheran Church in America. 12 July 1981.
8. McCormick, R., "Notes on Moral Theology" in *Theological Studies*. Vol. 43, 1982, p. 114.
9. *Time*. 118, 19 October 1981, No. 52.
10. *Nuclear Disarmament*, pp. 139–41. Interview from "Our Sunday Visitor" by Bruce Smith, 9 August 1981.
11. *The Tablet*. "Notebook". 5 February 1983.
12. *Time*. "Religion". No. 48, 29 November 1982.

13. *Nuclear Disarmament*, p. 183. The statement by 29 bishops, that possession of nuclear weapons is immoral. October 1981.

14. *New York Times*, 13 September 1981, p. 37.

15. *Nuclear Disarmament*, p. 161. Archbishop John R. Quinn's Pastoral Statement: *Instruments of Peace – Weapons on War*. 4 October 1981.

16. United States bishops statement: *To Live in Jesus Christ*. 11 November 1976, pp. 90 and 91.

17. *Origins*, Catholic Institute for Justice and Peace, US Catholic Conference 1982.

18. *The Tablet*, 20 November 1982, p. 1158.

19. Some 51 million people.

20. *Time*, 29 November 1982, p. 43.

21. *Second Draft*. "Limited Nuclear War" in *Origins*. 28 October 1982, Vol. 12, No. 20, C3, p. 315.

22. *Second Draft. Ibid.*, C3, p. 316.

23. *Second Draft. Ibid.*, IV, No. 3, B, p. 325.

24. *Ibid.*, No. 1, p. 307.

25. *Ibid.* Here the pastoral is quoting from Vatican II. "Pastoral Constitution on the Church in the Modern World", para 80.

26. *Ibid.*, No. 11, A, p. 313.

27. *Ibid.*

28. *Ibid.*, No. 11, B, p. 315.

29. *Ibid.*, No. 11, D, p. 316.

30. John Paul II. Address to the United Nations Special Session, 1982, 8.

31. McDonnell, Killian. *The Tablet*. 12 February 1983. "US Bishops Challenged", p. 126.

32. *Second Draft*. C1, p. 314.

33. Grisez, Germain. *Some Questions and Answers of the Proposed NCCB Collective Pastoral on War and Peace*. This is a private document circulated to the bishops of the United States.

34. *US Military Posture Statement for F.Y.* 1983, Washington (D.C.), 1982, p. 19.

35. *Some Questions and Answers of the Proposed NCCB Collective Pastoral on War and Peace*, p. 2.

36. *Ibid.*, p. 3.

37. *Second Draft*, p. 317.

38. *Some Questions and Answers of the Proposed NCCB Collective Pastoral on War and Peace*, p. 6.

39. McCormick, R. and Ramsey, P. (eds.), *Doing Evil to Achieve Good*. Loyala University Press, Chicago (Ill.), 1978.

40. *Octogesima Adveniens*. CIJP 1972, para 49.
    Evangelisation in the Modern World. Catholic Truth Society, para 62 and 66, (not dated).

41. *Time.* "Religion", 29 November 1982.
42. Kiernan, J.V. and Himes, K.R., "Pluralism in Moral Evaluation of War". *The Month*, February 1983, p. 43.
43. *The Tablet*, 12 February 1983, p. 126.
44. Curran, C., *Politics, Medicine and Christian Ethics*. A dialogue with Paul Ramsey. Fortress Press, Philadelphia (Penn.), 1972, p. 100.
45. *Evangelii Nuntiandi* Part 4. Catholic Truth Society, Article 29, (not dated).
    Ogesima Adveniens. This is Action. The Justice and Peace Commission, London, 1972, para 46.
46. Reagan, Ronald. "Address to the National Association of Evangelicals" 8 March 1982. *The Economist*, May 1982, p. 45.
47. *The Tablet*, 4 December 1982, p. 1223.
    The Times, 7 February 1983, p. 12.
48. *Catholic Herald*, 4 February 1983.
    The Economist, February 1983, p. 21.
49. *The Times*, 28 March 1983.
50. Camara, H., *Structures of Injustice*. The Justice and Peace Commission, 1972, p. 7.
51. The position of Christians and political involvement is clearly and forcefully developed by Professor J.G. Davies, *Christians, Politics and Violent Revolution*. SCM, London, 1976, pp. 9–43.
52. *Time.* "Religion", 9 August 1982.
53. *Origins.* 28 October 1982, Vol. 12, p. 326.
54. "Pluralism in Moral Evaluation of War", *The Month*, February 1983.
55. *The Tablet*, 4 December 1982, p. 1223.
56. *Catholic Herald*, 7 January 1983.
57. *The Economist*, 5 February 1983, p. 21.
    The Democrat, No. 5, 20 December 1982, Vol. 1, p. 23.
58. Winter, F.X., "US Bishops and the Arms Race" in *The Month*. August 1982, p. 265. F.X. Winter is Associate Professor of Moral Theology in the School of Foreign Service, Georgetown University, Washington (D.C.), Lecturer on Ethics of Military Leadership at the Army War College, Carlisle Barracks (Penn.).
59. *Ibid.*, p. 260.
60. *Ibid.*, p. 263.
61. *Listener*, 3 March 1983, p. 14. Interview on BBC Radio 4 with Michael Charlton.
62. *The Tablet*, 29 January 1983, p. 92.
63. *Second Draft*, 28 October 1982. "Introduction", p. 306.
64. *Ibid.*, p. 312.
65. *Ibid.*, 2, C3, p. 315.
66. *Ibid.*, 2, C, p. 314.

67. It is interesting to note that the Working Party of the Church of England used the same moral criteria, a point which will be discussed in the next section.

68. *Second Draft*, pp. 307–25, 28 October 1982, Vol. 12.

69. *Ibid.*, 11, Section A, p. 313.

70. *Origins*, 28 October 1982, Vol. 12, No. 20, pp. 305–28. Referred to above as *Second Draft*.

71. *Origins*, 14 April 1983, Vol. 12. Hereafter referred to as the *Third Draft*.

72. *Third Draft*, p. 698.

73. *Ibid.*

74. *Ibid.*, Section 2, para 2.

75. *Ibid.*, Section 2, para 1.

76. *Ibid.*, p. 715, Section D.2.

77. *Ibid.*, p. 699, Section B.

78. *Ibid.*, p. 712, Section C.2.

79. *The Tablet*, 16 April 1983, p. 359.

80. *Third Draft*, p. 689, Section A, No. 1.

81. *Third Draft*, p. 715 ff.

82. *Third Draft*, pp. 709 and 718.

83. *Third Draft*, p. 718. Apart from nuclear war, many Christians would still reject the absolute pacifist position on the argument made by Ramsey that, for love to be effective, it may be necessary to employ force.

84. *Ibid.*

85. *Third Draft*, p. 723.

86. *Ibid.*, p. 722.

87. *Ibid.*, p. 722.

88. *Catholic Herald*, 29 April 1983, p. 2.

89. *The Tablet*, 30 April 1983, p. 411.

90. *Ibid.*

91. *Third Draft*, p. 714.

92. Clark, Wm. to Cardinal Bernardin. 15 January 1983. *Third Draft*, p. 728 (Footnote 74).

93. Weinberger, Casper, *Annual Report to Congress*. 1 February 1983, p. 55.
Letter from Weinberger to Bishop O'Connor. 9 February 1983. *Third Draft*, p. 728 (Footnote 75).

94. *Third Draft*, p. 714.

95. *Third Draft*, p. 715.

96. *The Tablet*. The representatives were from the United States, France, Federal Republic of Germany, England, Wales and Scotland, Belgium, Italy and the Netherlands. Also present were Cardinals J. Ratzinger and A. Casaroli.

97. Rome Constitution on Peace and Disarmament. *A Vatican*

Synthesis, 7 April 1983.

Origins. National Documentary Service.

98. Abbott, W.M. (ed.), "Decree on the Bishops" *Documents of Vatican II*. Geoffrey Chapman, London, 1966, p. 425, para 38.

99. *The Tablet*, 30 April 1983, p. 401.

100. *Origins*. National Documentary Service. 7 April 1983.

101. Schneiders, Sandra "New Testament Reflections on Peace and Nuclear Arms" in *Catholics and Nuclear War*. G. Chapman, London, 1983, p. 91.

102. *The Challenge of Peace: God's Promise and Our Response*. This is the final text of the Pastoral Letter which was published after the debate. Catholic Truth Society with SPCK, London, 1983.

103. *Third Draft*, p. 709.

104. Douglass, J.W., *The Non-Violent Cross: A Theology of Revolution*. Chapman, London, 1968, p. 175.

105. Justin *Dialogue with Trypho*. Chapter 20.
The First Apology. Chapters 14 and 39 quoted in *Third Draft*, p. 709.

106. *Third Draft*, p. 718.

107. *Ibid.*

108. Zahn, Gordon. "Afterwards" in *War or Peace – The Search for New Answers*. Thomas A. Shannon (ed.), Orbis Books, Maryknoll, 1980, p. 234.

109. *Third Draft*, p. 713.

110. *The Church and The Bomb*. The Report of the Working Party of the Church of England under the Chairmanship of the Bishop of Salisbury. Hodder & Stoughton, 1982, p. 98.
Ruston, Roger. *Nuclear Deterrence – Right or Wrong?* Catholic Information Services, 1981, p. 31 ff.

111. *The Times*, 4 May 1983, p. 6.
The Tablet, 7 May 1983, p. 436.

CHAPTER FIVE: *The Response of the Church of England*

1. Quoted from the official text provided by Lambeth Palace, p. 2. Quoted by Winters, F.X. *Theological Studies*. September 1982, No. 3.

2. *The Church and The Bomb*. Nuclear Weapons and Christian Conscience. The Report of the Working Party of the Church of England under the chairmanship of the Bishop of Salisbury. Hodder & Stoughton, London, 1982. Hereafter referred to as *The Report*.

3. *The Report*, Introduction, p. vii.

4. *The Report*, p. 77.

5. *Ibid.*, p. 96.
6. *Ibid.*, p. 97.
7. *The Times*, 25 October 1982.
8. *The Report*, p. 98.
9. *Ibid.*
10. *Ibid.*, p. 153.
11. *Ibid.*, p. 99.
12. *Ibid.*
13. *Ibid.*, p. 153.
14. *Ibid.*, p. 122.
15. *Ibid.*, p. 120.
16. *Ibid.*, p. 124.
17. *Ibid.*, p. 159.
18. *Ibid.*, p. 159. Enoch Powell believes that our nuclear deterrence policy is sheer madness and suicidal. *The Times*, 1 June 1983, p. 4.
19. *Ibid.*, pp. 159 and 160.
20. *Ibid.*, p. 160. The Chevaline is a British system designed to improve the penetrative capability of the warheads of a Polaris missile.
21. *Ibid.*, p. 154.
22. *Ibid.*, p. 155 (No. 3).
23. *Ibid.*, p. 161.
24. *Ibid.*, pp. 163 and 164.
25. *The Times*, 7 February 1983.
26. *The Times*, 9 February 1983.
27. *Ibid.*
28. *The Times*, 7 February 1983.
29. *The Times*, 9 February 1983.
30. *The Times*, 10 February 1983.
31. *The Times*, 29 January 1983, p. 8.
32. Langan, J., "The American Hierarchy & Nuclear Weapons" in *Theological Studies*. September 1982, No. 3, p. 462.
33. *Ibid.*
34. *The Times*, 8 February 1982. This point was also made by Alexander Solzhenitsyn in an interview with Bernard Levin in *The Times*, 23 May 1983, p. 11.
35. *The Times*, 20 November 1982.
36. *The Times*, 19 October 1982.
37. *Guardian*, 16 May 1983.
38. *The Times*, 10 January 1983.
39. *Observer*.
40. Shannon, Thomas A. (ed.), *War or Peace: The Search for New Answers*. Orbis Books, Maryknoll, 1980, p. 27ff.
41. Hollinbach, D., "Nuclear Weapons and Nuclear War: The

Shape of the Catholic Debate" in *Theological Studies*. December 1982, Vol. 43, No. 4, p. 600.

There is a valuable discussion by Professor R. McCormick, SJ, on possession/threat/intention "Notes on Moral Theology" in *Theological Studies*. March 1983, Vol. 44, No. 1.

42. *Guardian*, 30 March 1983.

The German Bishops in their Pastoral Letter (*Righteousness Creates Peace* – 18 April 1983) referred to the ethics of deterrence and explicitly accepted the three criteria of the United States bishops:

(1) War must not become more probable; (2) Weapons are reduced to lowest level; (3) Military choices must facilitate progressive disarmament. *cf. Third Draft*, p. 715.

43. Murnion, P.J. (ed.). *Catholics and Nuclear War*. Chapman, London, 1983, p. 179.

44. Andropov, Y.V., *The Sixtieth Anniversary of the Union of Soviet Socialist Republic*. Novosti Press, 1982, p. 39 (no place). Rostow, E., *The Listener*, 3 March 1983, p. 14.

45. "American Foreign Policy in a Cold Climate" in *Encounter*. November 1983, p. 24.

46. *The Sixtieth Anniversary of the Union of Soviet Socialist Republic*, p. 39.

47. Mogg, William Rees, *Guardian*, 16 May 1983, p. 9.

48. Evans, G., *The Yellow Rainmakers*. Verso/New Left Books, London, 1983.

49. *Guardian*, 19 May 1983.

50. Chamberlain, O., Conference for Nobel Prizewinners on *Science and Peace* at Sorbonne University, 26 October 1983 (unpub. papers).

51. *The Report*, p. 99 and p. 154.

52. Winter, F.X. "U.S. Bishops' Arms Letter: a compromise?" in *The Month*, September 1983, p. 296.

53. *Catholics and Nuclear War*, p. 180.

54. This other document was also called *The Church and the Bomb*: a Report by the Board For Social Responsibility. Church Information Office, London. (This Report is known as GS.542 and will be referred to as such in the following observations.)

55. GS.542, p. 4.

56. *Ibid.*, p. 9.

57. *Ibid.*, p. 12.

58. *Ibid.*, p. 13.

59. *Ibid.*, p. 15.

60. *Ibid.*

61. *Ibid.*, p. 18.

62. The General Synod Debate, February 1983. Church Information Office, London, 1983. Entitled *The Church and The Bomb*, p. 39. (Hereafter referred to as the *Synod Document*.)
63. *Synod Document*, p. 40.
64. *Ibid.*, p. 8.
65. Bishop Leonard seems implicitly to accept the well-known slogan "Better dead than red". Not everyone would agree with this thinking and some categorically believe in the other slogan "Better red than dead". This is a position Christians have already experienced when they lived and progressed in the context of the Roman Empire.
66. *Synod Document*, p. 7.
67. GS.542, p. 93.
68. *Synod Document*, p. 64.
69. *Ibid.*, p. 66.
70. *Ibid.*
71. *Synod Document*, p. 5.
    Third Draft, p. 700, para. 1.
72. *Third Draft*, p. 716, III.
73. *The Report*, No. 3, p. 155.
74. Letter to the author dated 16 May 1983.
75. Letter from the Bishop of Salisbury to *The Times*, 5 September 1983.
76. *Der Speigel*, 9 May 1983, p. 122. See also *The Tablet*, 21 May 1983, p. 485.
77. *The Tablet*, 21 May 1983, p. 485.
78. *Synod Document*, p. 65.
79. *NATO Facts and Figures*. NATO Information Service, Brussels, 1978, p. 108.

CHAPTER SIX: *The Response of a Local Church – Field Research*

1. *The Church and The Bomb* – Nuclear Weapons and Christian Conscience. The Report of the Working Party of the Church of England under the chairmanship of the Bishop of Salisbury. Hodder & Stoughton, London, 1982, p. 158.
   Third Draft, Section iv, B1, p. 722.
2. Young, Nigel, *Problems and Possibilities in the Study of Peace*. No. 3 in Peace Studies Papers. The School of Peace Studies, Bradford and Houseman, London, 1980.
3. The relationship between worship and mission is very clearly developed by Professor J.G. Davies in *Worship and Mission*, SCM Press, London, 1966.
4. Eckhardt, William, "Cross-National Measurements of Compassion" in *Peace Research*, Vol. 8, No. 4, 1976, p. 110.

5. *International Developments* 1977, Vol. 1.
6. Balasuriya, Tissa, *The Eucharist and Human Liberation*. SCM Press, London, 1979, p. 132.
7. Paxton, N., "The Liberating Eucharist" in *New Blackfriars*. April 1983, p. 180.
    Moreland, David, OSB, discussion document for the Justice and Peace Commission of England and Wales entitled *The Eucharist and Justice*, p. 1 to p. 8.
8. Gutierrez, G., *A Theology of Liberation*, English edition. SCM Press, London, 1974, p. 265.
9. Paxton, N., "The Liberating Eucharist" in *New Blackfriars*, April 1983, p. 183.
10. This point is graphically and interestingly treated by W.J. Hollenweger in his *Missa Discipulorum*, Disceplei Mass *Jungermess/Gomer: Das Gesicht des Unsichtbaren*. Munich, Chr. Kaiser Verlag, 1983.
11. De Clercq, B., "Political Commitment and Liturgical Celebration" in *Concilium*, V. 4, No. 9, April 1973, p. 115.
12. Davies, J.G. *New Perspectives on Worship Today*. SCM Press, London, 1978, p. 68.
13. Moreland, D., *The Eucharist and Justice*. The Justice & Peace Commission of England and Wales (no date given), p. 13.
14. Davies, J.G. *Worship and Mission*. SCM Press, London, 1966, p. 95.
15. *Ibid.*, p. 138. Davies shows how Koinonia in Paul's writings signifies not only the collection but also the fellowship, self-giving and grace.
16. Joint Mission Hospital Equipment Board Ltd., 4 West Street, Ewell, Surrey, 1UL KT17.

CHAPTER SEVEN: *Can Man Live with the Technology of Death?*

1. General Synod Debate, p. 17.
2. *Third Draft*, p. 701. *The Church and The Bomb*.
3. *Third Draft*, p. 703.
4. Hollenweger, W.J., Missa Discipulorum *Junger Messe/Gomer Das Gesicht des Unsightbaren*. Munich Chr. Kaiser Verlag, 1983.
    Davies, J.G., *New Perspectives on Worship Today*. SCM Press, London, 1978, pp. 52–75.
5. *Third Draft*, p. 704.
    New Perspectives on Worship Today, p. 55.
6. *The Church and The Bomb*, p. 113.
7. Davies, J.G., *Christians, Politics and Violent Revolution*. SCM Press, London, 1976, p. 3.

8. Barth, K., *The Church and The Political Problem of our Day*. Hodder & Stoughton, 1939, pp. 16–21.
9. *The Times*, 15 May 1983, p. 1.
10. *Christians, Politics and Violent Revolution*, pp. 9–43. There is a useful reflection on Christianity and political relevance in *Concilium* (Vol. 4, No. 9, April 1973). The contributors are: T. Steeman, E. Schillabeeckx, Ludwig Rutti and B. De Clercq.
11. Cullinan, T., *Eucharist and Politics*. CIIR (no date given), p. 2.
12. Hastings, A., *Mission and Ministry*. Sheed & Ward/Stag Books, 1971, p. 49.
13. Kung, Hans, *The Times*, 28 January 1980. Kung, Hans. *On Being a Christian*. Collins, London, 1977, p. 555ff.
14. *Peace and Disarmament*. Documents of the World Council of Churches. CCIA 1982, PCIP.
15. Camara, Helder, *Structures of Injustice*. Justice and Peace Commission, 1972, p. 7.
16. Exodus 3 : 7f; 13 : 30. *Mission and Ministry*, p. 48.
17. O'Mahony, Patrick. *The Fantasy of Human Rights*. Mayhew-McCrimmon, Essex, 1978, pp. 41–61.
18. Ward, B. and Dubos, Renè, *Only One Earth*. Pelican Books, 1972, p. 23ff.
19. Wolff, H.W., *Anthropology of the Old Testament*. SCM Press, London, 1974, pp. 159–65.
20. The Brandt Report attempted to demonstrate that peace, development, population and conservation are closely connected. To endanger one is to threaten the others.
21. Article, "Slaughter for Sport", by the editor. *The Tablet*, 22 October 1977.
22. Davies, J.G., *Christians, Politics and Violent Revolution*. SCM Press, London, 1976, p. 38.
23. Morris, C., *Captive Conscience*. Amnesty International, London, 1977, p. 7.
24. *Third Draft*, p. 718.
25. General Synod Debate, p. 17.
26. Latey, Maurice, "Church, State and Bomb" in *Encounter*, June 1983, p. 86.
27. Lakeland, Paul, "God in the Nuclear Age" in *The Month*, April 1984, p. 121ff.
28. *Ibid*.
29. Levinson, D.J., "Authoritarian personality and foreign policy" in *Journal of Conflict Resolution*. 1, 1957, p. 43.

30. I = Introvert (as distinct from extrovert); N = Neurotic (as distinct from stable). The IN Scale is the means by which these are measured.
31. Factors of War and Peace Attitudes: *Peace Research Reviews.* Vol. 1, No. 5, October 1967.
    Allport, G.W., *The Nature of Prejudice.* Addison Wesley, London, 1954, p. 444ff.
    Chester, M. and Schmuck, R., "Participant Observation in a Super Patriot Discussion Group" in *Journal of Social Issues.* Vol. 19, 2, 1963, pp. 18–30.
    Newmeyer, J.A., "Measurement of Racial Conservatism" in *Journal of Social Psychology*, Vol. 67, 1965, pp. 357–69.
    Ferguson, L.W., "The Isolation and Measurement of Nationalism" in *Journal of Social Psychology*, 16, 1942, pp. 215–28.
32. Levinson, D.J., "Authoritarian Personality and Foreign Policy" in *Journal of Conflict Resolution.* 1, 1957, p. 44.
33. *The Nature of Prejudice*, p. 451.
34. Bierler, Ludwig, *Ireland, Harbinger of the Middle Ages.* Oxford University Press, 1963, pp. 1–137.
    Godfrey, C.J., *The Church in Anglo Saxon England.* Cambridge University Press, pp. 67–107.
    Churchill, W., *A History of the English Speaking Peoples*, Vol. 1, Cassell, London, 1976, p. 56ff.
35. Ferguson, J., *War and Peace in the World's Religions.* Sheldon Press, London, 1977, p. 157.
36. Friedli, Richard, *Frieden Wagen – The Contribution of Religion to the Work of Peace and to the Analysis of Power.* Fribourg University, 1981.
37. *Ibid.*, pp. 179–99.
38. The same questions arise about the church and human rights. In a new study, Evans, R. and A., *Human Rights – A Dialogue between the First and Third Worlds.* Orbis Books in collab. with Lutterworth Press, Surrey, 1983, the editors, Robert and Alice Evans select eight from twenty or more case-studies from six continents with commentaries by prominent theologians. In his reflections Dr R.A. Evans concludes: "The Christian Church was generally perceived by those interviewed in all six continents as predominantly a negative or inhibiting factor in the genuine promotion of human rights."
39. *Frieden Wagen – The Contribution of Religion to the Work of Peace and the Analysis of Power*, p. 191.
40. Calcutta Project – which was outlined in the last chapter.
41. O'Mahony, Patrick, *Brandt: The Christian Connection.* Catholic Truth Society, 1982, p. 2.
42. Channel 4 television, 29 May 1983.

43. Lentz, T.R., "Elite Opinions in the U.S.", and Eckhardt, W., "Factors of War/Peace Attitudes" in *Peace Research Reviews*. Vol. 1, October 1957, No. 5.
44. *Christians, Politics and Violent Revolution*, p. 29.
45. Private and original files, Amnesty International – Archives of Our Lady of the Wayside Church, Shirley. March–October 1978.
46. Aquinas, Thomas, *Summa Theologica*, 11–11, Q. 26, Art. 4.
47. Tillich, Paul, *Love, Power and Justice*. Oxford University Press, London, 1976, p. 34.
48. *Ibid.*, p. 125.
49. *Ibid.*, p. 116.
50. Cammileri, J.A., *Civilisation in Crisis*. Cambridge University Press, 1976, p. 232ff.
    The American Federation model is discussed by Prof M.Q. Sibley in "Coercion of States and World Peace" *Foundations of Peace and Freedom*. Dunn, T. (ed.), Christopher Davies, Swansea 1978, p. 315. The idea of international law and world government is also developed by Clark, G. and Sohn, L.B. *World Peace Through World Law*. Cambridge (Mass.), Harvard University Press, 1966.
51. *Peace Research Reviews*, p. 36.
52. O'Brien, D.J., "Catholic Opposition to the Vietnam War" in *War or Peace?* Shannan, Thomas (ed.), Orbis Books, Maryknoll, New York, 1980, p. 121.
53. Heater, D., *World Studies: Education for International Understanding in Britain*. Harrap, London, 1980.
    Heater, D., "World Affairs, Public Opinion and Education" in *Teaching Politics*. Politics Association, London, 1983.
54. *Third Draft*, p. 718.
55. Zahn, G., "Total War and Absolute Pacifism" in *Concilium*. April 1983, p. 30.
56. *Ibid*.
57. Schillebeekx, E., "Eager to Spread the Gospel of Peace" in *Concilium*, April 1983, p. 81.
58. Ambler, R., "The Christian Ethic in a Nuclear Society" (unpub. paper), April 1983, pp. 18–23.
59. *Ibid.*, p. 22.
60. Randle, Michael (ed.), *Defence without the Bomb*, Taylor & Francis, 1983, pp. 208–43.
61. *Ibid.*, pp. 208–43.
62. *Ibid.*, p. 241.
63. *Ibid.*, p. 243.
64. *Ibid.*, p. 244.
65. *Ibid.*

66. *Ibid.*, p. 9. The Commission also believes that Britain should concentrate on a conventional frontier-based military strategy involving investment in air and naval defences and a small professional mobile army. *Cf.* p. 144.
67. *Ibid.*, p. 8.
68. *Ibid.*, p. 24.
69. *Ibid.*, p. 266.
70. *Third Draft*, p. 717, Section 3.
71. Though Robert McNamara thinks they would cost less than nuclear weapons. *The Times*, 17 September 1983, p. 6.
72. Pope John Paul II, Coventry 1982. *The Pope in Britain*. St Paul's Press, 1982, p. 9.
73. *Defence without the Bomb*, pp. 113, 139–40, 163.

Bibliography

PUBLISHED SOURCES

Abbott, William (ed.), "Pastoral Constitution of the Church in the Modern World" in *Documents of Vatican II*. Chapman, London, 1966.

Acta Apostolicae Sedis (AAS)

Address to the VII Congress *Peace and Disarmament* – Documents of the World Council of Churches. Presented by the Commission of the Churches on International Affairs and the Pontifical Commission, 1982.

Aiken, W.M. and La Follette, Hugh (eds.), *World Hunger and Moral Obligation*. Prentice Hall Inc., Englewood Cliffs, N.J., 1977.

Allport, G.W., *The Nature of Prejudice*. Addison Wesley, London, 1954.

Ambrose Book 1. "On the Martyrdom of St Agnes". Quoted in The Divine Office, Collins, London, 1974.

Ambrose, de Officiis Ministorum. PL. 16, 74–78; 81–86.

Andropov, Y.V., *The Sixtieth Anniversary of the Union of Soviet Socialist Republic*. Novosti Press (no place) 1982.

Aquinas, T., *Summa Theologica*.

Augustine, Epistle. 47, 5 PL 33, 186–187.

Augustine, Epistle Ad Marcellinum (138) 11, 9.

Augustine, Epistle Ad Bonifacium, 189, VI.

Augustine Sermon, "On the Martyrdom of St Lawrence". Quoted in *The Divine Office*, Collins, London, 1974.

Bainton, R.H., *Christian Attitudes towards War & Peace*. Hodder & Stoughton, London, 1983.

Balasuriya, Tissa, *The Eucharist and Human Liberation*. SCM Press, London, 1979.

Barth, K., *Church Dogmatics*. T. & T. Clarke, Edinburgh, 1958.

Barth, K., *The Church and the Political Problem of our Day*. Hodder & Stoughton, London, 1939.

Basil, Epistle 101, PG. 32, 682.

Bauer, P., *Reality and Rhetoric*. Weidenfeld & Nicolson, London, 1984.
Benton, P., *One Man against the Drylands*. Collins & Harvill Press, London, 1972.
Berlin, Isaiah, *Four Essays on Liberty*. Oxford University Press, London, 1969.
Bernstein, H. (ed.), *Underdevelopment and Development*. Penguin Books, London, 1973.
Beyond Conflict or Compromise. UN Development Programme (not dated).
Bhagwati, J., *The Economics of Underdeveloped Countries*. Weidenfeld & Nicolson, World University Library, London, 1966.
Bieler, Ludwig, *Ireland, Harbinger of the Middle Ages*. Oxford University Press, 1963.
Birch, C. and Cobb, J.R. (Jr.), *The Liberation of Life*. Cambridge University Press, London, 1981.
Bombs for Breakfast. COPAT, 1978.
Bonhoeffer, Deitrich, *Ethics*. Collins (Fontana), London, 1970.
Bouscaren, T.L., *Ethics of Ectopic Operations*. Bruce Publishing Co., Milwaukee, 1944.
Bridger, F. (ed.), *The Cross and the Bomb*. Mowbray, London, 1983.
Brown, David, *Choices – Ethics and the Christian*. Blackwell, Oxford, 1983.
Brown, F., Driver, S.R. & Briggs, C.A., *Hebrew and English Lexicon of the Old Testament*. Oxford Clarendon Press, London, 1977.
Buhlmann, W., *The Chosen Peoples*. St Paul's Press, Slough, 1982.
Buhlmann, W., *The Coming of the Third Church*. St Paul's Press, Slough, 1976.
Burke, E., *Reflections on the Revolution in France*. Penguin Books, Harmondsworth, 1980.

Cadoux, C.J., *The Early Christian Attitude to War*. George Allen & Unwin, London, 1940.
Camara, Helder, *Structures of Injustice*. The International Commission for Justice & Peace, London, 1972.
Camara, Helder, *Interview with Jose dé Broucker*. Collins, London, 1977.
Cammileri, J.A., *Civilisation in Crisis*. Cambridge University Press, 1976.
Caro, J., *Shulhan Arukh, Yoreh De'ah*.
Cavadino, P., *Get Off their Backs*. Hazelmere Group & Third World First, Oxford, 1972.
The Challenge of Peace: God's Promise and Our Response. Revised Text of Pastoral Letter. CTS/SPCK, London, 1983.

Cheshire, Leonard, *The Nuclear Dilemma: A Moral Study*. The Third of a series of studies on Peace, Defence and Disarmament by various authors. Justice and Peace Commission, England and Wales, London, 1983.

Childress, J.F., "Just War Criteria" in Thomas A. Shannon (ed.), *War or Peace? The Search for New Answers*. Orbis Books, N.Y., Maryknoll, N.Y., 1980.

Childs, B.S., *Exodus*. SCM Press, London, 1974.

Christo, Carlos, *Letters from a Prisoner of Conscience*. Lutterworth Press, London, 1978.

The Church and The Bomb: Report of a Working Party under the Chairmanship of the Bishop of Salisbury. Hodder & Stoughton, 1982. Referred to as *The Report*.

The Church and The Bomb: A Report by the Board for Social Responsibility. CIO, Church House, London, SW1P. (Referred to as *GS.542*.)

Churchill, W., *A History of the English Speaking Peoples*. Vol. 1. Cassell & Co., London, 1976.

Clark, C., *Starvation or Plenty?* Secker & Warburg, London, 1970.

Clark, G. and Sohn, L.B., *World Peace through World Law*. Harvard University Press, Cambridge, Mass., 1976.

Clark, M.B. and Mowlam, M. (eds.), *Debate on Disarmament*. Routledge & Kegan Paul, London, 1982.

Clark, R., *The Great Experiment*. UN, N.Y., 1971.

Cleaver, Eldridge, *Soul On Ice*. Jonathan Cape, London, 1969.

Colonnese, L.M. (ed.), *Conscientization for Liberty*. Division for Latin America. U.S. Catholic Conference, Washington, 1971.

Common Crisis: North–South. The Brandt Commission, Pan Books, London, 1983.

Connery, J., *Abortion: The Development of the Roman Catholic Perspective*. Loyala University Press, Chicago, 1977.

Considine, J.J., *The Religious Dimension in the New Latin America*. Catholic Inter-American Co-operation Programme, Notre Dame, 1966.

Considine, J.J., *The Church in the New Latin America*. Catholic Inter-American Co-operation Programme, Notre Dame, 1964.

Cranson, Maurice, *What are Human Rights?* Bodley Head, London, 1973.

The C.T.C. Reporter. Centre on Transnational Corporations. Vol. 1, No. 6, April 1979. U.N., N.Y.

Cullinan, T., *Eucharist and Politics*. CIIR (no date given).

Curran, Charles, E., *Politics, Medicine and Christian Ethics*. A Dialogue with Paul Ramsey, Fortress Press, Philadelphia, 1972.

Davies, J.G., *Worship and Mission*. SCM Press, London, 1966.

Davies, J.G., *New Perspectives on Worship Today*. SCM Press, London, 1978.

Davies, J.G., *Christians, Politics and Violent Revolution*. SCM Press, London, 1976.

Davis, Angela, *If They Come in the Morning*. Orbach & Chambers, London, 1971.

Davis, H., *Moral and Pastoral Theology*. Vol. 2. Sheed & Ward, London, 1943.

De Chardin, Teilhard, *Man's Place in Nature*. Collins Fontana Books, London, 1971.

Defence without the Bomb. Report sponsored by the University of Bradford Peace Studies, Taylor and Francis, London, 1983.

Desmond, Cosmas, *Christians and Capitalists*. The Bowerdean Press, London, 1978.

Deutsch, K.W., *Nationalism and Social Communication*. MIT Press, Massachusetts, 1966.

Dixon Long, T. and Wright, C., *Science Policies of Industrial Nations*. Praeger Publishers, New York, Washington and London, 1975.

Douglass, J.W., *The Non-Violent Cross: A Theology of Revolution and Peace*. Chapman, London, 1968.

Duchacek, T., *Nations and Men*. Dryden Press, Illinois, 1975.

Dunn, T. (ed.), *Foundations of War and Peace*. Christopher Davies, Swansea, 1978.

Edwards, Bob, *Multinational Companies and Trade Unions*. Spokesman. Bertrand Russell Peace Foundation, Nottingham, 1977.

"The Eightieth Year" *This is Action*. The Justice and Peace Commission, London, 1972.

Ethics of Business in Developing Countries. International Christian Union of Business Executives, Brussels, 1980.

Euthanasia and Clinical Practice. The Linacre Centre, London, 1982.

Evangelii Nuntiandi. Part 4, CTS, Article 29 (not dated).

Evangelisation in the Modern World. CTS, London (not dated).

Evans, G., *The Yellow Rainmakers*. Versa/New Left Books, London, 1983.

Evans, R. and A., *Human Rights – A Dialogue between the First and Third Worlds*. Orbis Books with Lutterworth Press, Surrey, 1983.

Falconer, Alan (ed.), "Theological Reflection on Human Rights" in *Understanding Human Rights*. Irish School of Ecumenics, Dublin, 1978.

Falk, R.A., *This Endangered Planet: Prospects and Proposals for Human Survival*. Random House, N.Y., 1971.

Falk, R.A., *Human Rights and State Sovereignty*. Holmes & Meier Publishers Inc., London, 1981.

Fannon, Frantz, *The Wretched of the Earth*. Penguin Books, London, 1967.

Ferguson, J., *Disarmament – The Unanswerable Case*. Heinemann, London, 1982.

Ferguson, J., *War and Peace in the World's Religions*. Sheldon Press, London, 1977.

Fitzgerald, Garratt, *Unequal Partners*. United Nations, N.Y., 1979.

Fletcher, J., "Give if it helps but not if it hurts" in *World Hunger & Moral Obligation*. Prentice Hall Inc., Englewood Cliffs, N.J., 1977.

Freidli, R., *Friden Wagen – The Contribution of Religion to the Work of Peace and to the Analysis of Power*. Fribourg University, 1981.

Freire, P., *Education, the Practice of Freedom*. Writers & Readers Publishing Co-operative, London, 1974.

Galbraith, J.K., *The Nature of Mass Poverty*. Penguin Books, Harmondsworth, 1979.

Gallett, P., *Freedom to Starve*. Penguin Books, Harmondsworth, 1972.

George, S., *How the Other Half Dies*. Penguin Books, N.Y., 1976.

George, S., *The Church and Human Rights*. Working Paper No. 1. PCJP, Rome, 1975.

Godfrey, C.J., *The Church in Anglo-Saxon England*. Cambridge University Press, 1962.

Grisez, G., *Abortion: The Myths, The Realities and the Arguments*. Corpus Books, Washington, D.C., 1970.

Gula, R.M., *What are they saying about Moral Norms?* Paulist Press, N.Y., 1982.

Gutierrez, G., *A Theology of Liberation*. (English edition), SCM Press, London, 1974.

Hardin, G., "Lifeboat Ethics – The Case against helping the Poor" in *World Hunger and Moral Obligation*. Prentice Hall Inc., Englewood Cliffs, N.J., 1977.

Haring, B., *Medical Ethics*. St Paul's Publication, Slough, 1972.

Haring, B., *Free and Faithful in Christ*. St Paul's Publication, Slough, 1972.

Haslam, D. and Ambler, R., *Agenda for Prophets*. The Bowerdean Press, London, 1980.

Hastings, A., *Mission & Ministry*. Sheed & Ward Stag Books, London, 1971.

Hayter, T., *Aid as Imperialism*. Pelican Books, London, 1971.

Heater, D., *World Studies for International Understanding in Britain*, Harrap, London, 1980.

Heater, D., "World Affairs, Public Opinion & Education" in *Teaching Politics*. Politics Association, London, 1983.

Hehir, J.B., *The Church and the Arms Race*. Document prepared by the Commission for International Justice & Peace, England and Wales, Catholic Information Office, Abbots Langley, 1982.

Hensman, C.R., *Rich Against Poor*. Allen Lane, The Penguin Press, London, 1970.

Hesselbach, W., *Commonweal Enterprise*. Series No. 4, Frankfurt, 1970.

Heyer, R. (ed.), "Report on War and Peace", US Bishops' Annual Meeting. *Nuclear Disarmament*. Washington, D.C., November 16 to 19, 1981.

Hirsch, F., *The Social Limits to Growth*. Routledge & Kegan Paul, London, 1977.

Hollenbach, David, *Nuclear Ethics*. Paulist Press, N.Y., Ramsey, 1983.

Hollenweger, W.J., Missa Discipulorum. *Junger/Messe/Gomer Das Gesicht des Unsightbaren*. Munich Chr., Kaiser Verlag, 1983.

Howard, Michael, *War and the Liberal Conscience*. Temple Smith, London, 1978.

Huxley, T.H., *Man's Place in Nature and Other Essays*. Dent, London, 1906.

Hyatt, J.P., "Exodus" in *New Century Bible Commentary*. Grand Rapids & Marshall, London. Morgan & Scott, London, 1980.

Illich, I.D., *Deschooling Society*. Calder & Bowers, London, 1970.

International Development, 1977. Vol. 1.

International Development Review. Vol. XVIII. No. 4, 1976. Society for International Development, Washington, D.C.

Jacobitz, I., "Euthanasia" in *Encyclopaedia Judiaca*. Vol. 6.

Jennings, A. and Weiss, T.G. (eds.), *The Challenge of Development in the 80s: Our Response*. Pergamon Press, Oxford, 1982.

John Paul II, Address to the 2nd Special Session of the UN General Assembly on Disarmament, N.Y., 11 June 1982. *Peace & Disarmament*, p. 247.

John Paul II, *The Pope in Britain*. Coventry 1982. St Paul Publication, London, 1982.

Johnson, J.T., *Ideology, Reason and the Limitation of War*. Princeton University Press, Princeton, N.J., 1981.

Johnson, J.T., *Just War Tradition and the Limitation of War*. Princeton University Press, Princeton, N.J., 1981.

Johnson, K.R., *Britain and the Common Market – A Christian View*.
British Council of Churches, London, 1971.
Justin, *Dialogue with Trypho*, Chapter 20.
Justin, *The First Apology*, Chapters 14 and 39.

Kaldor, Mary, *The Disintegrating West*. Penguin Books, London,
1978.
Kedourie, E., *Nationalism*. Hutchinson University Library, Lon-
don, 1960.
Kelly, G., *Medico-Moral Problems*. Burns, Oats & Washbourne,
London, 1955.
Kirby, P., *Lessons in Liberation*. Dominican Publications, Dublin,
1981.
Kolakowski, L., *Religion*. Fontana Paperbacks, London, 1980.
Kolko, G., *The Politics of War*. Weidenfeld & Nicolson, London,
1969.
Krieger, D., *Disarmament and Development*. Foundation Reshaping
the International Order. Rotterdam, 1981.

Latey, Maurice, *Tyranny: A Study in the Abuse of Power*. Pelican
Books, London, 1972.
Lehmkukl, *Theologia Moralis*. Vol. 1. No. 1010.
Levinson, D.J., "Authoritarian personality and Foreign Policy" in
Journal of Conflict Resolution, 1, 1957.
Lifton, R.J., *Home from the War*. Wildwood House, London, 1974.
Linacre Papers No. 2. London, 1978, p. 5.
Liverpool 1980, Official Report of the National Pastoral Congress. St
Paul Publication, Slough, 1980.
Lowler, J.G., *Nuclear War, the Ethics, the Rhetoric and the Reality*.
Newman Press, Westminster, Maryland, 1965.

Mackay, L. and Fernbach, D., *Nuclear Free Defence*. Heretic Books,
London, 1983.
MacQuarrie, John, *The Concept of Peace*. SCM Press, London, 1973.
Maimondes, *Mishneh Torah, Yad Hazakah*, Roze'ah, 2 : 7.
Marcuse, H., *One Dimensional Man*. Abacus Sphere Books, Lon-
don, 1974.
Maritain, Jacques, *Man and the State*. Hollis & Carter, London,
1954.
Mark, J., *The Changing Role of British Aid to Education in Develop-
ing Countries*. Foreign and Commonwealth Office, London, 1972.
Marshall, John, *Ethics of Medical Practice*. Darton, Longman &
Todd, London, 1960.
Mater et Magistra. Pope John XXIII. CTS, London, 1963.

Mayr, E., *Animal Species and Evolution*. The Bellknop Press of Harvard University, 1963.

Mboya, T., *Freedom and After*. Andre Deutsch, London, 1963.

McCabe, H., *Law, Love and Language*. Sheed & Ward Stag Books, London, 1968.

McCormack, A., *Multinational Investment – Boon or Burden for the Developing Countries?* W.R. Grace & Co., N.Y., 1980.

McCormack, A., *The Population Explosion and World Hunger*. Burns Oats, London, 1963.

McCormick, R. (ed.) *et. al.*, *Doing Evil to Achieve Good: Moral Choice in Conflict Situations*. Loyala University Press, Chicago, 1978.

McCormick, Richard, *How Brave a New World*. SCM Press, London, 1981.

McDonagh, E., *Invitation and Response*. Gill & McMillan, Dublin, 1972.

McDonagh, E., *Violence and Political Change*. Catholic Institute for International Relations, London, 1978.

McGregor, I., *Human Rights*. Batsford, London, 1975.

Medawar, Charles, *Social Audit – Insult or Injury*. Social Audit, London (not dated).

Merton, T., *Faith & Violence: Christian Teaching and Christian Practice*. University of Notre Dame, Notre Dame, Indiana, 1968.

Moreland D., *The Eucharist and Justice*. The Justice & Peace Commission of England and Wales (no date given).

Morris, C., *Captive Conscience*. Amnesty International, London, 1977.

Multinational Charter, International Confederation of Free Trade Unions, Brussels, 1975.

Murnion, Philip, J. (ed.), *Catholics and Nuclear War*. Geoffrey Chapman, London, 1983.

Myrdal, G.M., *The Challenge of World Poverty*. Penguin Books, London 1970.

Narveson, J., "Morality and Starvation" in *World Hunger & Moral Obligation*. Prentice Hall Inc., Englewood Cliffs, N.J., 1977.

Newmeyer, J. A., "Measurement of Racial Conservation" in *Journal of Social Psychology*. Vol. 67, 1965. pp. 357–369.

Neibuhr, Reinhold, *Nations and Empires*. Faber & Faber, London, 1959.

Neibuhr, Reinhold, "Christians, Politics and Communist Religion" in John Lewis *et. al.*, *Christianity and the Social Revolution*. Scribners, New York, 1936.

Neibuhr, Reinhold, *Moral Man & Immoral Society*. T. & T. Clarke, Edinburgh, 1963.

Newbegin, L. *The Other Side of '84*. British Council of Churches, London, 1983.

New Light on Social Problems. Mater et Magistra. CTS 1961.

Noonan, John T., *The Morality of Abortion*. Harvard University Press, Cambridge, Massachusetts, 1970.

North – South: A Programme for Survival. Pan World Affairs, London, 1980.

Nute, B.R., *Camara's Latin America*. Non-Violence in Action Series. Friends' Peace and International Relations Committee, London, 1974.

O'Brien, D.J., "Catholic Opposition to the Vietnam War" in *War or Peace*. Shannan, Thomas (ed.), Orbis Books, Maryknoll, N.Y., 1980.

Octogesima Adveniens. CIJP, 1972.

O'Mahony, Patrick, *Multinationals & Human Rights*. Mayhew-McCrimmon, Essex, 1980.

O'Mahony, Patrick, *The Fantasy of Human Rights*. Mayhew-McCrimmon, Essex, 1978.

O'Mahony, Patrick, *Brandt: The Christian Connection*. CTS, London, 1982.

O'Mahony, Patrick, *Investment: a blessing or a curse?* Mayhew-McCrimmon, Essex, 1979.

O'Mahony, Patrick, *Money: The Christian Dilemma*. CTS, London, 1981.

O'Neil, O. "Life Boat Earth" in *World Hunger and Moral Obligation*. Prentice Hall Inc., Englewood Cliffs, N.J., 1977.

Our World and You. The World Conference of Bishops, C.A.F.O.D., London, 1972.

Owen, David, *Negotiate and Survive*. Campaign for Labour Victory. London, 1980.

Owen, David, *Human Rights*. Jonathan Cape, London, 1978.

Paine, T., *Rights of Man*. Penguin Books, Harmondsworth, 1971.

Palmstierna, H. *The Future Imperative for the Human Environment*. United Nations, 1972.

Peace and Disarmament. Documents of the World Council of Churches. Presented by CCIA, Geneva, 1982.

Peace Defence Disarmament. Statement and Correspondence, Bishops of England & Wales, 1983–84 Catholic Information Services, Abbots Langley, 1984.

Pearse, E. and Kahn, R., *The White Tribes of Europe*. Action for World Development. London, 1970.

Plamenatz, J., *Man and Society*, Vol. 2. Longman, London, 1963.

Plato, *The Last Days of Socrates*. Penguin Books, Harmondsworth, 1982.

Plato, *The Laws*. Penguin Books, Harmondsworth, 1970.

Polany, M., *The Tacit Dimension*. Routledge & Kegan Paul, London, 1967.

The Pope In Britain, St Paul Publication, London, 1982.

Pope John XXIII, *Mater et Magistra*. "New Aspects of the Social Question", CTS, London, 1963.

Pope John XXIII, *Pacem in Terris*. Encyclical Letter, CTS. London, 1980.

Pope Paul VI, *Address to the United Nations General Assembly*, 4 October 1965, CTS, London.

Pope Paul VI, *Populorum Progressio*, CTS, London, 1967.

Pope Paul VI, *Evangelisation in the Modern World*. CTS, London (not dated).

Pope Paul VI, *Appeal for Peace to U.N.* CTS, London, 1965.

Powell, E., *Wrestling with the Angel*. Sheldon Press, London, 1977.

Prins, G. (ed.), *Defended to Death*. (A Study of the Nuclear Arms Race from Cambridge University Disarmament Seminar), Penguin Books, Harmondsworth, 1980.

Quigley, T.E. (ed.), *Freedom and Unfreedom in the Americas*. IDOC, N.Y., 1971.

Quinn, A., *The Church and the Option for the Poor in Peru*. CIIR Papers No. 3, London, 1982.

Rachels, H., "Vegeterianism and other Weighty Problems" in *World Hunger & Moral Obligation*. Prentice Hall Inc., Englewood Cliffs, N.J., 1977.

Ramsey, Paul, *War and the Christian Conscience* – How shall modern war be conducted justly? Duke University Press, Durham, N.C., 1961.

Ramsey, Paul, *The Just War: Force and Political Responsibility*. Charles Scribners' Sons, New York, 1968.

Real Aid. A Strategy for Britain. The Independent Group on British Aid, London, 1982.

Responsible Investment. Young Friends Central Committee, Birmingham, 1980.

Riddell, R. (ed.), *Adjustment or Protectionism?* CIIR London, 1980.

Roberts, J., *From Massacres to Mining*. War on Want, London, 1978.

Robson, J.M., *The Improvement of Mankind*. Routledge & Kegan Paul, London, 1968.

Roight, Dorothy, *Ride with the Sun*. McGraw-Hill International Publications.

Ruede, E., *The Morality of War*. STD Thesis, Rome, 1970.

Rummel, R.J., *Understanding Conflict and War. Vol. 3. Conflict in Perspective*. Sage Publishing, Beverley Hills/London, 1977.

Russell, F.H., *The Just War in the Middle Ages*. Cambridge University Press, 1975.

Ruston, Roger, *Nuclear Deterrence – Right or Wrong?* Catholic Information Services, Abbots Langley, 1981.

Sampson, A., *The Sovereign State*. Coronet Books, London, 1973.

Sanger, Clyde, "Disarmament and Development in the 80s" in *Safe and Sound*. Zed Press, London, 1982.

Schell, Jonathan, *The Fate of the Earth*. Pan Books, London, 1982.

Schmidt, Elizabeth, *Decoding Corporate Camouflage*. Institute for Policy Studies, Washington, 1980.

Schwartz, A., *The Starved and the Silent*. Gollancz, London, 1967.

Segunda, Juan Luis, *The Liberation of Theology*. Gill & McMillan, Dublin, 1977.

Seton-Watson, H., *Nations and States*. Methuen, London, 1977.

Sevard, Ruth Leger, *World Military and Social Expenses*. World Priorities, Virginia, 1982.

Shannan, Thomas A. (ed.), *War or Peace: The Search for New Answers*. Orbis Books, Maryknoll, 1980.

Shannan, Thomas A., *What are they saying about Peace and War?* Paulist Press, N.Y./Ramsey, 1983.

Sheed, F.J., *God and the Human Condition*. Sheed & Ward, London, 1966.

Sheed, F.J., *Man The Forgotten*. Sheed & Ward, London, 1948.

Sheed, F.J., *Society and Sanity*. Sheed & Ward, London, 1954.

Sider, R.J., *Rich Christians in an Age of Hunger*. Hodder & Stoughton, London, 1973.

Simon, A., *Bread for the World*. Paulist Press, N.Y., 1975.

Simon, J.G. (ed.) et. al., *The Ethical Investor*. Yale University Press, New Haven & London, 1972.

Singer, P., "Famine, Affluence and Morality" in *World Hunger & Moral Obligation*. Prentice Hall Inc., Englewood Cliffs, N.J., 1977.

Slote, M.A., "The Morality of Wealth" in *World Hunger & Moral Obligation*. Prentice Hall Inc., Englewood Cliffs, N.J., 1977.

Smith, A.D., *Theories & Nationalism*. Duckworth, London, 1971.

Snyder, Louis, L., *The Meaning of Nationalism*. Rutgers University Press, New Jersey, 1954.

Solzhenitsyn, A., *The Oak and the Calf*. Collins Harvill Press, London, 1980.

Stamm, J.J. and Andrew, M.E., *The Ten Commandments in Recent Research*. SCM Press, London, 1967.

Stares, R., *Black Trade Unions in South Africa: The Responsibilities of British Companies*. Christian Concern for South Africa, London, 1979.

Stratmann, F., *The Church & War – A Catholic Study*. P.J. Kennedy & Sons, New York, 1928.

Terraine, J., *The Mighty Continent*. British Broadcasting Corporation with Hutchinson, London, 1974.

Thiemeyer, T., *Principles of Theory and Commonweal Economy*. Series Commonweal Economy No. 3, Frankfurt, 1970.

Thompson, C.S. (ed.), *Morals and Missiles*. James Clark & Co. Ltd., London, 1959.

Thompson, E.P., *Beyond the Cold War*. Merlin Press, London, 1981.

Thompson, E.P., *Zero Option*. The Merlin Press, London, 1982.

Thompson, Robert (ed.), *War in Peace*. Orbis Publishing Co., London, 1981.

Tillich, Paul, *Love, Power and Justice*. Oxford University Press, London, 1976.

Tolstoy, L.N., *War and Peace*. Vols. 1 & 2. Penguin Books, London, 1957.

Toynbee, A., *Mankind and Mother Earth*. Oxford University Press, London, 1976.

Transnational Corporations. CIO Publishing, Church House, London, 1983.

Universal Declaration of Human Rights. United Nations Office of Information. Article 3. N.Y., 1976.

Van Asbeck, F.M., "The Church and the Disorder of the International Society" in *The Church and International Disorder*. Vol. 4. of the Amsterdam Series on *Man's Disorder and God's Design*. Harper Bros., N.Y., 1948.

Walker, D. *Power to End Poverty*. Action for World Development, London, 1969.

Ward, Barbara, *The Rich Nations and The Poor Nations*. Hamish Hamilton, London, 1982.

Ward, Barbara, *Space Ship Earth*. Hamish Hamilton, London, 1966.

Ward, Barbara, *The Angry Seventies*. PCJP, Rome, 1970.

Ward, Barbara, *A New Creation*. PCJP, Rome, 1970.

Ward, Barbara and Dubos, Rene, *Only One Earth*. Pelican Books, London, 1972.

Wehr, P. and Washburn, M., *Peace and World Order Systems*. Teaching & Research, London, 1976.

Westow, Theo., *Who is my Brother?* Sheed & Ward, London, 1966.

Whittaker, Ben, *The Foundations*. Pelican Books, Harmondsworth, 1979.

Whittaker, Ben, *The Fourth World*. Schoken Books, N.Y., 1973.

Who is Theatening Whom? Peace Council of the German Democratic Republic, Dresden (not dated).

Wolff, H.W., *Anthropology of the Old Testament*. SCM Press, London, 1974.

World Goodwill Commentary No. 14. New International Economy Order, London, 1980.

World Health Organisation. *The First Ten Years of the World Health Organisation*. WHO 1958.

Yoder, J., *The Politics of Jesus*. Eerdmans; Grand Rapids, 1972.

Young, Nigel, *Problems and Possibilities in the Study of Peace*. No. 3 in Peace Studies Papers. The School of Peace Studies, Bradford and Houseman, London, 1980.

Zahn, Gordon, "Afterwards" in *War or Peace – The Search for New Answers*. Thomas A. Shannan (ed.), Orbis Books, Maryknoll, 1980.

Zahn, Gordon, *War, Conscience and Dissent*. Chapman, London, 1967.

REPORTS

A Healing Touch. Introduction to the 1983 Report of the Commonwealth Secretary-General, Shridath S. Ramphal, Commonwealth Secretariat, London.

Attack on Mass Poverty and Unemployment. A Report of the Committee for Development Planning, UN, N.Y., 1972.

Britain's Role in the Second Development Decade. Report by the Society for International Development and the Overseas Development Institute, London, 1972.

The Church & The Bomb. Report of a Working Party under the Chairmanship of the Bishop of Salisbury. Hodder & Stoughton, 1982 (*The Report*).

The Church & The Bomb. A Report by the Board for Social Responsibility, CIO House, London SW1P (*GS.542*).

CCIA Annual Report. Commission of the Churches for International Affairs. 1950/51.

CINI – Child in Need Institute – Annual Report 1983. West Bengal.

Commonwealth Heads of Government. The New Delhi Communique, November 1983. Commonwealth Secretariat, London.

Defence without the Bomb. Report sponsored by the University of Bradford Peace Studies. Taylor & Francis, London, 1983.

De Gaspar, D. (ed.) *et al.*, *World Hunger: A Christian Reappraisal.* Report of the Fourth Meeting of the Advisory Group on Economic Matters held in Washington, D.C., USA, October 5 to 8 1981. Commission on the Churches' Participation in Development, World Council of Churches, Geneva.

Disarmament and Development. The United Nations, New York, 1972.

Economic & Social Consequences of the Arms Race & Military Expenditure. Report of the Secretary-General, UN, N.Y., 1972.

Food, Work and Justice. WCC Geneva, 1983.

McNamara, Robert S., *Address to the Board of Governors at Nairobi*, 24 September 1973. International Bank for Reconstruction & Development, Washington, 1973.

NATO Facts and Figures. NATO Information Service, Brussels, 1978.

Overseas Development Institute. Briefing Paper No. 1. July 1982.

On Making Peace in a Nuclear World. British Council of Churches, Nineteenth Assembly, 83rd Meeting of the Council. 21 to 23 November 1983. Division of International Affairs.

Partners in Development. A Report of the Pearson Commission in International Development. Pall Mall Press, London, 1969.

Peace and Disarmament. Arms Control and Disarmament Research Unit, Foreign & Commonwealth Office, London, 1982.

Political Imprisonment in South Africa. An Amnesty International Report, London, 1978.

Sao Paulo: Growth and Poverty. A Report by the Justice & Peace Commission of the Archdiocese of Sao Paulo. Bowerdean Press in Association with CIIR, London, 1978.

Sharing. Bulletin No. 3 September 1980, WCC Programme on Transnational Corporations, Geneva, 1980.

Social & Labour Practices of Some European Based Multinationals in the Metal Trades. ILO Geneva, 1976.

"Towards a New Economic & Social Order" in the *ICFTU Development Charter.* Adopted by the 70th Meeting of the ICFTU Executive Board (Hamburg – 17 to 19 May 1978). International Confederation of Free Trade Unions, Brussels.

A Third Force for the Third World. Report of a Working Party sponsored by Christian Aid and the Catholic Fund for Overseas Development, Overseas Development Institute, London, 1972.

Towards Accelerated Development. Report of the Committee for Development Planning, UN, N.Y., 1970.

Towards the Elimination of Poverty in Britain and the Third World. Report by the Labour Party, London, 1975.

Tripartite Declaration of Principles Concerning Multinational Enterprises and Social Policies. ILO, Geneva, 1976.

UNCTAD 3, *Make or Break for Development* – A Report of the World Development Movement, London, 1972.

The US Congress Senate, Committee of Foreign Relations, *THE SALT II TREATY.* Hearings on ex, 96–1, 96th Congress, 1 September 1979. Part 4.

U.S. Military Posture Statement for F.Y. 1983. Washington, 1982.

Weinberger, Casper, *Annual Report to Congress,* 1 February 1983.

World Bank, Washington, D.C. World Development Report. The International Bank for Reconstruction and Development, 1978.

PERIODICALS

Urban – Kilpatrick Interview. "American Foreign Policy in a Cold Climate". *Encounter.* November 1983. p. 9.

Arupe, Pedro, "Christ Hungering in the World". *The Month.* January 1977.

"Accusation from Prison". *New Blackfriars.* December 1970. p. 549ff.

Childress, J.F., "Just War Theories". *Theological Studies.* 1959. 20. pp. 40–61

Chester, M. & Schmuck, R., "Participant Observation in a Super Patriot Discussion Group". *Journal of Social Issues.* Vol. 19. 2. 1963.

Chekhutov, A., "Socialist and Newly Free Countries: Monetary Relations". *Social Sciences.* Vol. XIII. No. 2. 1982.

Concilium. Vol. 4. No. 9. April 1973.

The Democrat. No. 5, 20 December 1982. Vol. 1. p. 23.

Der Speigel. 9 May 1983. p. 122.

De Clercq, B., "Political Commitment and Liturgical Celebration". *Concilium.* Vol. 4. No. 9. April 1973. p. 115.

Derrick, P., "What Happened to Brandt?" *The Month.* January 1984. p. 16.

The Economist. 5 February 1983. p. 21.

Eckhardt, William, "Cross National Measurements of Compassion". *Peace Research*. Vol. 8. No. 4. 1976. p. 110.

Ford, J.C., "The Hydrogen Bombing of Cities". *Theology Digest*. Vol. 5. No. 1. Winter. 1957. pp. 6 & 7.

Ferguson, L.W., "The Isolation and Measurement of Nationalism". *Journal of Social Psychology*. 16. 1942. pp. 215–28.

Hollenbach, David, "Nuclear Weapons and Nuclear War". *Theological Studies*. December 1982. Vol. 43. No. 4. p. 594.

Hollenbach, David, "Nuclear Weapons and Nuclear War: The Shape of the Catholic Debate". *Theological Studies*. December 1982. p. 600.

Hume, Basil, "Address to the National Conference of Priests". *Briefing*. Catholic Information Services, Abbots Langley. September 1983.

Harriott, J.F.X., "Justice in the World". *The Month*. October 1971. pp. 104ff.

Johnson, J.T., "On Keeping Faith: The Use of History for Religious Ethics". *Journal of Religious Ethics*. 1979. pp. 112–13.

John Paul II, Address at Drogheda. *Origins*. 9. 1979. p. 272.

Kiernan, J.V. and Himes, K.R., "Pluralism in Moral Evaluation of War". *The Month*. February 1983. p. 43.

L'Osservatore Romano. 5 December 1963.

L'Osservatore Romano. 21 June 1982.

The Listener. 3 March 1983. p. 14.

The Listener. 26 May 1983. p. 2.

Langan, J., "The American Hierarchy & Nuclear Weapons". *Theological Studies*. September 1982. No. 3. p. 462.

Latey, Maurice, "Church State and Bomb". *Encounter*. June 1983. pp. 79 & ff.

McCormick, R. and Ramsey, P., "Notes on Moral Theology". *Theological Studies*. Vol. 43. 1982. No. 1 & Vol. 44. March 1983. No. 1.

Murray, J.C., "Remarks on the Moral Problems of War". *Theological Studies*. 1959. 20. pp. 40–61.

McDonnell, Killian, "U.S. Bishops Challenged". *The Tablet*. 12 February 1983. p. 126.

The New Scientist. 21 October 1982. p. 138.

New Statesman. 20 January 1984. p. 13ff.

Origins. 28 October 1982. Vol. 12 (Second Draft) Catholic Institute for Justice and Peace, 14 April 1983. Vol. 12 (Third Draft) Official National Documentary Service.

O'Brien, W.V., "Just War Doctrine in a Nuclear Contest". *Theological Studies*. June 1983. Vol. 44. No. 2. p. 197.

Oskov, E.R., "Possible Paths to Real Development". *New Scientist*. No. 1393. 19 January 1984. p. 28ff.

Paxton, N., "The Liberating Eucharist". *New Blackfriars*. April 1983.
Peace Research Reviews. Vol. 1. No. 5. October 1967.
Reagan, Ronald, "Address to the National Association of Evangelicals". 8 March 1982. *The Economist*. May 1982.
Rostow, E., *The Listener*. 3 March 1983. p. 14.
Roszak, Theodore, "The Dilemma of the Just War". *Nation*. 14 April 1983. p. 328.
Surle, Paul, "The Challenge of Peace – The US Bishops Pastoral on War and Peace. *The Furrow*. Vol. 43. No. 4. Furrow Trust, Maynooth, August 1983. p. 485ff.
Schillebeek, E., "Eager to Speed the Gospel of Peace". *Concilium*. April 1983. p. 81.
The Tablet. 22 October 1977.
   April 1980. p. 334.
   20 November 1982. p. 1158.
   4 December 1982. p. 1223.
   29 January 1983. p. 92.
   5 February 1983. "Notebook".
   12 February 1983. p. 126.
   12 February 1983. p. 127.
   16 April 1983. p. 359.
   30 April 1983. pp. 411 and 401.
   7 May 1983. p. 346.
   21 May 1983. p. 485.
   9 July 1983. p. 648.
T.V. Times Magazine. 3 to 9 October 1981.
Time. 19 October 1981. Vol. 118. No. 52.
   9 August 1982. Vol. 43. pp. 39 and 43.
   29 November 1982. "Religion". No. 48. p. 47.
   4 June 1983. p. 9.
Udagama, P. "The Problem of Education and Training in Developing Countries". *International Development Review*. No. 1. 1973. p. 3ff.
Ward, Barbara, "Peace Through Justice". *The Tablet*. 20 January 1973. p. 51.
Winter, F.X., "Nuclear Deterrence Morality". *Theological Studies*. September 1982. No. 3. p. 429.
Winter, F.X., "U.S. Bishops and the Arms Race". *The Month*. August 1982. p. 265.
Winter, F.X., "U.S. Bishops' Arms Letter; a compromise?" *The Month*. September 1983. p. 296.
Windass, S., "Non-Nuclear Europe". *New Statesman*. 20 January 1984. p. 13.
Zahn, Gordon, "Total War and Absolute Pacifism". *Concilium*. April 1983. p. 30.

UNPUBLISHED SOURCES

Ambler, R., "The Christian Ethic in a Nuclear Society", paper April 1973.

Chamberlain, O., Conference for Nobel Prize Winners on "Science and Peace" at Sorbonne University, papers 26 October 1983.

Donohue, T.C., "Warfare & Justice in 16th Century Scholasticism", Ph.D. Thesis. St. Louis University, 1960.

Fox, Robert J., "The Limitations of Warfare according to the Just War Theory", Ph.D. Thesis. Catholic University of America, 1963.

Grisez, G., "Some Questions and Answers of the Proposed UCCB Collective Pastoral on War and Peace". Private document circulated to the bishops of the United States.

Hartigan, R.S., "Non-Combatant Immunity: An Analysis of Its Philosophical and Historical Origins", Ph.D. Thesis. Georgetown University, 1964.

Lammers, Stephen, "The Just War Tradition – An Examination of Some Modern Claims to that Tradition", Ph.D. Thesis. Brown University, 1971.

McFadden, W., "A Theological Evaluation of Nuclear Pacifism as held by Selected Christian Thinkers", Ph.D. Thesis. Boston University of Theology, 1966.

O'Connor, D.T., "War in a Moral Perspective: A Critical Appraisal of the Views of Paul Ramsey", Ph.D. Thesis. Claremont Graduate School, 1982.

Potter, R. B., "The Structure of Certain American Christian Responses to the Nuclear Dilemma", Ph.D. Thesis. Harvard University, 1965.

Tonks, H., "Faith, Hope and Decision Making", Ph.D. Thesis. University of Birmingham, 1981.

Walters, Leroy, "Five Classic Just War Theories. A Study in the thought of Thomas Aquinas, Vitoria, Surez, Gentili and Gratius", Ph.D. Thesis. Yale, 1971.

Private Letters to the Writer from the Chairman of the Working Party, the Bishop of Salisbury (*The Church and The Bomb*) also from a member of the Working Party, Canon Paul Oestreicher.

INDEX OF NAMES

Index of Names